Brain Damage,
Behaviour,
and the Mind

Brain Damage, Behaviour, and the Mind

MOYRA WILLIAMS

Department of Clinical Psychology,
Cambridge Area Health Authority

JOHN WILEY & SONS

Chichester · New York · Brisbane · Toronto

Library of Congress Cataloging in Publication Data:

Williams, Moyra.
  Brain damage, behaviour, and the mind.

  Revision of the 1970 ed. published under title: Brain damage and the mind.
  Includes index.
  1. Brain damage.   2. Psychology, Pathological.
I. Title. [DNLM: 1. Brain damage, Chronic.
2. Mental disorders. 3. Cognition disorders.
4. Speech disorders. 5. Psychomotor disorders. WL354
W725b (P)]
RC386.2.W55   1978   616.8   78–16370

ISBN 0 471 99704 8

Photosetting by Thomson Press (India) Limited, New Delhi, and printed in Great Britain at The Pitman Press, Bath

Acknowledgements

I would like to express my gratitude to those who have made this book possible by encouraging and allowing me to work in this field, in particular Professor W. Ritchie Russell and the late Professor Sir Hugh Cairns who first enticed me into it; to Professors O. L. Zangwill and the late R. C. Olfield, the pioneers of neuropsychology in this country; Dr L. Z. Cosin for the opportunity to work in geriatrics; and finally the consultants of Littlemore Hospital, Oxford, and Addenbrooke's and Fulbourn Hospitals, Cambridge, who have enabled me to study some of the cases mentioned here.

I would also like to thank Dr R. T. Wilkinson, Dr Karl Pribram, the late Dr Grey Walter, and Dr Elizabeth Warrington for allowing me to read and quote from papers of theirs which are difficult to obtain in this country.

Finally, my most sincere thanks to Glenna Dixon for preparing the manuscript, and to Mrs Marcia Thorburn for providing the illustrations.

Contents

List of Tables

List of Figures

1
General Principles

There are two different ways in which one can look at brain–behaviour correlations: from the standpoint of the brain or from that of the mental mechanisms themselves. That is to say one can take the different areas of the brain as a starting point and analyse the impairments of function which follow their destruction, or one can take the different mental functions as the starting point, and see how they are affected by disorders in different cerebral areas. If the evidence is reliable, both attitudes should lead to the same conclusions so to do both in the same volume is unnecessary.

This book, being written primarily for psychologists whose main concern is with the analysis of mental functions, will adopt the second of the above procedures. Each section will open with a description of clinical observations and continue with some of the experimental investigations which have been based on them. Finally, the cerebral areas involved in their dissolution will be discussed.

When the study of neuropsychology, as it has now come to be called, was first initiated it was hoped that it would not only help to elucidate the connection between brain and behaviour, but would also increase man's understanding of mental activity itself. By selectively cutting out individual mental functions, the others would, it was hoped, be thrown into relief and become more open to scrutiny. Nature herself would perform the experiment and its consequences would be open to scientific scrutiny. That this has not always happened is now generally coming to be accepted; why it has not happened is another matter whose consideration had better be deferred until after the examination of the evidence itself.

In a field as large as this one cannot hope to include all the relevant data within the confines of a few hundred pages. The author's selection has been based on three principles. In the first place the work reported here is almost exclusively confined to that dealing with human beings. For obvious reasons this means observations in the clinical setting. Animal experiments, important though they are, have been mentioned only if directly relevant to the clinical observations.

In the second place mental activity is considered only in relation to the gross anatomical areas of the brain involved. The effects of variation in the biochemical and electrophysiological activity of this complicated organ are only referred to briefly. Again this is not because such factors are considered unimportant: on the contrary, they are of such vital importance that whole books have been devoted to them alone.

In the third place the literature covered here has been restricted almost entirely to that published in the English language. Further selection of this vast bulk of literature has again been necessary and most of the work referred to will be that with which the author has some personal connection and hence some basis on which to form a judgement.

For those not familiar with neuroanatomy and physiology, a brief description of the brain might be useful. It is customary to consider neurological control of the body as mediated by two separate systems: the central nervous system (CNS) comprising the brain and spinal cord together with their incoming (afferent) and outgoing (efferent) fibres, and the autonomic (ANS) comprising the sympathetic and parasympathetic systems. While the former is concerned mainly with the exterior world, the latter monitors and is affected by internal bodily events.

Nerves from the autonomic system, however, interact with those from the CNS at many levels. The brain—the structure which will concern us most closely here—consists of four major portions arranged around four spaces or ventricles which themselves form the upper regions of the spinal canal (see Fig. 1). At the point where the spinal cord emerges from the spine and enters the skull through the *foramen magnum*, it widens out into the *brain stem*. This area is far from homogeneous, being divisible into a great number of different centres and nuclei each subserving a different function. The areas receives many of the large nerves connecting the brain to the sense organs, the *cranial nerves*. At the back or dorsal side of the brain stem is the *fourth ventricle* the area on top of which develops and branches out to form the *cerebellum*, a structure largely concerned with motor control. At the front or anterior part of the brain stem is the *pons*. In between these the *medulla* contains all the ascending and descending fibre tracts interconnecting brain and spinal cord, together with a complicated network of

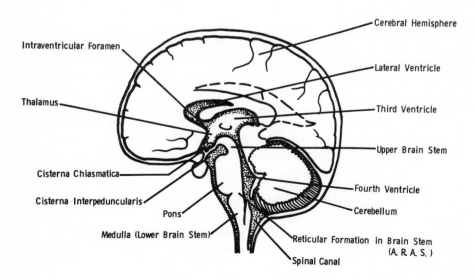

Figure 1. Lateral view of section through brain and brain stem

interconnecting fibres known as the *ascending reticular activating system* (ARAS).

At the top of the brain stem and surrounding the *third ventricle* are the *thalamus, hypothalamus, basal ganglia,* and other important relay centres which will be considered in greater detail in later chapters. From here both the spinal cord and the central canal around which it is built divide into two large lobes comprising the cerebral hemispheres surrounding the *lateral ventricles* (see Fig. 2). The hemispheres are joined by a band of fibres running the length of the third ventricle known as the *corpus callosum*. The hemispheres are themselves composed of two distinct layers, (1) the convoluted surface composed largely of grey cell bodies, *the cortex*, and (2) the lighter coloured myelin covered neural sheaths together with surrounding glial cells, the *white matter*. Each hemisphere is divided by deep fissures or sulci into four lobes, *frontal, parietal, occipital,* and *temporal* (see Fig. 3).

The cerebral hemispheres are supported by and separated from the brain stem and cerebellum by a fairly rigid layer of tissue which stretches across inside the skull, the *tentorium cerebelli*. This divides the brain into two large areas, the anterior (or frontal) and posterior (back) fossae which will be referred to again in Chapter 2.

The neural tissues of the brain and spinal cord are themselves covered by three layers (or laminae) of tissue, the *meninges*; the pia mater (soft), arachnoid (fibrous), and dura mater (hard) (see Fig. 4). It is these which carry the blood vessels.

Oxygen, nutrients and other substances are circulated throughout the brain by the blood. The brain uses a great deal of oxygen (i.e. about 8% of the total body consumption) and most of its energy is derived from carbohydrate metabolism.

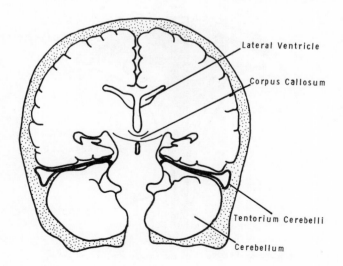

Figure 2. Transverse section through brain

4

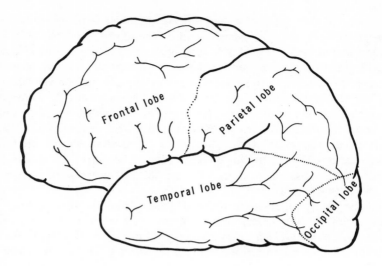

Figure 3. Exterior view of brain

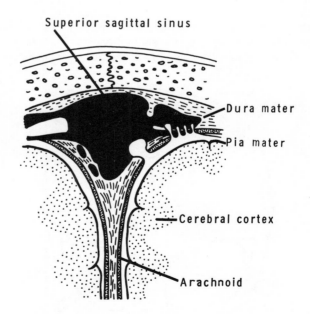

Figure 4. Diagram of meninges and dural sinus

Three major arteries serve the brain, the anterior, posterior, and middle cerebral arteries. The venous drainage from the brain takes place mainly through the largely vascular channels in the dura, the *dural sinuses*. The other body fluid surrounding the brain and supplying it with vital substances is that contained in the ventricle and spinal canal—the cerebrospinal fluid (CSF). Blood and CSF pass close to one another in the *choroid plexus*, vascular fringe-like processes of pia mater projecting into the ventricles. However, the thin membranes separating blood and CSF form a very effective barrier to many substances preventing them passing from one to another, the *blood-brain barrier*.

Each nerve cell (neuron) consists basically of three sections (see Fig. 5), the cell body containing the nucleus, the axon (a long fibre which carries the message from the cell body to its terminal endings), and the dendrites which receive impulses from other nerve cells. The interconnections between the nerve cells—the *synapses*—consist of fluid-filled areas in which various chemicals are formed, degraded, and reformed, these processes probably being the cause of the electrical energy which results in the 'nervous impulse'.

Nervous impulses normally occur so fast and emit so little energy that they are not observable except by very sensitive instruments. Electrodes attached to the scalp can, however, pick up patterns of electrical activity produced by the neurons, which if amplified many times can be recorded by pen and form the electroencephalogram—the *EEG* (see Fig. 6). These patterns vary with the mental state and condition of the subject, as will be described later. The structure, arrangement, and possibly even biochemical constituents of the neurons vary in different parts of the brain, the variations probably being associated with different functions as will be described and discussed in the appropriate sections later.

Since most of this book will be concerned with attempts to relate mental activity and brain damage, some indication may be given of the means by which the nature and location of the latter are verified. Direct surgical intervention is of course the surest method, but this is not always possible or desirable.

The EEG can provide useful data about the gross presence and location of damaged tissue, as the pattern of impulses from the skull over such areas tends to be slower and more rhythmical than over active cerebral tissue.

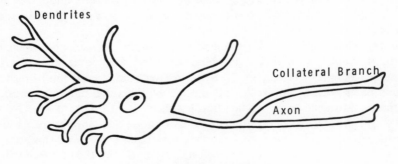

Figure 5. Diagram of a neuron

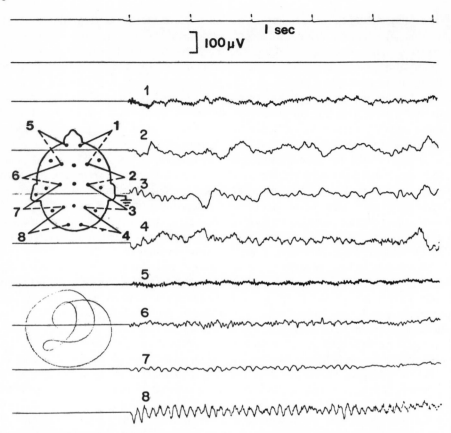

Figure 6. EEG record of waking brain, showing absence of activity in leads over frontal lobes

Straight X-rays of the skull can give a great deal of information to skilled observers. The pineal body, a small mass lying in a depression at the base of the brain tends to become calcified quite early in life, and stands out as a small lighter coloured mark in an X-ray. The position of this in relation to landmarks on the skull can give valuable clues to the presence of space occupying lesions such as tumours or blood clots.

Air-encephalography (or Pneumoencephalography) consists of replacing a measured quantity of CSF by air which being less dense than fluid offers less resistance to the X-rays (see Fig. 7). By tilting the head, the air can be moved to various parts within the skull, and outline of the subarachnoid spaces, the ventricles and the cisterns can be photographed.

Angiography consists of injecting an X-ray opaque substance into an artery in the neck (the carotid artery) and allowing it to circulate around the brain (see Fig. 8). X-ray pictures taken at various time intervals after the injection will give clear pictures of all blood vessels in that hemisphere.

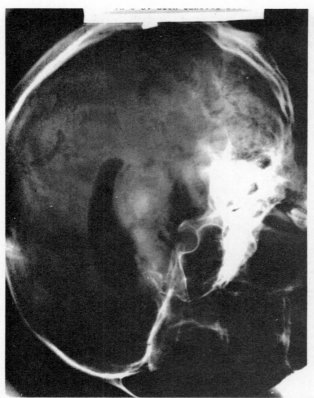

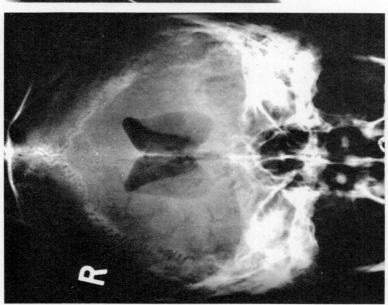

Figure 7. Air pictures of normal brain, showing outline of ventricles

8

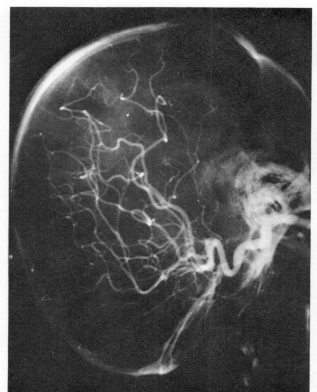

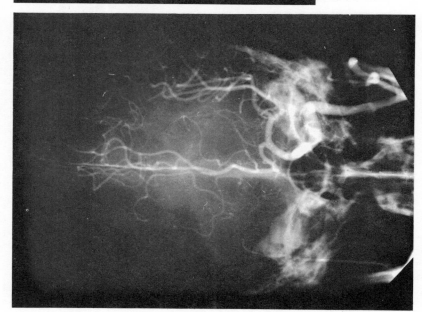

Figure 8. Angiograms of normal left hemisphere, showing position of blood vessels

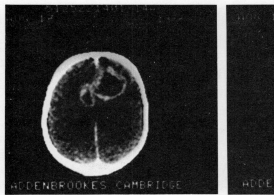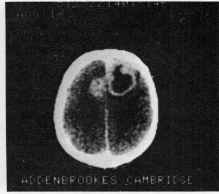

Figure 9. CAT scan of brain, showing bi-frontal lesions

Radioisotopic encephalography is a recent technical innovation which is proving useful. More of the radioisotope is taken up by tissue in a state of high metabolic activity (such as tumours) than in others; so by scanning the skull for concentrations of radioisotope, after carotid injections of it, such areas can be located.

Computerized axial tomography (CAT) is based on X-rays linked to a computer which calculates the absorption coefficient of the tissues in different areas at different levels of the brain and presents these as a picture (see Fig. 9). Areas of abnormal density are shown up clearly as paler than normal tissue.

Although the data presented in the following pages has been grouped under different functional headings, it cannot be stressed too strongly that there is a great deal of overlap between these categories and they are distinguished by name only. Moreover, a patient showing a disorder falling into one of these categories usually shows some in others as well. The distinction is based, however, not only on the nature of the functions themselves but also, as will become apparent in the text, on the common finding that discrete anatomical lesions are often involved in disorders of the different functions.

2
Disorders of Consciousness

Responsiveness to outside events is not the prerogative of man or even of animals. Plants respond to light and to the proximity of other plants, while even stones may break up in frost and rain. Where consciousness begins and ends is a philosophical question but in the clinical field argument is overcome by a strict adherence to the measurement of behaviour. Consciousness is defined by the clinician in terms of the changes in behaviour which follow sensory stimulation, and in this sense it is closely connected, in man and other mammals, with activity within the brain.

Clinical consciousness is by no means an all-or-none phenomenon. Behaviour of different degrees and complexity is seen in different conditions, and in this chapter an attempt will be made to examine the relationship between the level of consciousness observed and the activity of specific areas within the brain.

The levels of consciousness defined in clinical terms are: (1) simple reflex activity; (2) restless and purposeless movements; (3) purposeful movements but no speech or understanding of speech; (4) restless movements and the ability to utter a few words or phrases, often explosive; (5) uninhibited speech and action but disorientation and amnesia for current events; and (6) full orientation and social decorum (Russell, 1959, p.51).

These may also be referred to as coma, stupor, delirium, confusion and clouding of consciousness (Plum and Posner, 1972). It is important to distinguish them from the 'locked-in syndrome' or 'de-efferented state' described by Feldman (see Plum and Posner, 1972) where the patient may be unable to move anything other than his eyes, but can still be taught the Morse code, and by means of eye movements communicate complex ideas and signify consciousness of all that is going on around them.

The different levels of consciousness tend to shade into one another and the transition from one to the next is often difficult to define. Thus, describing one patient suffering from tuberculous meningitis Williams and Smith (1954) report

For the first week in hospital he remained drowsy, confused, and unable to feed himself. During the second week the acute confusional state lightened. He began to sit up in bed and gradually learnt to feed himself until by the end of twelve days he was alert, friendly and co-operative, but with a gross amnesia for all recent events. Thus he could never remember having seen the ward sister before in spite of the devoted care she gave him. When the trolley was brought for his daily lumbar puncture he would obediently roll over on his side, but as soon as the needle was withdrawn he would deny that he had ever had anything done to his back. He was fully awake all day and occupied himself with handwork or reading the comic strips in the papers, but the moment he was distracted from his occupation, he would have no recollection of what he had been doing the moment before.

Although during the return of consciousness, orientation for person, time, and place usually recovers before the ability to retain recent experiences (memory), this is not always the case. Patients often describe 'waking up and not knowing who or where I was', indicating that they have retained a recollection of the situation they were in before regaining all other past memories.

Unconsciousness is differentiated from unwakefulness in that in the former condition the patient can never be fully aroused by external stimuli whereas in the latter he can. There are a number of clinical conditions in which wakefulness rather than consciousness is impaired, a patient tending to fall asleep or to drowse in abnormal circumstances (see Section 2.7).

The connection between the levels of behaviour mentioned above and activity of the brain can be followed on the electroencephalogram—EEG (see Chapter 1)—which records the electrical activity of the brain by means of electrodes placed on the surface of the skull.

Clinical consciousness may be impaired by a variety of different causes, divided by Plum and Posner into supratentorial lesions, subtentorial lesions and metabolic disorders.

2.1 SUPRATENTORIAL LESIONS

As has been described briefly in Chapter 1, the tentorium cerebelli separates the cerebral hemispheres from the cerebellum and divides the brain into two large areas. It contains an opening in the centre through which the brain stem passes (see Fig. 2). The uncus and a small part of the hippocampus normally overhang this opening to some extent. If pressure builds up on one side or the other of the tentorium, these structures become compressed and interfere with nerve and blood supplies.

The commonest supratentorial lesions causing loss of consciousness are concussional head injuries, cerebrovascular lesions and intracranial tumours.

Head Injuries

In concussional head injury the patient is rendered unconscious immediately, but from then on his degree of responsiveness increases in the way already described. A typical case may be quoted as follows.

A housewife, aged 44, who had two children aged 10 and 8 was knocked off her bicycle on 2.3.51. On admission to hospital she was found to have severe lacerations on the back of her head, fixed and dilated pupils and apparent weakness over the left side. She was responding to painful stimuli but the following day her conscious level deteriorated and her temperature and blood pressure rose. 5.3.51, three days after admission, further examinations were carried out to exclude a blood clot and obstruction to the circulation of the cerebrospinal fluid which might have resulted in raising the pressure inside the brain (raised intracranial pressure). 7.3.51, conscious level began to improve. She would open her eyes and mumble when spoken to but did not obey commands. 15.3.51, it was possible to recognize her mumblings as attempts to form such words as 'all right', 'I don't know'. She could count one and two fingers, but there was much perseveration, i.e. the repetition of one response to succeeding stimuli.

During the following two or three weeks she showed gradual mental improvement and became continent. She appeared to be slightly euphoric. Investigations were carried out which showed very slight dilation of the ventricles inside the brain, but nothing else. For the next five weeks she would talk readily but remained very confused and amnesic. Six weeks after injury there were signs of improvement in memorizing.

9.5.51, nine weeks after injury, she was able to date her accident correctly and believed that she had 'sorted out' most of the misplaced events in her remote past. 29.8.51, she had returned home and was able to lead a full social and domestic life although she still had a number of gaps in her memory for events which had occurred before her injury (Williams, 1954).

Loss of consciousness (and the accompanying amnesia) occurs only rarely in head injuries which are not caused by sudden violent changes of direction. Penetrating wounds of the head, even though they may cause severe cortical damage, seldom cause immediate unconsciousness or concussion (Russell, 1959, p. 75).

Intracranial Tumours (ICTs)

Consciousness may be impaired by ICTs either as a result of convulsions (see Section 2.6), of haemorrhage, of intracranial pressure, or of direct infiltration of areas around the thalamus and hypothalamus. The degree of responsiveness present at any one time depends mainly on the area of the brain affected. This point has been demonstrated very clearly by Cairns (1952). Lesions in the upper brain stem and around the thalamus, cause a state more like that of sleep. Sometimes these are short and may be accompanied by epileptic fits, the patient remaining fully awake between them and showing no disorders of mentality.

Dramatic examples are quoted by Cairns of patients with cystic tumours in and around the third ventricle, whose level of consciousness alternated as the cyst filled or was surgically emptied. When the cyst was full of fluid and causing local pressure on the floor of the third ventricle, one girl of 14

lay inert, except that her eyes followed the movements of objects or could be diverted by sound. As one approached her bedside her steady gaze seemed to promise speech, but no sound could be obtained from her by any form of stimulus. A painful stimulus would produce reflex withdrawal of the limb and, if the stimulus was maintained, slow feeble ineffective movements of a voluntary kind to remove the source of stimulation; but without tears, noise or other signs of pain or displeasure. She swallowed readily, but had to be fed; hard food would be swallowed whole, and she would take sugar, salt or quinine in her mouth without any signs of pleasure or distaste. There were also mild signs of bilateral pyramidal tract involvement, and she was totally incontinent of urine and faeces.

This patient's third ventricle cyst was aspirated without anaesthesia on several occasions. A needle was passed into the lateral ventricle, where the pressure of cerebrospinal fluid was found to be normal or nearly normal, and was then advanced into the region of the third ventricle. Cystic fluid in amounts of 12 to 18 cc was removed. On one occasion 5 cc of air were then injected to determine the site and extent of the cyst, which occupied the situation of the third ventricle.

On the first occasion, immediately the cyst was tapped the child roused and made the first loud sound we had heard from her, but she would not speak. However, within ten minutes she gave her name, age and address correctly, without any disorder of articulation and then asked where she was.

Attacks of hypersomnia, akinetic mutism (the condition described above in which the patient lies with eyes open appearing to follow moving objects but making not other responses) and petit mal (see Section 2.6) may also occur in lesions around this area, which Cairns, by a process of deduction based on careful clinical records, claims must be due to direct involvement of the area affected by the lesion and cannot be due to generalized cerebral impairment either from anoxia (due to restricted bloodflow) or to increased intracranial pressure.

2.2 SUBTENTORIAL LESIONS

Lesions of the posterior fossa may be caused by cellular destruction (due to cerebral vascular disease, nutritional deficiency, neoplasms, etc.) or by compression. Lesions in the lower brain stem may cause sudden, short, intermittent attacks of deep unconsciousness, usually followed quickly by alterations of breathing, irregular pulse, fluctuations of blood pressure, and increased tonus of the limbs which together frequently result in death. Those lying outside the pontine-midbrain reticular formation may destroy large areas of the brain without causing coma, leaving the patient as 'a mind . . . encumbered by a body over which it has lost the power of compelling obedience' (Plum and Posner, 1972, p. 127), i.e. the 'locked-in syndrome'. This must be distinguished from the akinetic mutism just described above, which condition arises from much more extensive impairment of the arousing systems of the hemispheres.

2.3 METABOLIC DISORDERS

Cerebral metabolism has three major functions to perform: (1) to maintain the electrical potentials necessary for the transportation of sodium and potassium; (2) to synthesize the transmitter substances (such as acetylcholine); and (3) to replace the catabolized enzymes and repair cellular damage. Its main requirements are glucose (100 mg of brain tissue uses 5.5 mg of glucose every minute, all but 15% of which is oxidized); oxygen (100 mg of brain tissue uses 3.3 cc of oxygen every minute, whether awake or asleep), and vitamins (mainly thiamine and pyridaxine) to act as catalysts in the oxidation process.

Lack of glucose (hypoglycemia), most commonly seen in diabetics after overdoses of insulin or in those who do not eat sufficient sugar after taking insulin, causes abnormalities mainly in the cerebral cortex and hippocampus. Impaired consciousness is usually its first sign.

Lack of thiamine, most commonly found in alcoholics on inadequate diets specifically affects the mamillary bodies and the periaqueductal grey matter; its effects are seen in memory impairment (see Chapter 4).

2.4 HORMONE DISORDERS

These do not usually affect consciousness so much as other aspects of behaviour such as aggression or irritability. In the case of the thyroid, however, the situation may be different. Since hormones from the thyroid affect all metabolic functions, thyroid dysfunction can cause impaired consciousness and even coma.

2.5 TOXIC INFECTIVE DISORDERS

That consciousness may be disordered from toxic and infective states has long been known. The mental confusion that accompanies any high fever is described in most psychiatric textbooks, and is characterized not so much by loss of responsiveness as by the inappropriateness of the responses made. The patient is disorientated, misinterprets his sensory environment or sees things that are not there (hallucinates), and becomes unable to keep track of time. Of special interest, however, are the disorders which have both a specific effect on discrete cerebral areas and cause selective impairments of consciousness and wakefulness. Of these encephalitis lethargica and tuberculous meningitis are the best known. Describing the condition of patients in the acute stages of encephalitis lethargica Mayer-Gross, Slater, and Roth (1960) point out that disorders of sleep rhythm and mental changes are the most common characteristics. There is:

Irresistible somnolence which continues for days or weeks. The patient can be aroused to have his meals and often carry on a rational conversation, and if stimulation is maintained he can be kept awake for periods of half to one hour, but left to himself, lethargy soon overpowers him. During sleep there is a marked restlessness and myoclonic jerking. More rarely there is total sleeplessness and inversion of the sleep rhythm. (p. 415).

Accompanying these in the acute phase of the illness may be delirium

> marked by vivid, terrifying hallucinations ... states of delirium may alternate with periods of somnolence, the combination rather characteristic of encephalitis lethargica. Acute stupor is not uncommon and may take a typically catatonic form with negativism and flexibilitas cerea (the tendency to hold the limbs in any position in which they are placed) ... more universal is a curious affective change ... marked by emotional immobility with poverty of affective response to all stimuli even when the patient is at his most alert; the death of a wife, a child or a friend is passed by without comment or apparent reaction. (p. 416).

In tuberculous meningitis (TBM) an illness which has been recognized for much longer than encephalitis lethargica, Williams and Smith (1954) quote Whytt as noting in 1768 that in the early stages in children 'Their spirits being low they incline mostly to lie in bed, although they are more often disposed to watching than sleep'. This state usually gives way after a short time to an 'amnesic' state which may persist for many months (see Chapter 3), during which patients are often rather euphoric but sufficiently alert and rational to occupy themselves and cope adequately (though not yet quite normally) with intellectual problems, but have difficulty in retaining any new impression for more than a few minutes. More will be said about this stage in Chapter 3, but here it may be noted in passing that, in TBM, as in encephalitis lethargica, the brunt of the disease falls on the base of the brain and particularly on the more anterior of the basal cisterns.

The mental state in tuberculous meningitis and encephalitis lethargica is distinguished from that seen in other toxic illnesses involving the brain by affecting wakefulness and memory more severely than perception, sensation, and intellectual functions. Williams and Smith quote the case of a patient who had every sign of tuberculous meningitis and was treated unsuccessfully for such until his mental condition led to some suspicion. Thus, in this man orientation and memory were relatively well preserved in the face of gross disorders of intellect and over-active, aggressive behaviour. Re-examination showed him to have neurosyphilis rather than tuberculous meningitis and when treated for this he made a good recovery.

2.6 EPILEPSY

Epileptic seizures are among the commonest causes of disordered consciousness though not all seizures are followed or accompanied by loss of consciousness. Epilepsy is indeed a term used to describe a great variety of cerebral disorders, whose only common characteristics are, in the words of Hughlings Jackson, 'an occasional, an excessive, and a disordered discharge of neural tissue' (see Schmidt and Wilder, 1968).

Epileptic disorders are usually classified into focal, generalized, petit mal and psychomotor seizures. In *focal seizures*, the disorder starts at a local area of damaged (but not completely destroyed) cortical tissue in the cerebral hemispheres.

If it remains confined to this or adjacent areas, its only outward manifestation may be disordered sensation or movement of circumscribed body parts—the twitching or tingling of an arm or leg. If the dysrhythmia radiates outwards and reaches the deep midline structures of the diencephalon, mesencephalon, reticular formation and nuclei of the thalamic projection system (the area called by Penfield (1952) the 'centrencephalic integrating system') loss of consciousness will ensue. From here, the attack tends to be rebroadcast to the whole brain, and the seizure becomes *generalized*.

Petit mal attacks, which are characterized by sudden, and usually quite short periods of arrested activity and consciousness, are taken to start and remain confined to the centrencephalic region. These are distinguished from myoclonic attacks (which consist of bilateral clonic movements of parts of the face or body) and from akinetic attacks (where all muscular tone may be lost but consciousness retained), in that voluntary movements and consciousness stop. They are invariably accompanied by the typical 'spike and wave' pattern seen in EEG. *Psychomotor* attacks usually have their origin in the temporal lobes. These are characterized by altered but not necessarily complete loss of consciousness, and 'automatic' behaviour, for much of which the patient may be completely amnesic afterwards. Preceding the onset of such attacks, patients often describe 'auras' of hallucinatory experiences or *déjà vu*, in which all that is going on around them seems to have happened before. Perceptual distortions (things appearing smaller or larger than normal), changes of mood (terror, anxiety), and changes of self-awareness (depersonalization) have also commonly been reported.

The pattern of returning consciousness after epileptic seizures varies. After petit mal the return is usually sudden and complete, the patient being able to carry on with an interrupted task exactly where he left off. After generalized or grand mal seizures, the patient is usually drowsy or hazy for a considerable time (often going into a deep sleep). He may, on finally awakening, also have amnesia for some events actually preceding the onset of the fit.

Whether epilepsy is also associated with permanent between-fit disorders of mental behaviour or personality is a much debated question. Patients commonly show lability of mood, poor control over their impulses and disorders of perception which are difficult to distinguish from those seen in schizophrenic illness (Slater *et al.*, 1963), but in general it seems to be the conclusion that such disorders are related to the extent and localization of cerebral damage rather than the incidence of seizures. (Schmidt and Wilder, 1968).

The clinical disorders causing epilepsy are varied and have been classified by Schmidt and Wilder as follows.

Trauma. Gun-shot wounds penetrating the cerebral hemispheres are followed by one or more epileptic seizures in 30–50% of cases (though in those involving the occipital area only, the incidence is rather less). In closed head injuries the incidence is only 5%.

The cerebral areas most commonly damaged in 'acceleration trauma' are the under surface and tips of the temporal lobes and the base of the frontal lobes, i.e. those parts of the cerebral hemisphere in closest contact with the skull. If there is no fit within one year of the trauma, the likelihood of fits appearing later is extremely small, but against this, the incidence of one or more fits within 24 hours of injury does not mean that further attacks will follow. In general the incidence of attacks decreases with time, especially if the attacks are generalized rather than focal.

The causes of post-traumatic epilepsy are probably scarring and adhesions of the dura and meninges which in turn stretch and damage nerve cells; direct damage to the blood vessels; or cellular atrophy and glial reactions following contusions and haemorrhage.

Tumours. Epilepsy of late onset is associated with intracranial tumours in 53% of focal and 10% of generalized seizures. Slow-growing tumours, especially those involving the central areas are more likely than fast-growing tumours to have this effect; but an apparent paradox is that tumours directly involving the basal ganglia, thalamus and other deep midline structures seldom produce seizures. *Cerebrovascular disease* is found in 15% of those people over 50-years who suffer a fit for the first time. In those who suffer infarcts of the cortex, the incidence is even higher. Focal epilepsy starting in adolescence is often associated with arteriovenous malformations.

Metabolic Disorders. Hypoglycemia, disorders of lipid metabolism, kidney diseases and the withdrawal of certain drugs, may all be followed by epileptic seizures.

Febrile conditions are a common cause of convulsions in young children, especially those with a strong family history, and may be due to an imbalance of water and electrolytes similar to the condition following metabolic disorders.

In addition to the causes listed above, epileptic attacks may be triggered off by certain sensory stimuli. Thus in those people who have a low threshold to fits, frequent rhythmical flashes of light (stroboscope) are a common stimulant. Patterns of horizontal and vertical lines have been identified as the trigger in a number of cases (Wilkins *et al.*, 1975), sensitivity being decreased if vision is restricted to one eye only. Loud noises may fire off fits in a number of people, and even some words (written or spoken) may be sufficient in certain sensitive individuals (Sherwin, 1966). At the same time the onset of a fit may be checked in some subjects by mental effort or by conditioning (see Ervin, 1967).

The passage of electric currents through the brain will also cause seizures, and this last mechanism is often used for therapeutic purposes in the treatment of depression (electroconvulsive therapy) as will be discussed in greater detail in Chapter 3. In many cases, however, the cause is never discovered.

During the seizure itself, certain activities and changes occur throughout the brain which may have a profound influence on mental behaviour. The blood flow to the brain itself is increased; sodium enters and potassium leaves the discharging cells; bound acetylcholine decreases while free acetylcholine and serotonin increase; and several alterations occur in the nature and distribution of amino acids.

2.7 SLEEP

Although all the instances of disordered consciousness described above occur under conditions of cerebral dysfunction, periodic loss of consciousness in sleep is an essential to normal waking behaviour. Indeed, at one time it was believed that if an animal was prevented from sleeping for too long, death would inevitably result. Even with slighter degrees of sleep deprivation, mental activity is usually impaired. 'The sleep-deprived man of whom sustained attention is demanded makes frequent errors of omission and commission. He fails to do the right thing at the right time, does the right things at the wrong time or the wrong thing at the right time.' (Oswald, 1966, p. 54).

In recent years, however, the adverse effect of sleep deprivation as such has been doubted. Not only have some people managed to keep awake for several days and nights without showing any ill-effects (mental or physical) but others have been located all over the world who habitually only sleep for 3–4 hours per night as compared to the usual 7–8 hours. (Dement, 1972).

The nature and function of sleep are still largely unknown, but the weight of opinion now regards them as 'an active brain process, controlled by the bio-genic amines' (Williams, 1971) rather than as a cessation of cerebral activity.

A regular cycle of sleep and waking—the circadian rhythm—accompanied as it is by other biochemical changes within the body, seems to be more essential than prolonged periods of sleep as such. In general, sleep is divided into two types: rapid eye movement (REM) or paradoxical, and non-REM (NREM) or orthodox. The NREM is further divided into four stages, differentiated mainly by the EEG activity recorded in them, the proportions of which vary throughout the night with a variety of normal (e.g. age) and abnormal conditions, and can be experimentally manipulated by the ingestion of various pharmacological compounds. In paradoxical sleep the EEG is desynchronized, the body muscles lose tone and bloodflow and protein synthesis within the brain are increased. In orthodox, NREM sleep, there is synchrony of the EEG, muscle tone is maintained, and there is a release of growth hormone. It has been suggested by Lewis (1976) that in paradoxical or REM sleep, repairs take place in the brain; in orthodox or NREM sleep they take place in the body.

During sleep, as in many other conditions where consciousness is altered, awareness is not completely absent. The sensory system is continually monitoring incoming data, rejecting the insignificant and picking out the significant or rare in response to which the subject makes appropriate actions, even if necessary awaking (e.g. the mother wakes when she hears her child cry; the man used to traffic wakes when it ceases). In between the two extremes of rejection and selection, there is a phase wherein sensory data or preoccupations are woven into a strange half-world of experience called dreams.

Dreams and the physiology associated with them have been considered in a number of works (see Oswald, 1966) and will therefore not be discussed any further here.

That the rhythm of sleep is fundamentally under the control of small areas within the brain has been recognized for a number of years. The clinical observations of Gélineau on narcolepsy in the nineteenth century and von Economo on encephalitis lethargica early in the twentieth century pointed to the hypothalamus and midbrain as crucial centres. Furthermore, clinical cases have been reported of human beings born with only the midbrain and thalamus whom Cairns (1952) describes as follows.

Some of these individuals may survive for years, in one case of mine for 20 years. In them, the cerebral cortex is absent or has virtually disappeared, and the brain stem and sometimes the thalamus remain relatively intact. From these cases, it appears that the human brain stem and thalamic 'preparation' sleeps and wakes; it reacts to hunger, loud sounds and crude visual stimuli by movements of eyes, eyelids, and facial muscles; it may see and hear; it may be able to taste and smell, to reject the unpalatable and accept such food as it likes; it can itself utter crude sounds, can cry and smile, showing displeasure when hungry and pleasure, in a babyish way, when being sung to; it may be able to perform spontaneously crude movements of its limbs.

A point which has constantly been observed and must be borne in mind is that even when in fairly deep coma, patients still show EEG sleep-waking cycles, but the more normal the sleep pattern in these cases, the better the prognosis (Williams, Karocan, and Hursh, 1974).

Experimental work on animals in the 1940s by Moruzzi and Magoun drew attention to the part played by the ascending reticular formation (ARAS) of the brain stem (see Fig. 1) in cortical arousal, which suggested that unless impulses from this area were able to reach the higher cerebral centres, 'wakefulness' could not occur. However, the actual connection between activity of the ARAS and consciousness is far from simple. As pointed out by Thompson (1967):

it is almost axiomatic in the field of brain function and behaviour that whenever a clear picture relating a given structure to particular functions emerges, additional research will tend to complicate or obfuscate this picture. Such has been the fate of the classical view of the ARAS. However, . . . the original observations of Moruzzi and Magoun, namely that activation of the ARAS produces cortical EEG arousal, still stands . . . It is the interpretation of these experiments that has been altered by the newer information (p. 434).

20

In summarizing the attitude of the late 1960s to the function of the **ARAS**, Thompson stresses the following points:

1. The reticular formation is recognized as being subdivided in both anatomical and functional organization into discrete areas.
2. Cortical EEG and behavioural arousal are not always concomitant; either can occur without the other.
3. Sleep-waking cycles and 'attentive behaviour' can occur in animals with virtually complete destruction of the ARAS, while conversely animals with lesions limited to sensory pathways may be much impaired in attentive behaviour.
4. To conclude 'that the ARAS has a clear or paramount unitary function would seem at present to be somewhat premature' (Thompson, 1967, p. 457).

From 1970 onwards, increasing attention has been paid to the connection between different nuclei within the ARAS and the different neuro transmitter substances which may be associated with them. For example, the connection between the locus coeruleus (one of the areas recognized by its coloration, see Fig. 10) and serotonin (5HT) has received much consideration; and the concept that this substance may be involved in the perpetuation of behavioural patterns, will be discussed further in the next chapter.

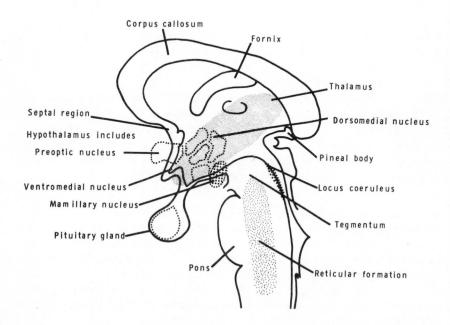

Figure 10. Areas of the brain concerned with wakefulness and consciousness

2.8 OVERAROUSAL

Up till now, all impairments of consciousness have been considered in relation to the number and range of environmental events to which the subject does not respond. But obviously there are a great many events occurring in our environment the whole time to which responses would be inappropriate and might even reduce efficiency. In fact, consciousness seems to include some mechanism by means of which these stimuli are 'filtered out' before we ever become aware of them. When listening to a conversation in a noisy room, we reject all sounds except those made by the speakers to whom we are attending. When listening to a concert, we remain almost unaware of the coughs, creaks, and rustles of our neighbours. When walking across a field, we do not notice the daisies growing on it until we start looking for a golfball among them.

There are some clinical conditions in which the filtering mechanism described above seems to go wrong or fails to work. This is particularly noticeable in autistic children—children whose behaviour is characterized by withdrawal (especially from social stimuli) stereotyped, repetitive gestures, and an absence of exploratory activity. The behaviour of such children and their EEG records are found to be less disturbed the less stimulating their environment (Hutt *et al.*, 1964), and there is a mounting volume of evidence to suggest that some of the illnesses grouped under the general heading of schizophrenia may show the same tendencies (see McGhie, Chapman, and Lawson, 1965).

For many years it has been recognized that one characteristic of schizophrenic patients is their tendency to respond to all aspects of a stimulus instead of 'abstracting' from it those elements most relevant to the immediate situation and ignoring the others. Described in detail by Goldstein, and called by him 'concreteness', Payne and Friedlander (1962) rechristened the characteristic 'over inclusiveness'; but the mechanism responsible for the condition was not considered by those investigators. In the 1960s, however, it was this aspect of schizophrenic 'thought disorder' which received most attention.

From analysing the situations in which this lack of abstraction or rejection becomes most pronounced, Marchbanks and Williams (1971) concluded that the rate at which incipient reactions are scanned and compared with external requirements is slowed up; so that too few dimensions are scanned adequately and reactions which would normally be rejected as inappropriate are accepted. Cromwell (1975) reviewing a great deal of the experimental work carried out in this decade, came to a similar conclusion. Slow processing would, in his words, lead to 'inability to reject an appropriate association, once elicited, in order to recycle a search for a more appropriate one' (p. 613). At the same time, Cromwell stressed that this mechanism could only be identified in those schizophrenic patients whose condition was of gradual, insidious onset, who did not demonstrate florid paranoid symptoms, and who responded well to phenothyazine therapy. Those with opposite symptoms (usually referred to as acute or paranoid schizophrenia) might, on the contrary, have a fast rate of processing. The term 'overarousal' in these conditions might be rather misleading. Indeed, as

Cromwell stresses, even the term arousal has little real usefulness. It can mean different things in different conditions and bears little consistent relationship to any physiological measures.

Although the majority of clinicians accept that schizophrenic symptoms have a biochemical (probably metabolic) basis, direct evidence of this is still awaited. Even longitudinal studies relating ups and downs in symptomatology to neurochemical metabolism is scarce; but in one study Phillipson et al. (1977) did find a close correlation between over-inclusive thought disorder, clinical symptoms, and plasma drug levels, in a group of five schizophrenic patients studied before, and four weeks after the instigation of chemotherapy.

2.9 PSYCHOLOGICAL FACTORS IN ALTERED CONSCIOUSNESS

During states of altered or lowered consciousness a number of behavioural characteristics have been identified.

Loss of Vigilance

As might be expected vigilance is lowered. If a subject is placed in a situation in which he has to watch out for intermittent signals, he begins missing some out. This can be of great importance in military and industrial concerns, where a lapse on the part of a fatigued nightwatchman might cause the loss of a country or of a million-pound machine. The connection between vigilance and wakefulness has therefore been studied in detail, and a number of correlated variables have been established. For example, in order for the fatigued subject not to miss signals, he needs longer between the signals to make his response. The signals have to be greater in intensity in relation to the background noise to be registered, and a preliminary alerting signal often helps. Incentive is also of importance. The physiological mechanisms which may explain these finds will be discussed later.

Altered Thinking and Imagery

As has been described in Section 2.7, mental activity becomes altered in character. External stimuli are reacted to in the form of images, but the type of imagery aroused in the patient's mind varies with the level of cerebral activity.

However, in illnesses which affect wakefulness, the roused patient may still be capable of logical thinking. He can carry out learnt behaviour patterns (e.g. use language) appropriately. He can work out quite complex perceptual problems (e.g. play a game of draughts). Moreover, after recovery of the condition causing impaired consciousness, even if this has lasted for many months, intellectual ability seems to return to its previous level. Thus, patients who remained 'unconscious' after head injury, cerebral tumours, and tuberculous meningitis, for weeks on end have been shown to be capable of resuming their previous occupations or passing intellectual tests at the same level as before.

Loss of Retentiveness

The connection between lowered levels of consciousness and inability to retain impressions is a consistent finding in all clinical conditions. After concussional head injuries (as opposed to penetrating ones that do not cause loss of consciousness) memory is always to some extent (even if only temporarily) impaired. After illnesses affecting wakefulness, the same phenomenon is seen. Even during sleep and especially after dreaming, there is a very strong tendency to 'forget'. The connection between consciousness and memory will be considered further in Chapter 4.

Disorders of Mood

These are again a most common finding in clinical conditions. A heightening of mood (euphoria) is the most common concomitant of altered consciousness but flattening of it has also been reported in encephalitis lethargica; and depression is not uncommon in the early stages of both intracranial tumours and tuberculous meningitis. This subject will be dealt with more fully in Chapter 3.

Aggressiveness

'Behaviour disturbances', especially in children, very frequently accompany disorders of sleep. The fact that children who recovered from the Spanish 'flu epidemic of 1917 (encephalitis lethargica) very frequently grew up to show uncontrolled outbursts of aggression is well known. Clardy and Hill (1949) studied the sleep patterns of children with no history of cerebral injury but whose behaviour problems has led to institutionalization, and found a markedly abnormal number of sleep disturbances amongst them characterized by restlessness and nightmares.

2.10 PHYSIOLOGICAL MECHANISMS IN ALTERED CONSCIOUSNESS

In the clinical material discussed in this section, note has already been made of the point that cerebral lesions causing impairment of consciousness tend to be subcortical and to be centred around the midbrain, the diencephalon and the reticular formation (see Fig. 1). Evidence that sleep is also controlled and mediated by these areas comes from the work on the ARAS and from studies of those unfortunate human beings born with only the midbrain and thalamus.

While lowered consciousness is associated with lesions in and around the midbrain causing impaired activity of these areas, there is also evidence that overarousal is due to altered activity within the reticular system (Hutt *et al.*, 1964) and there is some evidence that in animals, behaviour disturbances of the type associated with disordered consciousness may arise from experimental lesions in the ventromedial area (see Herberg, 1967, p. 105). Herberg suggests that these latter findings point to a conclusion that the hypothalamic excitatory drive mechanisms are normally opposed by inhibitory mechanisms sited in the ventromedial area of the brain.

The manner in which these areas interact with the cortex and thereby influence mental activity has yet to be established. Some clues to this may come from the studies being conducted on evoked cortical responses. It has long been recognized that sensory signals (e.g. clicks) are accompanied by cortical activity which although not detectable to the human eye, can be measured on the EEG if the waves from this are passed through computers. Wilkinson and Morlock (1967) summarize some of the early work on evoked potentials as follows: 'If attention is distracted from a stimulus the over-all amplitude of the evoked responses to that stimulus usually falls; if, on the other hand, attention is concentrated on the stimulus by requiring the subject to make some discriminatory response to it, the amplitude of the evoked response becomes much larger'. From further analysis of the EEG records of subjects asked to listen to runs of clicks and respond to each one by pressing a button with a thumb, it has become apparent that there are four components to the auditory evoked response—two positive and two negative. During normal waking alertness the second of these negative responses (N2) can hardly be seen, but as a person becomes drowsy this component becomes more and more noticeable, and as he moves into sleep its amplitude increases considerably.

Following the first four components and the signal itself, there may be a further positive and negative wave (P3, N3) associated with the act of making a motor response. Wilkinson believes that these records reflect sensory activity which occurs preparatory to an effector action.

Other studies which may one day throw light on the connection between activity in subcortical areas of the brain and mental activity, come from the pharmacologists. Evidence is accumulating that different nuclei in and around the thalamus control and are controlled by different neurochemical transmitters; that each nucleus is the centre of a complex neural network mediating these transmitters to and from the cerebral hemispheres, and that these networks interact with one another. Thus depletion of forebrain noradrenaline (NA) in the network arising from the locus coeruleus by injections of 6-hydroxydopamine (6-OHDA) into the dorsal NA bundle in the rat, while not affecting the animal's ability to acquire new behaviour patterns in response to food rewards, does reduce their ability to suppress this behaviour after punishment (Mason and Iverson, 1975, 1976), a point which will be discussed in greater detail in Chapter 4, but relevant here to the question of over-inclusive and stereotyped behaviour consistently observed in states of lowered consciousness.

2.11 CONCLUSIONS

In this chapter it has been pointed out that consciousness is not only influenced by physical events occurring in the brain, but that the areas of the brain most closely involved are closely related to one another and are situated along the brain stem and in the diencephalon. Whether the effect is directly due to activity within these cerebral areas or is due rather to the activation of the cortex by them is less clear.

It has also been pointed out, however, that the relation between consciousness and brain stem activity is complex. It is not simply a question of the more stimulation the better. Over-stimulation causes as much discomfort and disruption of mental processes as under-stimulation; blocking of sensory input is often as vital to effective survival as reaction. Indeed as one famous anatomist put it many years ago, 'The main object of the synapse is not to assist transmission but to block it'. While most clinicians regard the main function of the cortex as reacting to external stimuli it may be that this is not the whole truth. It may be that what the alert wakeful cortex is also doing is playing the part of a complicated synapse—delaying the response until after a number of different sensory impressions have been processed. The intimate connection between consciousness, wakefulness, mood, and memory, however, suggests that before speculating any further on the physiological basis for the first of these states, it would be wiser to consider the others.

3
Disorders of Mood

Fluctuation of mood in relation to changes in both physiological and psychological conditions are completely normal. It is when mood does not reflect these
changes but remains fixed at either too high a pitch (mania) or too low
(depression) or fails to move at all (flattened) that it is said to be abnormal. For
instance, if the thought of winning the football pools does not make a person feel
elated or the thought of the loss of a near relative does not make him depressed,
something is wrong.

The measurement of mood is not easy. As mood constitutes essentially the
subjective colouring of behaviour rather than behaviour itself, it can only be
evaluated subjectively. Attempts to quantify these judgements by, for example,
asking subjects to rate their feelings or by saying whether certain statements
apply to them or not have been made, and are included in several well-known
scales, such as the MMPI, the Foulds symptom–sign inventory; and the
Hamilton rating scale (see Anastasi, 1970).

Disorders of mood are frequently accompanied by physiological and mental changes of a more objective and therefore quantifiable nature; and most
of what we know about the causes (and indeed about the nature of mood
itself) comes from a study of these and the methods of treatment which
seem to affect them.

There are many possible ways of classifying mood disorders. The most obvious
classification is according to the nature of the mood itself, and whether this is
elated (manic) or depressed. In a great many cases, swings occur from one to the
other (manic-depressive or bipolar disorders) but in others the abnormalities
always fluctuate in the same direction (unipolar).

The most common and distressing of the disorders is depression. Clinicians
usually differentiate between (1) those depressive states which seem to have their
origin in psychological events—the reactive depression; (2) those whose origin
cannot be related to psychological events and tend to be accompanied by
physiological disorders—endogenous depression; (3) those occurring in association with endocrine changes—the menopausal and involutional depressions;
and (4) those which may be traced to an initial psychological episode but persist
long after normal sadness or mourning should have stopped—precipitated
depression. In this chapter these distinctions will be overlooked, not because they
are considered unimportant but because there is no evidence that the depressive
mood is different in the different conditions. Disorders of mood and their
accompaniments will be considered under four sections:

3.1 THE PSYCHOLOGICAL ACCOMPANIMENTS OF MOOD DISORDER

A depressed person does not just feel sad—full stop! His sadness usually colours his reactions to all other events and particularly to the way in which he regards himself and his own deeds. He may feel that he is unworthy of the things he has and of the people around him. He has an overwhelming sense of guilt. He may feel that the whole world is in a mess and heading for destruction, and that he himself is responsible for all that has gone wrong in it. He may even feel that his body is contaminated. In the same way the manic person often projects his sense of well-being and happiness into all he does. He dresses in flamboyant clothes. He goes out and buys unnecessary objects—usually in duplicate or triplicate. He throws his money around feeling that he will never need it again, that a power greater than himself will look after him. He feels filled with unaccustomed strength, is convinced that he can carry out great deeds, that he has been chosen for rare honours, and that his intellectual powers are better than they ever were. It is a common finding, however, that a patient's intelligence and memorizing ability is in direct contrast to his subjective judgement when mood is disordered. The depressed patient although he feels himself to be incapable and may take time to think out a problem or to recall a past event, is still able to function at a higher intellectual level than the manic who usually functions at a very low level of efficiency.

On standard intelligence tests, depression thus tends to lower performance on all timed tests but does not affect those requiring logical thought. Mania, on the other hand, produces a more general 'organic' picture (see Chapter 2). If asked to judge how they themselves think they are doing, the depressed patient will underestimate his performance, while the manic will overestimate it.

3.2 PHYSIOLOGICAL ACCOMPANIMENTS OF MOOD DISORDER

Motor

One of the most striking and consistent accompaniments of a depressive state is psychomotor retardation—a slowing up of reaction time, a reluctance to act and a paucity of the actions made. Conversely, in the manic state reaction time is shortened and there is an abundance of (often irrelevant) motor behaviour. These alterations are particularly common in the sphere of spontaneous speech, and may even precede the onset of subjective and objective mood changes. Thus one patient who showed marked and regular mood swings was studied over a two-month period by Hutt and Coxon (1965). She showed quite consistent changes in both the speed of her spontaneous utterances and the length of sentence uttered, and the measured changes in these not only correlated closely with her mood but also preceded by a few days each mood swing.

Autonomic Activity

Inability to sleep, loss of appetite and a decrease in sex drive are frequent accompaniments of both heightened and lowered mood, although less often seen in the reactive than in the endogenous depressive states. It is a further characteristic of endogenous depression that the mood follows the diurnal rhythm, the patient frequently reporting that he feels worse in the morning and better towards evening.

3.3 FACTORS AFFECTING DISORDERS OF MOOD

Since the essence of a mood disorder is its failure to respond to environmental changes, or to psychological pressures, it is not surprising that attempts to alter it by manipulation of the environment or by psychological methods are usually ineffective. On the other hand, disorders of mood do often respond dramatically and gratifyingly to various forms of physiological treatment. The lifting of depression by those physiological measures which also induce epileptic seizures is probably the best known.

Convulsive therapy for the treatment of mental—and specifically mood—disorders was first introduced by von Meduna in 1933, following observation that schizophrenic patients often became accessible and tractable after induced seizures. The clinical agents used by von Meduna (1937) in the early days were replaced in 1937 by electric currents passed through two electrodes placed on the forehead, an innovation due to Cerletti and Bini. While relieving the schizophrenic symptoms to some extent, however, the effect of this treatment on depressive states is far more dramatic and electric convulsive treatment (ECT) is now used almost exclusively for this purpose.

The usual method of administering the treatment is described in most psychiatric textbooks. Briefly, alternating electric current of 70–120 V. is applied through temporal electrodes for 0.3–0.6 s, the aim being to produce a clinical seizure with minimum amount of electric current. Treatments are usually given two to three times a week for two to four weeks depending on symptoms. While this treatment is very effective in relieving endogenous and precipitated depression, one serious disadvantage is that it leaves the patient temporarily confused and amnesic.

Whether the amnesia is an essential part of the cure, or just an unwanted side-effect, has been much debated. Ottosson (1960) and Cronholm and Ottosson, (1963) in a careful study involving three different strengths of electric current, showed that while the memory impairment was related to the amount of current flowing through the brain tissue, the therapeutic effect on depression depended on the occurrence of an epileptic fit alone, which points to the latter conclusion. A search has thus been going on for agents which will induce epileptic seizures without affecting memory.

Chemical agents such as indoklon seem to produce even more post-ictal confusion and memory loss than electric stimulation, but variations in the placement of the electrodes in ECT can reduce it considerably. The comparison between the effects of shocks administered bilaterally with those administered to one side of the head only (unilateral ECT) has been investigated in a number of recent projects (see Fig. 11). Lancaster, Steinert, and Frost (1958) compared the effect of unilateral ECT applied to the non-dominant hemisphere in 28 patients with the conventional bilateral treatment in 15 patients, and found that whereas the unilateral treatment certainly cut down the incidence of confusion and amnesia, improvement of the depression was slightly greater and more complete in those who had received bilateral treatment. Later workers, however, did not substantiate this finding and believed that no significance in the therapeutic effectiveness of the two forms of treatment was seen.

Bilateral frontal placement of the electrodes has also been tried in a few cases, but although minimizing memory loss does not seem to be so epileptogenic or therapeutically effective (Abrams and Taylor, 1973).

Although most of the literature indicates that it is the occurrence of the convulsion as such which influences depression, there are still many who believe that the therapeutic effect of the ECT lies more in the attitude of the hospital and

Figure 11. Showing placement of electrodes in unilateral ECT

in the ritual surrounding it than its physiological effects. Watts (1976) relates an anecdote in which two years after a new machine had been installed in one hospital, it was found not to be working; yet the 'treatment' given by it seemed to all connected to have been effective. Watts further argues that, despite all evidence to the contrary (see Cronholm and Ottosson, 1963) the anaesthesia given routinely to patients before application of the electric current, may be the curative agent.

Other psychological theories to explain the effectiveness of ECT have been discussed by Miller (1967). He divides them into those deriving from psychoanalytic and those from learning theory. The psychoanalytic theories seek to explain the effect on regression (the subject in the post-convulsive stage being reduced to an infantile state of total dependency), fear (fear of the treatment itself taking over from and displacing all other emotions), and punishment (the subject feeling that by suffering in this way he is atoning for all his past sins). The learning theory explanations are based on neural consolidation and response competition. The latter are largely based on animal experiments and their implications to an understanding of memory is greater than that for depression, as will be discussed in Chapter 4.

Connections between the physiological effects of ECT and alterations of mood are still largely speculative; and whether one accepts them or not is a matter for personal choice. Convulsions—whether spontaneous or electrically induced—are known to be followed by a number of physiological alterations in brain metabolism (see p. 14), and most theories attribute mood alterations to alterations in the concentration of the brain monoamines.

The connection between the relief of depression by ECT and self-stimulation by means of implanted electrodes in the hypothalamus of rats (the so called 'pleasure centre') has never been systematically studied, but also leads to speculation. With electrodes placed in the posterior part of the hypothalamus (except for the mamillary bodies) electrical stimulation seems to act as a 'reward' in that in order to obtain it an animal will overcome considerable hardship (i.e. cross an electrified grid) and work hard. An animal allowed to stimulate itself will continue to do so at the rate of 4500 times an hour, showing no satiation with the passage of time. As the electrodes are moved forward into the anterior hypothalamus and tegmental hypothalamus, the rate of self-stimulation begins to decline. 'Rates rise again slightly in the preoptic region and posterior forebrain, but they are not as high as in the posterior hypothalamus, and they fall sharply to about 200 an hour as the electrodes are moved forward into cortical parts of the rhinencephalon' (Olds, 1958).

While these findings suggest a 'pleasure centre' in the posterior hypothalamus in rats, the extent to which self-stimulation is carried out depends on many factors, including the animal's internal environment. The changes of self-stimulation rate under conditions of hunger and endocrinological disorders are very complex and depend on both the strength of current and precise electrode placement.

This is not the place to try to summarize or evaluate the work being done on this subject, much of which is still ongoing (see Wauquier and Rolls, 1976); but in passing it might be pointed out that doubts are being raised about concluding that self-stimulation is necessarily carried out because of the pleasure engendered by it. It may, indeed, be merely due to the reinforcement of the act itself—the formation of a motor habit (Valenstein, 1976). This possibility will be discussed further in Chapter 4.

In humans, suffering from epilepsy, dyskinesia, and intractable pain, stimulation of areas around the medial forebrain bundle by implanted electrodes do sometimes seem to arouse pleasurable sensations—even occasionally states of euphoria (Delgado, 1976)—but the effects vary in different people, and even in the same people at different times. Moreover, when humans are allowed to stimulate themselves, they never do so at the high rates shown by rats unless consciousness is disturbed (Sem-Jacobsen, 1976). Cerebral stimulation via implanted electrodes for the relief of depression does not appear to have been attempted as yet.

Chemotherapy

Although this book cannot consider the part played in mental activity by biochemical factors, enough will have been said in the last few paragraphs to indicate the likelihood of pharmacological agents affecting the functions of the hypothalamus and so affecting mood. This is indeed the case. While ECT is a very effective (and possibly the only effective) agent in relieving depression in a number of patients, radical relief of symptoms can also be achieved in many by appropriate drugs.

The chemical formulae of the effective compounds and the part they play in the cycle of events occurring in the transmission of nervous impulses, are described in a number of textbooks.

3.4 CAUSES OF MOOD DISORDERS

The term depression has come to be used in common parlance to replace that of 'nervous breakdown' as a euphemism for any memory or mental disorder which makes a person incapable of working or looking after himself.

Clinical depression is a clearly defined and easily recognizable syndrome, though its basic cause is still largely unknown. The symptoms are almost certainly due, as has been stressed, to an imbalance of amines throughout the brain, this in turn being regulated by diencephalic and especially hypothalamic nuclei. The imbalance may be caused by psychological factors or physiological ones.

Psychological theories of aetiology have been classified by Becker (1974) into two groups: (1) those deriving from psychoanalytic theory; and (2) those deriving from cognitive and behavioural psychology. Psychoanalytic theories postulate the loss of a deeply loved object (this can be a person, an ideal, a skill, or a body-part) which cannot be compensated for by the normal mourning process.

Indeed, according to Freud, while for the mourner it is the outside world which is impoverished, for the depressive it is the ego. According to some of Freud's successors, in particular Melanie Klein, the loss is sensed in early infancy and carries with it a degree of self-blame or guilt. Hence, the normally outgoing aggressive impulses are turned inward, causing loss of self-esteem and later self-destructive tendencies.

In the congitive and behavioural theories, attention is focused more on the 'here and now'. Attempts to avoid anxiety due to cognitive dissonance (Festinger's name for the effect experienced when an event or stimulus simultaneously arouses two opposing desires: approach and avoidance) usually lead to the devaluation of a goal or a role. This leads to a sense of loss and incompetence which may develop further into immobility and inertia. Seligman's (1973) theory of 'learned helplessness' suggests another possible aetiology of a somewhat similar nature. Seligman noted that dogs faced with a painful situation from which there was no escape assumed an attitude of withdrawal, inertia, and indifference, which was liable to persist even after removal of the precipitating situation. The attitude of helplessness was only 'cured' by encouraging the animals to learn some adequate method of escape or avoidance. Seligman was impressed by similarities between the attitudes of such dogs and those of patients suffering from depression.

Physiological causes are usually looked for in biochemical factors. These may be precipitated by stress, dietary deficiency, or infection. Viruses which directly attack the diencephalon can trigger acute depressive episodes. On the other hand, head injuries causing direct mechanical injury to this area, more often result in euphoric mood changes.

Heredity appears to play an important part, if not in the actual aetiology of the particular illness, at least in determining an individual's susceptibility. Thus, although all people subject to continued psychological stress may develop metabolic disorders which become fixed and irreversible except through physiological means, those individuals with an apparently genetic predisposition are triggered more easily into such episodes.

Where the onset of abnormal mood can be traced to a definite cerebral insult, it does not always follow that the incident causes the mood disorder. On realization that he has lost some of his former intellectual faculties such as occurs with the onset of dementia, and after some head injuries, an individual is likely to become severely and understandably depressed, but when all judgement and self-criticism are lost in the later stages of dementia, a manic carefreeness may take over.

3.5 CONCLUSIONS

The difficulties inherent in the measurement of mood disorders does not reduce their importance. Indeed to the individual suffering from depression, the affective component of the illness is its overriding symptom. Difficulties of measurement do, however, somewhat reduce the 'scientific' attention paid to the symptom, and hence the number of 'respectable' studies which have been made of it. This is reflected in the shortness of this chapter as compared to others in this book.

Where objective scientific measurements are made, they usually concentrate on the physiological and behavioural changes accompanying mood disorders rather than on assessment of mood *per se*; and from the studies of these, it seems clear that mood is controlled primarily by nuclei within or close to the thalamus. The neural networks from these to the cerebral cortex, on whose functioning efficient mental activity depends, are maintained by a complex breaking-down and resynthesis of biochemical compounds; processes which also influence (and are influenced by) sleep, motor activity, memory, and many other aspects of behaviour.

4
Disorders of Memory

Defects of memory (amnesia) are a common symptom of cerebral disorder. As a transient phenomenon they occur in a wide variety of diseases, both those intrinsically cerebral and those of a more generalized nature affecting the brain directly. They are often but one part of a more widespread cerebral dysfunction such as in manifested in diffuse intellectual impairment, delirium, stupor or coma. Sometimes they are the predominant, and occasionally the only recognizable features of the dysfunction.

The range of memory defect is considerable. It may be partial loss of registration, appearing simply as exaggerated forgetfulness; a severe inability to recall or record all current events, with preservation of more distant memories; a limited but complete amnesia for a sharply defined period; repeated episodes of such amnesia with hazy and inaccurate recollection. (Whitty, 1966, p. 72).

Whitty, in the above paragraphs, summarizes succinctly the great range of problems confronting the psychologist in this sphere. In the past great emphasis was laid on distinguishing 'organic' from 'functional' memory impairment. Long and embittered wrangles ranged over such questions, one particularly famous case being that of 'B', summarized by Zangwill (1967), about whom papers filled the German literature and international congresses from 1926 (the year 'B' was first described by Grünthal and Störrung) to 1958. Zangwill points out at the end of his account that 'we appear to have reached the limits of usefulness of this particular dichotomy' and in 1977 Pratt confirms this, concluding a chapter on 'psychogenic loss of memory', in the following way: 'A sharp distinction between the various categories of psychogenic loss of memory . . . seems unwarranted. Their explanation must be sought in psychological terms; the organic element is limited to providing a fertile ground for their growth.' (Pratt, 1977, p. 232). Nevertheless, it is still important to recognize the components of memory which may reflect organic or psychogenic aspects of a disorder.

In order to impose some order on the data collected to date and to provide a framework for classification, psychologists have usually tried to concentrate on answering two questions:

1. What aspects of the memory function are affected by what organic conditions?
2. What areas of the brain are involved?

Classical psychology divides memory into three stages—registration, retention, and recall or recognition (renamed in the computer-age encoding, storage, and retrieval)—but where memory defects are present it is often difficult, if not impossible, to say in which of these stages the breakdown has occurred. Clinicians usually prefer to consider memory defects from a practical point of view as:

1. Retrograde amnesia—the difficulty of recalling events preceding the onset of the amnesic period.
2. Anterograde amnesia—the difficulty of learning new skills and of retaining events that occurred after the onset of the amnesic period.

4.1 RETROGRADE AMNESIA (RA)

RA in Chronic Amnesic States

In conjunction with anterograde amnesia, patients with organic memory disturbances very often have difficulty in recalling events which preceded the onset of the amnesic period—retrograde amnesia (RA). These events, which were well recorded at the time, tend to be forgotten in inverse relation to their recency and led Ribot to postulate his famous 'law of regression' (Ribot, 1885).

For example, Milner's case H.M. who will be described in detail later. 'Did not remember the death of his favourite uncle three years before, nor anything of the period spent in hospital before the operation, but did recall a few trivial incidents that had taken place just before his admission to hospital. His early memories were seemingly vivid and intact.' (Milner, 1966, p. 113). A patient described by Talland

> was oblivious of everything since the time he had run a farm, long before his admission to the hospital at the age of 78. One woman in her seventies remembered in considerable detail the circumstances of her life in the parental and the family business, but apparently knew nothing about the several decades that had elapsed since, although they included her marriage and the death of her husband. So little did she take cognizance of the passage of years, of the wizened old woman bent in body she had become that, once asked what she would like to do if and when she left the hospital, she answered 'Go out to dances on Saturday nights'.
>
> Another woman in her seventies had no apparent recollection at all of the last three decades of her life, and remembered only a few landmarks of her youth. She believed her hospitalization followed an automobile accident in which her husband had been killed. He, in fact, had died only a couple of years prior to the interview, in ripe old age and many years after the patient's admission to hospital. Their oldest child, who the patient thought of as aged 24, was in her fifties. (Talland, 1965, p. 35).

In these patients, the loss not only covers recall of events and incidents, but may include generic images. Thus Zangwill (1950) describes a patient who, when asked to draw a public transport vehicle and a lady in modern clothes, produced illustrations of both dating from some 15 years before the onset of his illness.

How well Ribot's law of regression really holds up has, however, been questioned. Warrington and Sanders (1971), and Sanders and Warrington (1971 and, 1975) studied the memory of non-brain-damaged people between the ages of 16 and 80 years, and that of patients with organic amnesic syndromes. They used two different methods: (1) the recollection of finite events of major significance; and (2) the recognition of 'well-known faces'. In neither sphere did they find evidence for the sparing of remote memories in organic amnesia. Two more recent studies have, however, shown the opposite. Seltzer and Benson (1974) tested their subjects memory by questionnaires; Marslen-Wilson and Teuber (1975) tested theirs by their ability (with and without prompts) to put names to photographs of prominent people. Both these groups found that subjects with long-standing brain damage causing amnesia did better on the remote than on the recent items. The different findings may have been due to the slightly different techniques used, and also to fluctuations which may occur in the day-to-day behaviour of very amnesic patients.

RA After Concussional Head Injuries

RA not only follows chronic and irreversible conditions such as those mentioned above, but a gap for past events may remain in patients who have suffered from head injuries long after recovery of all other mental functions. Broadly speaking, it has been found that the extent of the amnesia varies considerably at different stages of the illness, and may be very much greater at the height of the illness than after full recovery. This 'shrinkage' of amnesia in the course of recovery has been described by many authors (Symonds, 1937; Russell, 1959; Williams and Zangwill, 1952). It is often believed (e.g. Russell, 1959) to occur in order of relative time sequence—i.e. the more remote events in memory being restored first—again following Ribot's principle, but exceptions to this are extremely common. Williams and Zangwill (1952) carried out a careful study of 32 cases of head injury. The patients were observed from an early stage after admission until the time of discharge from hospital. Follow-up studies after discharge were carried out wherever possible. Three grades of severity of head injury were arbitrarily defined on the basis of duration of the post-traumatic confusional state, and hence of the duration of the post-traumatic amnesia (PTA) as assessed after full recovery. In group 1 (nine patients), duration of PTA was under one hour; in group 2 (nine patients) it was one to 24 hours; and in group 3 (14 patients) over 24 hours.

In group 1 the patients 'last memory' after recovery of normal consciousness referred to an event which had preceded the moment of injury by under ten seconds (five cases) or by ten to 30 minutes (four cases). In the former cases there was always some haziness or amnesia for earlier events which cleared up rapidly over the next few hours or days. The order of recovery of memories, however, was not always in inverse ratio to their recency. In the latter cases there was progressive recovery of memory for events which had occurred both before and after that represented by the patient's 'last memory'. Again, no very clear direction of shrinkage could be ascertained.

In group 2, the pattern of recovery of pre-traumatic memory as a rule followed that displayed by the four cases in group 1 who had presented island of recent memory. In group 3, the study of recovery of memory was found to be complicated by defects in associated mental fields, especially by confusion, impaired conceptual grasp, memory defect for current events, disorientation, and confabulation. It is seen from these cases, however, that recovery from amnesia is shown not merely in the ability to recall more and more recent events with increasing ease or clarity; it involves above all the recall of events in orderly sequence, and the rebuilding of a coherent background of past experience. Although there is some tendency for the most recent events to be most often forgotten and to be restored latest, there are many exceptions to this principle. Availability of an event in memory is not wholly a function of its recency, and memory defects can be shown in ways other than in availability to voluntary recall. Russell (1959) has drawn attention to the fact that 'visions' for isolated events falling within the RA can occasionally be found during the early post-traumatic stages when the patient is still confused and amnesic, but not be recalled, after full recovery. This suggests that some forgetting due to time lapse may occur during the time the patient is in his PTA, and that as well as shrinkage, RA may show some extension due to lack of rehearsal—a point which will be taken up again in the discussion at the end of this section.

Some studies of the residual *retrograde memory defects* seen after recovery from head injury, when retrograde amnesia has attained its final brief and static duration have also been reported (Russell, 1959; Williams and Zangwill, 1952).

Williams and Zangwill's main findings were:

1. Some degree of residual memory memory defect (outside the short RA) for quite recent events preceding the head injury, is found in a majority of cases submitted to careful psychological interrogation. This defect may take the form of an actual memory gap, of hazy and ill-defined recollection, or of errors in temporal references. The phenomena observed are very reminiscent of those found in the recall of relatively remote events in normal individuals.
2. The more severe the head injury, the more likely were residual memory defects to occur.
3. The defects were apparently irreversible in the group of 24 cases studied.

In the light of these findings, it may be surmised that the process of shrinkage analysed in the earlier paragraphs is often less complete than is frequently supposed. Further, it may be suggested that the length of memory gap preceding the impact (RA in the conventional sense) is not necessarily a guide to the completeness of restoration of recent memory.

An important point to note is that RA is rarely, if ever, seen without some degree of amnesia for events following the trauma—post-traumatic amnesia or PTA (see Table 1). This is to say that unless the stream of consciousness is interrupted for at least some minutes, no preceding memory gap remains.

Table 1

Duration of PTA and RA compared in 1029 cases of 'accidental' head injury (gunshot wounds excluded). From W. Ritchie Russell, *Brain, Memory and Learning*, 1959, Oxford, Clarendon Press, reproduced by permission of the publishers

Duration of RA	Nil	1 hr	Duration of PTA				Total
			1–24 hrs	1–7 days	7 days	No record	
Nil	99	23	9	2	0	0	133
Under 30 minutes	—	178	274	174	80	1	707
Over 30 minutes	—	3	16	41	73	0	133
No record	—	4	14	14	15	9	56
Total	99	208	313	231	168	10	1029

RA After Tuberculous Meningitis

Much the same picture may be seen in patients after tuberculous meningitis (TBM) as in those after head injuries. As in the head injury cases it is found in many patients after TBM that apparently permanent retrograde memory defects are in evidence after otherwise complete recovery. These memory defects may extend over very long time intervals preceding the onset of the illness. As in the case of head injuries they are also far from complete losses of memory. An example can be quoted (Williams and Smith, 1954) as follows:

A soldier (reported by Cairns and Taylor in 1949) developed meningitis in March 1947 and streptomycin treatment was given for eight months, during most of which time the patient was confused and amnesic. In August 1947 when he became mentally clear, he had an almost complete amnesia for the two years preceding his illness. When interviewed two and a half years later, in December 1950, the patient was healthy and had been regularly employed at work as a clerk for about two years. His retrograde amnesia, however, showed little change from its condition on discharge from hospital. He said 'When I try to think back I am hazy about the whole time in Germany (two years). I couldn't chronicle events with any clarity, although some stand out. For example, I remember one instant when I fiddled a job to be appointed an officer's driver and we nearly had an accident. It would have been about Spring 1946, but I can't say what happened before or after it'. Shortly after the above episode the patient had been posted to a regiment in the Ruhr where he took a clerk's course. He learnt typewriting and apparently became very efficient; but he found that on recovery from his illness he had forgotten how to typewrite. All that he could recall of the course was a large plaque on the wall, the first letter of which were QWERT. Recently he had been shown a photograph of the men on the course. He found that he could name them all without difficulty, although he would have had no idea when or how he met them (Williams and Smith, 1954).

RA After Electro-Convulsive Therapy (ECT)

The RA caused by ECT allows for a more methodical examination of the defects than is possible in most clinical material, and this opportunity has been exploited by psychologists, in both animals and men.

The restitution of memory for past events after each individual treatment is gradual and parallels that for retention. Patients almost invariably regain personal orientation (knowledge of name, occupation, and home address) before that for place or time, the latter being the last to be restored in most instances (Lancaster, Steinart, and Frost, 1958; d'Elia, 1974). It is usually considered that those habits most firmly established and most often practised are the first to be regained. This principle applies even to the restitution of vocabulary. Rochford and Williams (1962) asked twelve patients to name a series of simple common objects, the names of which were acquired at different ages by children, and were found to present different degrees of difficulty to patients with organic dysphasia. The names themselves represented different degrees of frequency of usage in the language as a whole. It was found that a very close parallel existed between 'difficulty' or rarity of word, and time elapsing between treatment and recall of it by the ECT patients. Whereas a comb (a frequently used word learned by children at the age of four years) could be named by 90% of the patients within two minutes of being able to give their own names, the teeth of the comb (rarely used and not learned by children till the age of eleven years) could not be named, on the average, till twelve minutes later. Although this suggests a regression in terms of age, the authors suggest that age of acquisition and restitution of mental activity may both be related to, and dependent on, frequency of usage.

Although most patients usually deny any recollection of visual stimuli presented to them within a few seconds before the onset of the seizure, it has been noted that such stimuli can frequently be picked out on a choice recognition test (Mayer-Gross, 1943) or can be recalled with prompting (Williams, 1950). Even so, most patients still fail to remember where and when they had seen the material, and the sequential nature of picture-sets or numbers tends to be missed.

Material learned by repetition is affected in the same way as isolated stimuli. Zubin and Barrera (1941), using paired associates composed of common household commodities with different brand names, found that if two sets of word pairs were learned by subjects at twelve hour intervals and memory was tested some two hours after the second session, subjects remembered more of the second than of the first list. In a group of subjects given ECT immediately after the second learning task, no such differences were noted.

The degree to which an event or stimulus tends to be forgotten depends not only on the time of its occurrence, but also on (1) its nature, and (2) the efforts made to assimilate or 'encode' it (Dornbush and Williams, 1974). Familiar, easily retained word pairs are recalled more easily than unfamiliar ones (see Fig. 12, Williams, 1973), while pictures which a patient is expressly asked to remember are recalled more readily than those he is just asked to look at casually (Stones, 1970).

The effect of ECT on behavioural responses set up before it seems to be

˙somewhat equivocal, but in general verbal responses elicited by visual stimuli immediately before ECT are elicited again more easily afterwards, in spite of the fact that the original stimuli have been forgotten.

As well as amnesia for test stimuli, many patients complain of forgetfulness for remote personal events. 'Gaps' of memory, particularly for a period of disturbed mental activity, may remain permanently (Ebtinger, 1958). Names of persons and places and habits of work are also vulnerable (Brody, 1944).

Squire and his associates tested patients on multiple choice questionnaires for public events and TV programmes occurring one to three decades before ECT. Their scores 40 minutes and 24 hours after the first and fifth bilateral treatments compared with their pre-treatment scores, showed a significant drop, this being greatest for the most recent events and greater after the fifth than after the first treatment (Squire, 1975). The drop persisted for one to three weeks after completion of the treatment, and concerned especially the temporal sequencing of events (Squire, Chace, and Slater, 1976). Right unilateral ECT caused no such impairment (Squire, 1977). These memory losses resemble closely those following concussional head injuries (Williams and Zangwill, 1952), and fall outside the scope of RA as conventionally assessed.

In the restitution of personal memories following ECT, as in those after head injuries, there is nearly always a considerable 'shrinkage' with the passage of time. On first regaining orientation, patients may be unable to remember a large part of their past lives, but the gaps gradually close as normal mental functions

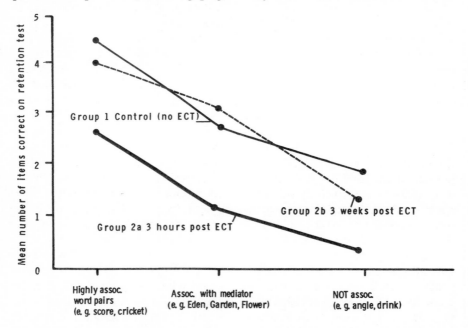

Figure 12. The mean number of correct easy and difficult word pairs recalled by control subjects and patients receiving ECT

are restored. The pattern of shrinkage is not always strictly from past to present (Ebtinger, 1958), and consists rather of a filling in between islands, as in the case after head injuries (Zangwill, 1964). Time may, however, be important in the recovery of the most recent pre-treatment memories. Cronholm and Lagergren (1959) found that stimuli shown to subjects 60 seconds before treatment were recovered before those shown 15 seconds before it, and the latter, before those presented only five seconds prior to the shock. Kehlet and Lunn (1951), however, found no such shrinkage. Their subjects were shown three series of pictures 16 hours, half an hour, and a few seconds before the shock. Examination half an hour and two hours after the shock showed no improvement in memory at the two retest sessions.

Although RA in animals cannot be studied in the same detail as in humans—i.e. the difference between subjective and objective memory disturbances cannot be ascertained—work with animals allows for greater control of the variables than is possible with man. The effect of electro–convulsive shock (ECS) on behaviour established prior to it has been studied in a number of experiments (see Weiskrantz, 1966). The procedure is usually to follow a single unique experience, such as stepping down off a raised platform, with an unpleasant experience such as electric shock to the feet. Rats learn avoidance, (not to step down) after a single such experience. If this foot shock is followed immediately by a convulsive shock (often administered through electrodes applied to the ears) they learn to avoid stepping down very slowly with repeated trials, but they do definitely learn, even when the interval between the response and ECS is very brief. The apparent amnesia for the foot shock is affected by: (1) the time elapsing between ECS and the retest; and (2) the number of times the animals are replaced in the original setting (equivalent perhaps to the number of cues provided for recall in the human situation) (Zinkin and Miller, 1967).

4.2 ANTEROGRADE AMNESIA

The Organic Amnesic Syndrome

Although the first clinical descriptions of this condition are usually attributed to Korsakov in 1889, Talland (1965) and Zangwill (1966) in their excellent historical reviews both note that even earlier writers had remarked on the existence of these clinical states. The condition described by Korsakov and which now bears his name includes among its symptoms, disorientation and confabulation as well as inability to retain information, but it is only the latter which will be considered in this section. The condition presented by such patients is described and analysed in detail by Talland (1965) in a group of chronic alcoholics, by Milner (1966) in a patient with bilateral mesial temporal lobe resection, by Williams and Pennybacker (1954) in a series of patients with tumours involving the third ventricle and by Williams and Smith (1954) in patients with tuberculous meningitis. Anterograde amnesia is also well known as a transitory state following concussional head injuries, as well as after ECT administered therapeutically for the relief of depression.

The condition is well illustrated in Milner's description of one patient (H.M.) who had undergone temporal lobe resection for the relief of epilepsy:

> He could no longer recognize the hospital staff, apart from Dr Scoville himself, whom he had known for many years; he did not remember and could not relearn the way to the bathroom, and he seemed to retain nothing of the day to day happenings in the hospital . . . Numerous illustrations of the severity of the amnesia could be given. Thus, ten months after the operation the family moved to a new house which was situated only a few blocks away from their old one, on the same street. When examined by Scoville and Milner nearly a year later, H.M. had not yet learned the new address, nor could he be trusted to find his way home alone, because he would go to the old house. Although he mows the lawn regularly, and quite expertly, his mother still has to tell him where to find the lawn-mower, even when he has been using it only the day before. The same forgetfulness applies to people he has met since the operation, even to those neighbours who have been visiting the house regularly for the past six years. He has not learnt their names and he does not recognize any of them if he meets them in the street. (Milner, 1966, p. 113).

Apart from the troubles mentioned above, H.M. showed no significant personality change

> remaining rather placid, but having occasional outbursts of mild irritability. Nor is there any evidence of general intellectual loss; in fact, his intelligence as measured by standard tests is actually a little higher now than before the operation (the Wechsler IQ of 117 obtained in 1962 comparing favourably with that of 104 reported in 1953), a paradoxical finding which may be due to the marked diminution in the number and severity of his seizures. (p. 113).

Talland subjected a group of 16 patients who showed chronic Korsakov states to a carefully controlled series of tests concerning reasoning ability, perception, learning and recall. On tests of intellectual and perceptual ability, and on tests of immediate recall, these patients did not show any marked deficit. It was only when the tests involved the serialization of data that defects were evident. In summarizing their performance, Talland states

> The patients are able to form new associations, but, once established, these dissolve very rapidly. Practice by repeated exposure or repetition does not advance their learning, and neither does the correction of errors. Multiple associations with the same response creates special difficulties; spatial cues can be helpful. While some verbal associations may last for an hour or even longer, conditioned responses extinguish almost instantly.

Interference as a cause of forgetting is more evident in the form of new task orientation than as new acquisition of which little enough is achieved. If Korsakov patients learn but little when instructed to, their incidental learning is scarcer still. Neither old nor recent learning seems to transfer in their formal tests of learning, although they can apply old skills to novel situations and tasks, especially if these involve simple routine operations. (p. 232).

The learning defect noted in such patients, nevertheless varies to some extent with the nature of the task. Talland's patients were able to acquire manipulative skills to a limited extent even though quite unable to learn the solution to spatial puzzles or to acquire verbal passages. In the latter, forgetting seemed to involve

Sheer loss of information, not just a distortion of the content. They learn or retain emotionally loaded reports no better than neutral accounts.

The patients' poor retention of connected verbal material cannot be explained by their inability to grasp its content. They tend to reproduce the story in its barest outline, retaining its gist rather than odd phrases, although the first few items are better remembered than the remainder. Of narratives crammed with incidents, they remember only a few snatches, not enough to convey the principal theme; but if this is reasonably prominent, descriptive details do not interfere with its recall, and are virtually ignored. (p. 256).

Amnesic states similar to the ones described above may be seen following concussional head injuries, in some infective disorders (tuberculous meningitis), in association with certain intracranial tumours, and following ECT. This last condition allows for more experimental study and will be considered in some detail.

AA Following ECT

For some time after the fit and before full orientation is established, patients pass through a confusional period very similar to that following concussion (see Chapter 2). At this time they tend to be disoriented and to forget sensory impressions as soon as the stimulation is withdrawn. The extent, duration and severity of the post ECT amnesic symptoms are found to vary with different individuals and to depend on a number of factors such as the time after treatment at which memory is assessed, how it is assessed (i.e. by recognition or recall) and the nature of the stimuli the subject is asked to remember. However, in the post ECT amnesic state, as in other organic amnesic states, the after effect of experience may often be seen in some form even though this may be difficult to categorize as 'memory'.

In two series of experiments conducted on subjects in the post ECT confusional period, Williams (1950) showed subjects a number of visual stimuli (pictures) and recorded their responses to them. It was found that:

44

1. The appropriate name for a picture could be elicited at its second appearance with less intensive stimulation than at its first appearance.
2. On the first occasion the appropriate name was often preceded by inappropriate verbal responses ('approximations') and these were also elicited by less stimulation the second time than the first—i.e. the whole sequence of behaviour leading up to correct naming was repeated but was triggered more easily a second time than a first.
3. Priming of a behavioural response (naming) by eliciting it in one context—e.g. by one picture—resulted in it being given more often and more quickly on later occasions and in response to other stimuli. This is in contrast to the behaviour of normal people, who, if they give a certain verbal response to one stimulus are less likely to give it to a second dissimilar one ('that's not as good a tree as the other was') (see Fig. 13).

These points seem to suggest that in the amnesic state, behavioural responses can be facilitated by prior arousal, but that they are not associated with the type of sensory image which constitutes the full aspects of a memory. Moreover, the

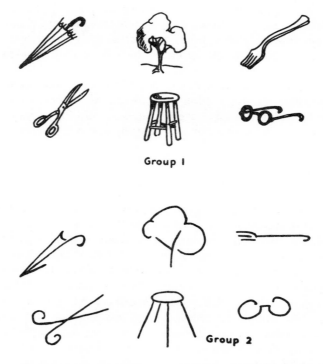

Figure 13. The material used by Williams (1950) to demonstrate the persistence of verbal response patterns after ECT. Reproduced by permission of the British Medical Association

emotions aroused by a stimulus may persist and become associated with other stimuli whilst the original stimulus is forgotten. Thus, Williams (1952) reports the case of a patient who was shown a series of pictures while in the confusional state after ECT, the first of which appeared to reawaken a forgotten traumatic incident from her youth. This picture was followed shortly afterwards by one of an innocuous chip basket. The following day the patient had no recollection of the traumatically-laden picture and indeed failed to recognize it. She was, however, deeply disturbed that day, attributing her depression to 'wondering why you had shown me the picture of the basket'.

Similar 'rationalizations' on the part of amnesic patients to account for emotional states due to forgotten experiences were demonstrated by Claparède (see McCurdy, 1928). A severely amnesic patient would always, on entering the presence of the professor, shake his hand and say how delighted he was to make his acquaintance. One day Claparède hid a pin in his hand which gave the patient a sharp jab as he clasped it. The next time the patient was ushered to the doctor's presence, he started forward with his hand outstretched in the usual manner, but then withdrew his hand and sat down. Asked by Claparède why he had done so, the patient replied that he suddenly had a stupid feeling that the professor might have a pin in his hand!

In the case of memory disorders following ECT, much attention has been paid to variations associated with the placement of the electrodes. After unilateral non-dominant ECT (UND see Chapter 2, and Fig. 12) word finding is not affected (Pratt and Warrington, 1972) and the early confusional state passes off quickly (Halliday et al., 1968; d'Elia, 1974). D'Elia in 1970 described a well-controlled trial in which he found that although the average number of treatments needed for the relief of depressive symptoms was slightly higher in the UND than in the BiECT group the ultimate therapeutic effect of both forms of treatment was the same. Both RA (assessed by the recall of personal data and word pairs) and AA (measured by ability to recall personal experiences, world news, and word pairs) were significantly less in the UND than the BiECT group. In a subsequent study comparing unilateral dominant (UD) with UND and BiECT, d'Elia (1974) found memory less disturbed even in UD than BiECT, although the difference did not reach significance in the verbal test (the learning of 30 word pairs). A similar difference was reported by Dornbush et al. in 1971. In considering the possible reasons for these differences much attention has been paid to the part played by verbalization in retention and retrieval. Although the ability to name objects from pictures or verbal descriptions of them tends to return sooner after right-sided UND than after BiECT in right-handed subjects (Pratt and Warrington, 1972) there is a good deal of variation (Pratt et al., 1971). Clyma (1975) found that using this task to determine dominance, 12% of a group of right-handed subjects referred for ECT showed a right hemisphere dominance. A point of interest was that this group consisted predominantly of subjects with personality disorders who did now show great relief from their depressive symptoms after the treatment, which raises speculations about the connections between mental illness and cerebral dominance as well as about the effect of ECT itself. Further discussion of the part played by the two hemispheres will be left till Chapter 9.

4.3 DIFFERENCES BETWEEN AMNESIA AND NORMAL FORGETTING

Retrograde Amnesia

The extent to which amnesia is similar to or different from normal forgetting is a question much debated by psychologists. The matter is particularly difficult to define in the case of RA, since adequate 'tests' for the assessment of recall of past personal experiences are very difficult to devise. The present author undertook one investigation into the matter which may be described briefly.

Twelve patients who had not been subjected to head injury or any other cerebral insult, were asked to describe a number of events in their past lives. Six of the patients had been admitted to hospital for illnesses of sudden onset (perforated ulcers, fractures, etc.), and six had been admitted for illnesses of gradual onset. Half of the patients in each group were interviewed the day after admission to be comparable with head injury patients suffering short RA and PTA, the other half were interviewed two to three weeks after admission to be comparable with the more severe head injury patients.
Each subject was asked to describe:

1. How he had spent the previous 24 hours.
2. How he had spent the last two hours before admission to hospital.
3. How he had spent some important day in his remote past, e.g. his wedding day.

It was noted that there was a big difference between the subjects' accounts of recent and remote events and of those preceding sudden trauma, and those preceding illness of gradual onset. Those preceding sudden trauma were recounted as sequences of isolated acts in which equal weighting was given to all events. For example, one patient in this group, describing the morning before an accident, said, 'At 8.30 the alarm went and I made a cup of tea. The post arrived at 8.54. Then I let the dog out . . .'. The events of his remote past were organized into meaningful and coherent schemes in which individual happenings could only be 'supposed' or 'guessed at' in recall. 'I know I *must* have had breakfast on the day I got married.' said one patient, 'but I can't really remember eating it'. Another, when asked to describe how he spent the evening before war was declared, said, 'I know what I must have been doing, but I can't really remember that particular evening as being different from any other'.

It is concluded that unless a comparatively routine and unimportant event is followed by some catastrophe, it normally becomes schematized and confused with other past memories. This conclusion is supported by the report of one patient who had broken his leg falling off a motor cycle, and was able to describe in detail the antecedent events: 'I always mend my own punctures, and had just mended one that day. I suppose I must have bungled it as going round a sharp corner the tyre burst—and that was it'. Asked when he had mended the puncture previous to this and what had happened subsequently, he looked quite offended and remarked, 'How could I possibly remember that, nothing happened to fix it'.

From these observations, it seems that it is not so much the short RA following concussion which needs explaining as the exceptionally vivid recollection of unimportant events when these are followed by important ones—a recollection which, in the words of a world-famous racing driver who recovered from severe burns, seemed to 'spread out in slow motion in front of me' every time he thought about them. Whether this is due to rehearsal—either intentional due to the necessity for explanation, or forced and unintentional—or whether it is due to fixation by the simultaneous arousal of an intense emotional reaction, is a question which will be considered in a later section of this chapter.

Anterograde Amnesia

In the case of anterograde amnesia, a comparison between normal and abnormal forgetting might seem to be easier. Many tests are available for the measurement of memory (see Williams, 1978) and it would seem a simple matter to apply these to amnesic patients and compare their performance with the norms. However, the matter is not really quite as simple as it sounds. In the first place, what aspect of memory is one going to measure?

Table 2
Aspects of memory requiring assessment in clinical practice

Aspect of memory	Means of measurement
Established skills	Tests of perception, naming, and manipulation of common objects (e.g. striking a match, tying a bow).
Memory span	The number of unrelated items (digits, words, tones, designs) that can be produced immediately after a single exposure.
Retention	The difference between the immediate and delayed (usually 5–10 min) reproduction of some task (story, address, visual design).
Learning (verbal)	The number of trials taken to give a perfect reproduction of a sentence, or word list.
Learning (motor)	The number of trials taken to make an error-free performance of a passage through a maze, etc.
Learning (associative)	The number of trials taken to learn associated word pairs.

The after effects of experiences (memory) are involved to some extent in just about every form of behaviour, but for the sake of simplicity, and to form a conceptual framework within which to study our problem it is customary among clinicians to divide memory into different sections (see Table 2) according to the aspect being assessed. Each of these sections has to be assessed independently but whatever aspect of memory one is assessing, the results obtained will be influenced by the following factors.

48

Events between Presentation of Stimulus and Test

Not only the length of time lapse, but also its content, are important. That preceding and subsequent events have an effect on the recall of target items (pro and retro active inhibition), the degree of interference being relative to the similarity between them, was demonstrated in some of the earliest psychological experiments ever conducted, and this effect is enormously exaggerated in organic amnesic states. A period of mental rest—especially sleep—after learning is said to assist consolidation, but dreaming may influence it adversely (Stones, 1974; Ekstrand, 1972; Idzikowski, 1977).

The effect of time alone is not clear cut. It is not disputed that recency plays a major role but exactly what the role is and how it works is unclear. By and large recent events are recalled more easily than remote ones, but if two sets of similar items (words or numbers) are learnt one after the other, reconstruction of the second list often involves intrusions from the first. Moreover, after the lapse of a certain time interval (i.e. the middle distance) remote events are often remembered better than recent ones.

The division of memory into two systems—one for short term and one for long term memory—was popular at one period, and gained great support from the amnesic studies which show that patients in these states are often able to recall strings of items immediately after a single hearing even when quite unable to recall any of them after a short time lapse. However, the common finding that in such patients patterns of behaviour may be reproduced, even if they lack the sense of familiarity; and that recall can often be instigated by partial reconstruction of the original stimulus (Williams, 1953; Warrington and Weiskrantz, 1971, (see Fig. 14) goes against this simple dichotomy.

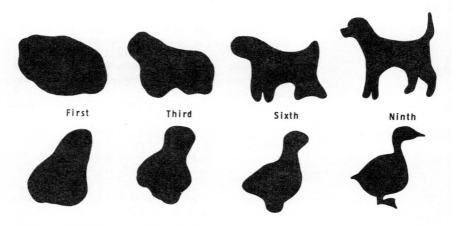

First   Third   Sixth   Ninth

Figure 14. Samples of the material used by Williams (1953) to demonstrate the effect of prompting on recall by amnesic patients. The ninth picture was the one originally shown to patients, but although they were often unable to recall it when originally asked, they often did so after being shown earlier item in the series

Context of Stimulus and Test

Even though a person may not consciously assimilate its context with a stimulus, it has been found that the presence or absence of original context at the time of recall influences performance (Godden and Baddeley, 1975). How far this extends is again unclear. It is obvious that if the context is closely associated with the stimulus—e.g. the background to the figure in a picture or, in the case of a word, a list of items from the same category—the two may be assimilated as a single unit; but the effect of context can extend to cover both place and time. Thus, items learned in one environment (e.g. under water or in one room of a building) are recalled better in that same environment than in another. Items learnt in one period of the day (early morning or late evening) are recalled better at that period 24 hours later than at a different stage of the diurnal rhythm twelve hours later.

Sensory Modality of the Stimulus

Most of the experimental work on memory in the clinical field has been confined to verbal and pictorial material, presented either visually or auditarily. Some experiments have been reported on haptic (touch) senses by O'Connor and Hermalin (1963), and on olfactory sensation (Butters *et al.*, 1973) but the data available is small in comparison. Moreover, the techniques for testing in these modalities have not been clearly standardized to date.

In the majority of experiments on normal subjects visually presented material is better recalled and recognized than that presented verbally (Paivio and Csapo, 1973) despite the concreteness or abstraction of its content. Easily 'imaged' words or stories are also better recalled than those which are not readily imaged.

Familiarity or Frequency of Stimulus

Whereas strings of items are best retained if the items themselves are familiar, easily named, and readily assimilated, a single rare or odd item will be better retained than the familiar one if it appears in a familiar surrounding (von Restorff effect). Thus the frequency with which an event has been experienced is, like recency, a variable which can work both for and against retrieval, depending on other variables in the total situation.

Method of Assessment

The methods used in the assessment procedure will have an important bearing on the scores obtained.

Three basic methods are available: recall, recognition, and reproduction. In recall, the subject is merely asked, after a specific time interval, what it was that he was asked to remember. In the case of reproduction, he is asked to reproduce it (i.e. repeat the sentence, tell the story, or draw the design) and in recognition he is either presented with the original item (target) alongside one or more other items and asked which he had been shown before (choice recognition), or shown the target and choices individually and asked to say for each one whether it was the target or not (yes–no recognition).

In scoring recall and reproduction, both accuracy, certainty and response latency have to be taken into consideration. In recognition, the number and similarity of alternatives offered (if the task is one of choice) are important variables.

Another method of assessment not in general use but which will be described in detail later is based on 'cued recall', where the score depends on the number of cues required to elicit the production of the item to be remembered.

Individual Variations among Subjects

That the attention and motivation of the person remembering are closely involved in the way he retains material will be obvious. Not quite so obvious is the fact that his manner of retention varies with chronological age. The three main spheres of learning—perceptual, motor, and linguistic—develop at different rates and reach their optima at different ages, as can be illustrated diagrammatically in Fig. 15. Hence tasks involving memory for location and those involving the learning of word pairs present different problems at different ages.

Not only is the nature (and sensory modality) of the task itself important however, the manner and situation in which it is given have different effects at different ages. With increase in age, there is a steady increase in 'selectivity', and the tendency to remember best those events or stimuli which fit in to existing conceptual schemata, ignoring others. Distracting, irrelevant, or 'incidental' details are omitted in recall in the adult as the 'drive towards organization'

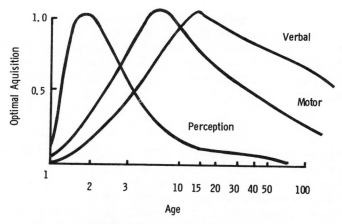

Figure 15. Different rates of learning in different
modalities in different age groups

increases. (In very old age, there may be a tendency to revert to more child-like tendencies, as will be mentioned in Chapter 10). An important factor in this process is the involvement of 'verbal mediators'.

Another important cause of individual variation is the intellectual capacity of the subject (IQ) which may determine strategies and the background against which new material is assimilated. IQ also enables retrieval methods to be developed and storage systems to be designed which may be involved in memory, although a direct connection between memory and intelligence is not always present. Luria (1969) described one subject who had an apparently limitless capacity to retain observations, which he made use of as a professional entertainer, but who showed no other outstanding intellectual skills.

No battery of tests is available in which all aspects of memory can be controlled for all variables. Even if there were, its administration would be too long and tiring for it to be applied to a sick or elderly person. Most of our knowledge about the nature of the memory disturbances in anterograde amnesia comes from experimental investigations designed to test specific hypotheses, which have been carried out on small groups of carefully selected patients and matched controls. The work has been carried out in three main centres; Boston, USA (by Cermak, Butters, and their associates), in London (by Warrington, Wyke, and their associates), and in Cambridge (by Baddeley, Piercy, Williams, and their associates). Some of the evidence has been conflicting and there is still clearly much to be learned, but the following points seem to be generally agreed on. (see Table 3).

Pattern of Breakdown. Compared to matched controls (i.e. non-amnesic people of the same age, IQ, and cultural background) patients with organic amnesia and no other defects such as dysphasia or dementia show no loss of established skills (perceptual, motor, or verbal), nor any impairment of immediate memory span. On learning tasks, there are considerable differences though these vary according

Table 3
Differences between amnesia and normal forgetting

Pattern of *breakdown*	Established skills—retained
	Memory span—retained
	Motor learning—some loss
	Verbal learning—great loss
	Associative learning—great loss
	Retention—great loss, especially of the sense of familiarity
Quality of *performance*	Fractionation
	Lack of associative spread
	Loss of localization
	Loss of sense of familiarity
Use of *strategies*	Poor use of semantic encoding
	Poor search of memory store at the time of recall

to the task given. Learning can occur in three spheres; perception, motor, and association. Perceptual learning, which is most active in the young child, shows little deterioration in amnesia. In the case of motor learning, manual skills may be acquired almost as quickly by the amnesic as the controls. The learning of routes through mazes presents rather greater problems, and there is a tendency in the amnesic to repeat errors (perseveration) instead of correcting them. Learning can be acquired, however, if the task is simplified by presenting it in small units or chunks. It is mainly in the learning of associations that the amnesic shows the greatest difference from the controls. While easy associations may be acquired without much difficulty, hard or distant ones present great problems.

It is also characteristic of the amnesic that even though his behaviour may indicate that he has learned, he will have little recollection of the learning sessions. Indeed, the greatest and most striking impairment in the amnesic lies in his inability to recall or recognize events after a short lapse of time; and it is in the spheres of recall and recognition that there are not only quantitative but also qualitative differences.

Quality of Performance. Normal forgetting involves some loss of detail, a certain confusion between items, resistance to recall, displacements, condensations, and 'closure' in the Gestalt sense. All of these are seen in an exaggerated form in the amnesic, but in the latter the memories actually evoked have characteristics which differ from normal. These can be summarized as follows.

1. Fractionation. As in the young child, each item tends to be isolated from its original context or associated with a faulty one. The normal adult, if asked to remember two lists of related items presented in a random order (cat, dog, chair, horse, table, wardrobe) will recall them in category 'clusters' (cat, dog, horse, table, chair, wardrobe). The amnesic seldom does this. If he manages to recall them at all, he tends to do so in a haphazard order or in the order in which he heard them.

2. Lack of associative spread. Related to the above and perhaps for the same reason, is another characteristic. If a normal person is asked to remember a list of words and is then read another list containing synonyms of or associations to the words (together with a group of new ones), he tends to be much slower at rejecting the former than the new words.

In some situations (e.g. if the words are presented in written as opposed to spoken form) the amnesics may make 'false positive' responses to associated words too, but they seldom do so to synonyms. Cueing by giving an association to an item to be remembered only helps the amnesic if the association is close or common, not if it is rare or distant.

3. Loss of localization. Although even normal people often find it difficult to say exactly when they experienced an event or if A came before B, this difficulty is greatly exaggerated in the amnesic, and may extend to his being unsure whether a picture of a common object that he is looking at now is one that he has just been shown before or is only familiar from his previous life experience. As against this,

most amnesic patients have little difficulty in telling whether a comparatively rare scene (such as a view in a picture post card) is one they have ever seen before or not. This has a parallel in clinical experience. The amnesic patient can often tell whether a person visiting him is one he has seen before; but whether the visitor is related to his present management or is a friend from the distant past, he may have difficulty in deciding.

4. Sensitivity to interference. All memory traces show some influence of previous or subsequent events, in the form of pro and retro active interference; but in the case of amnesia, this tendency is greatly increased. In the normal person different events and stimuli tend to become fused to some extent, so that what is remembered of any one time is determined by the 'set' or expectations derived from previous experiences. In the amnesic, such fusion is less evident. What is remembered is determined by the over-all familiarity of the item (due to the frequency with which it has occurred in the past) but not by its immediate antecedents.

5. Loss of sense of familiarity. As was originally pointed out by William James the real difference between memory and all other intellectual processes is a 'belief' that the present construction of the mind is attributable to the past; what McCurdy, following Claparède, called 'me-ness'. It is just this belief that is often lacking in the amnesic. Although, as mentioned above, he can often distinguish the absolutely new from the repeated experience, the frequently seen cannot be distinguished from the recently seen.

This tendency is most commonly seen in recognition situations, either those in which the subject is offered a choice of items, or the single yes–no condition ('was this the one I showed you?'). Here it is commonly found that the items must often picked out by the amnesic are those which he has most frequently seen in the past, regardless of their recency.

The rate at which the immediate sensory impressions fade or are lost varies with their nature. This is examined by presenting the subjects with two stimuli separated by short time intervals (1–30s) and asking them if the second is identical with the first, or not. Compared to controls, amnesic patients lose 'verbal' material (i.e. letters or words) more quickly than non-verbal (shapes or tones), regardless of whether the material is presented visually, auditarily, or by touch. In the normal or control subjects, the passage of time tends to cause 'closure' or 'name dependence'. (The original stimulus is identified with one more like the ideal than it is itself.) In the amnesic, this tendency is lacking.

Lack of familiarity also marks response to cues. Amnesic patients, like normals, can often recall more if they are given prompts or cues to the events than they can unaided; but the amnesic, in contrast to the normal, tends to accept the first item which the cue arouses in his memory, rather than continuing his search for something else.

Use of Strategies. Although evidence in this field cannot be observed directly, the qualitative differences observed above have been taken to indicate that amnesic patients either **cannot or do not use** the same strategies as normal people to retain information. If presented with a situation which he knows he is going to be tested on later, the amnesic's performance may improve to some extent (Fuld, 1976) but if asked how he managed to remember the events, he is seldom able to explain. Most normal people devise mnemonic systems based on either verbal mediators (such as remembering all the first letters and stringing them together to form a word, or making up rhymes to include the names), visual imagery (thinking of a familiar room and sticking each object or word in some part of it), or categorization (grouping the items into logical clusters). When asked for their recall, they reconstruct this system and work back through it. The amnesic patient typically makes no such attempt (Cermak, 1975, 1976), although if pressed to do so he proves himself perfectly capable of associating, imagining, and categorizing. Verbal tagging or labelling of items affects their recall (even to the extent of influencing their visual recognition (Owen and Williams, 1977), but when the time comes for recall, the strategy as well as the material seems to be missing to him.

As has been mentioned, cues or prompts provided either by the environment or the experimenter, are very effective in bringing back information which cannot be recalled spontaneously; but whereas in the normal person the recall of one item is used as a cue to others, the amnesic appears to stop his search as soon as a 'target' is reached, regardless of its fittingness.

To sum up, then, the organic amnesic patient is like the normal person in that the amount he is able to recall at any one moment is dependent on the same variables, but unlike him in that what he recalls is even more dependent on the situation of the moment (or very recent past events), and less on the integration of experiences with one another.

Where and why the amnesic defect exists is still unclear. Some people would place it is the first (encoding) phase, some in the second (storage) one, and some in the third (retrieval) one. It seems more likely, however, that some defects do occur in all three phases. For example, there is evidence that amnesic patients take longer than normals to assimilate or perceive stimuli (Huppert and Piercy, 1976); that they have greater difficulty in distinguishing details (Owen and Williams, 1977), that they are slower at processing information (Glosser *et al.*, 1976), and that they fail to use the normal semantic strategies (Cermak *et al.*, 1973). These suggest a defect of encoding. During the storage phase, however, there is an increased tendency to pro and retro active inhibition (Luria, 1971) and to stimulus competition (Winocur and Weiskrantz, 1976), while in the retrieval phase there is less active search in the memory store (Talland, 1965). Finally, there may be a fourth stage, that of decision ('This is, or is not, the item you showed me') where differences between amnesics and normals are also seen. Experiments using the usual measure of signal-detection theory have shown no differences here between amnesics and normals (Cutting, 1977), but this may be because the two groups are using different criteria on which to base their judgements (Riege, 1977). While the normal person probably bases his judgements on two factors—first the ease with which a response is aroused (the quicker, the more liable it is to be recent), and secondly the recall of its previous context (where he was at the time he experienced it)—the amnesic patient has to rely on the first factor alone as he can seldom recall contextual data.

4.4 THE RECOGNITION OF MINOR ORGANIC AMNESIC DISORDERS

The recognition of a patient with a fully fledged organic amnesic syndrome of the type described in the preceding section is not difficult; nor is it necessary to employ detailed tests to do so. Questions have been raised about whether the amnesic disorders arising from different clinical conditions all show identical characteristics, and it should be mentioned that most of the experimental work has been carried out on alcoholic Korsakovs only. Certainly those patients who show additional defects (e.g. dementia, dysphasia, or dyspraxia) present rather differently as will be described later; but the pure memory disorders following encephalitis or TBM seem to be similar to those following bitemporal lesions, Wernicke's encephalopathy and Korsakov conditions (Cermak, 1976). Moreover, the characteristics shown by these patients are paralleled by those shown by patients after concussional head injury and ECT. Within each of these states, individual variations are common, and all generalizations have to be made with caution.

Besides the patients mentioned above—i.e. those with clearcut organic amnesic syndromes—many patients may present with lesser degrees of memory impairment, the nature of which can have important implications for treatment and prognosis.

The distinction of these impairments which are due to organic causes from those due to other (e.g. psychiatric) ones is therefore important and has been the focus of most of the memory tests in current clinical use. Since the major defect in organic memory impairment is in the sphere of retention, it is in this sphere that measurement is usually concentrated.

A short, simple, and easily standardizable test has been described recently by Pratt (1977, p. 226). A series of photographs of well-known personalities is shown to the subject, and for each one not identified, the patient is given information about his name and occupation. Recall of this information is usually far more efficient in the patient with psychogenic (i.e. hysterical) amnesia, than would be expected if the personalities had been encountered for the very first time.

A common form of measuring retention in the clinical setting is to compare a patient's immediate reproduction of a story (e.g. the 'cowboy' story), or a 'name, address, and flower' ('Will you try to remember the name Joseph Spencer, of 15 Mills Drive, Dartford, and the flower bluebell'), or of a design, with that demanded some time later. The difference between the two scores (immediate and delayed) is taken as a measure of loss over time. So far, however, no published norms for loss over time on any of these tests are available.

Luria (1971) suggests that a measure of retention can be based on the difference between a subject's ability to recall three numbers (or names) after ten

Figure 16. Material used by Williams in set A of the delayed recall test

Object	Prompt	2 points each unaided	3 points each recall prompt	4 point each recognition
Apple	A common fruit	✓		
Axe	You use it when you want some wood for the fire	✓		
Dressing table	You find it in ladies' bedrooms	–	✓	
Violin	You would see it at a concert	✓		
Fish	Cats like eating it	–	✓	
Jug	You'd look for it if you were thirsty	✓		
Squirrel	It lives in the woods	✓		
Spoon	You see it on a well laid table	–	–	–
Spectacles	We see through them	✓		
		3 × 2 = 6	1 × 3 = 3	1×4=4
		Total raw score =13		

Figure 17. Sample score sheet for the Williams delayed recall test

seconds of unfilled time compared with his performance after 10 seconds filled with either an unlike or a like task. Standards for this could quite easily be established but again have not yet been published.

One particular aspect of memory which is important to recognize, especially for practical purposes and management, is the improvement in recall which may be seen to follow slight prompts. Williams has made use of this in standardizing her 'test of delayed recall', where the scoring procedure is based on both free and prompted recall of pictures after a ten minute interval filled by fairly standard verbal tests. (Williams, 1968).

The procedure consists of showing the subject a page containing nine pictures of common objects (Fig. 16), which he is asked to name (so that dysphasic and perceptual difficulties will be recognized if present) and try to remember since his memory for then will be tested later. He is then occupied in vocabulary or other verbal tests for 8–10 minutes, following which he is asked to 'Tell me as many of the items which were shown to you as you can recall'. If he asks about it, he is assured that the order in which he names them is not important.

For every item not recalled, he is then given a standard cue or prompt (see sample score sheet, Fig. 17). If after this he still fails to recall some of the items, he is shown a sheet of pictures containing the original nine together with nine others, and is asked to point to all the ones he saw before.

Three parallel sets of material are available, so that repeated testing can be carried out without the practice effects being too pronounced.

The total raw scores (consisting of two points for each item not recalled straight away, three additional points for each item not recalled after its prompt, and four additional points for each one not recognized) vary not only with the presence but also with the location of cerebral pathology. Thus lesions involving the cerebral cortex cause a far greater disturbance than subcortical ones

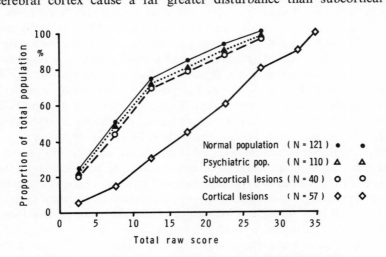

Figure 18. Showing the total raw scores on the Williams delayed recall test for adults in different diagnostic categories

involving the basal ganglia and cerebellum. The performances of normal people and of psychiatric patients are very similar and show little variation between the ages of 20 and 60 (see Fig. 18). This test has been used in a number of research projects. One of its main values is that patients do not find it tiring or distressing.

Of special importance in diagnosis is the quality of the patient's behaviour on tests of retention. Depression is characterized by retardation, and by little loss of retention. Cortical atrophy is characterized by a great tendency on the cueing tests to respond to the cue itself and treat this as the target, rather than using it as a signpost to a particular searchfield (see Table 4).

The distinction between organically-induced memory losses for past personal events and those due to emotional repression, can present difficulties.

The classical 'loss of memory' in which an individual may be found wandering around without any knowledge of who he is or what he has done up to that moment, is nowadays rare but does occasionally occur. Three characteristics mark this from organic conditions: (1) loss of personal orientation (especially for name) which is rare in organic cases except in the very early confusional state; (2) the all-embracing or global nature of the amnesia and its resistance to recovery by prompting; and (3) the persistence of inability to recall past events even when retention of recent ones is good. Thus a global amnesia for the past and disorientation for person in the presence of good retention, are strong indications of a hysterical amnesia.

A tendency to equate these conditions with malingering, or to assume that the sufferer is trying to cover up a misdeed are seldom justified. Although there is always an element of the desire to escape from emotional stress, the mechanisms responsible for fugue states are not under conscious control; nor is the cause of stress necessarily due to conflict with society.

In the case of children, defects are essentially similar to those seen in the adult but must be assessed against a background of normal childhood memorizing ability. The immediate memory span and ability to acquire new skills increases with age in childhood, so that mental age can be assessed by the amount and complexity of material a child can reproduce immediately after a single hearing. Retention of visual and non-visual skills also shows increase with age but as against this the ability to localize and recognize discrete visual stimuli (Kim's game) possibly reaches its optimum at the ages of eleven to 14, and begins to deteriorate at the same time that the reproduction of discrete experiences tend to be confused by 'sets' and expectancies derived from past experience.

It is particularly, therefore, in its effect on the recollection of discrete visual stimuli, that amnesia in childhood as in the adult can best be recognized. The responses of children to the test situation are, however, somewhat different to those seen in adults. Children with fewer past experiences and established habits or skills to fall back on are less inclined to confabulate when pressed for recall than are adults. They tend, instead, to remain mute. If given a prompt or a cue, children respond in a less related way to it than adults, and if forced to make a response may repeat what they have just done or heard instead of falling back on past personal idiosyncrasies (see Table 5).

Table 4
The main characteristics of different diagnostic groups in memory situations

Diagnostic group	Established skills	Immediate reproduction	Retention of incidental events	Cued recall	Learning
General cerebral deterioration	Patchy losses	Normal	Variable, but usually poor	Respond to cue as if it is a new stimulus—no memory search	Perseveration of faulty response
General physical illness	Normal	Usually poor	Depend on attention and arousal at time of experience	Normal	Poor, due to lack of effort
Organic amnesic (Korsakov) state	Normal	Normal	Very poor	Claim familiarity with response first aroused	Much perseveration, but motor skills can be retained
Depression	Normal	Normal	Normal	Normal	Poor, due to unwillingness to make effort
Anxiety	Normal	Tend to be poor and uneven	Normal	Normal	Uneven, often fluctuating performance

Table 5
The differences between adults and children in memory test
situations

Adults	Children
Reluctant to admit inability	Readily admit 'I forget'
Respond to cues by some act related to it	Respond to cues by some act often unrelated to cue
Repeat past individual habits or skills	Repeat last act done or last thing heard

4.5 NEUROPATHOLOGY

A thorough, but as he admits selective, review of the evidence associating amnesic defects with cerebral lesions has been made by Brierley (1966), as a result of which he concludes that

> the structures essential for the process of normal memorizing are the hippocampal formations within the temporal lobes, the mamillary bodies and possibly certain thalamic nuclei within the diencephalon. The anatomical connections of these regions suggest that a continuous pathway might be traced along the afferent fibres from the hippocampal gyrus to the hippocampus and out, via its efferent pathway the fornix, to the mamillary bodies. From these, the mamillo-thalamic tract leads to the anterior nuclear complex of the thalamus, which projects to the cingulate gyrus. The pathway is completed by the known connections between the cingulate and hippocampal gyri. This apparently continuous 'circuit' lies within the group of structures comprising the 'limbic lobe', to which Papez ascribed the elaboration of emotion and the control of visceral activity. (p. 173) (see Figs. 19 and 20).

In coming to these conclusions Brierley considers only those cases which presented with (1) clear-cut, isolated and well documented memory disturbances, and (2) well defined and isolated cerebral lesions. Thus cases with widespread vascular or neurological involvement have not been included. Brierley divides his material into two main groups:

1. Lesions in the mamillary bodies and the thalamus (usually showing a full Korsakov psychosis and predominantly due to metabolic disorders or dietary (vitamin B) deficiency, but may also be due to intracranial tumours.
2. Bilateral lesions of the hippocampal formation usually resulting from surgical intervention for the relief of epilepsy of psychosis. One of these latter cases, Scovile and Milner's case H.M., has already been referred to in this chapter. In these cases bilateral removal of the uncus and amygdaloid nucleus alone do not appear to cause amnesia, while unilateral interference causes only defects in the verbal skills if carried out in the dominant hemisphere, and passing and

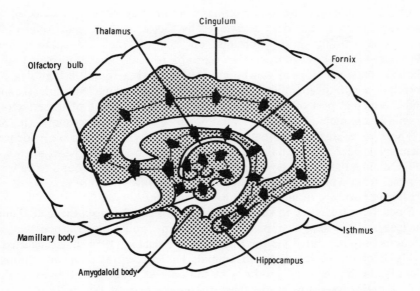

Figure 19. Hypothetical 'memory circuit' seen from the side

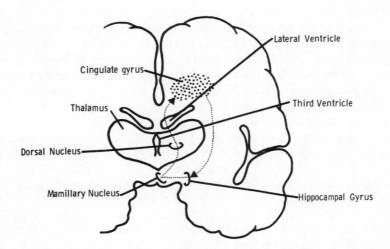

Figure 20. Hypothetical 'memory circuit' seen from the front

subjective sensations of forgetfulness if confined to the non-dominant hemisphere.

Brierley's memory circuit, which has long been accepted as connected with memory functions, has been questioned by Victor, Adams, and Collins (1971) who carried out post mortems on 82 of the 245 patients with Wernicke–Korsakov syndrome they were able to study intensively from both the clinical and psychological viewpoints. Although they found 'a high degree of correlation with the mamillary body, the medical dorsal nucleus of the thalamus and the medial part of the pulvinar', they conclude 'which of these factors is crucial in the memory function could not be decided with certainty' (p. 132).

There were, in fact, five patients in the series who showed no evidence of memory defect by severe damage of the mamillary bodies. In these patients, but in these only, the medial dorsal nucleus of the thalamus was found to be free of disease, from which the authors conclude that this structure may be of even greater importance in memory than the mamillary bodies.

Since there are as yet no known direct connections between the medial dorsal nucleus and the hippocampus, Victor, Adams, and Collins argue that connections may be routed via the forebrain as Mishkin (1954) has suggested.

Much of the recent work on animals has concentrated on attempting to identify the biochemical products of the different subcortical areas, and the neural pathways transmitting these to other areas of the brain. The exact relevance of these studies to human behaviour is still debated (see Chapter 11). There is no doubt that stimulation of certain thalamic nuclei in rats reinforces the behaviour which led up to it, whether the stimulation is initiated by the animal itself (self-stimulation) or by the experimentor. Interpretations of the data are usually based on the assumption that facilitation of behaviour patterns is due to 'drive reduction', so that it is necessary not just to identify the processes involved in reinforcement, but also to identify those involved in drive production. (Deutsch, 1976; Olds, 1976). Noradrenaline (NA) and dopamine (DA) have been much implicated, and while DA seems to be mainly responsible for the motivating component or drive, NA is held to be responsible for reinforcement or perpetuation of behaviour (Herberg et al., 1976).

The release of catecholamines (CAs) would account for the perpetuation of memories for events associated with intense emotional stimulation (see Section 4.1); but against this it must be remembered that production of CAs by an epileptic seizure, whilst altering both consciousness and mood, usually retards rather than improves memories for events surrounding it.

The fact, however, that epileptic discharges can be 'kindled' (i.e. become progressively prolonged, intense and widely propagated) by repeated stimulation of certain areas and not by intensifying the focal stimulation in the naïve animal (Goddard and McIntyre, 1973), indicates that the passage of an impulse across a synapse has some long lasting facilitatory effect. This has indeed been put forward by Akert and Livingston (1973) as the basis for repeated self-stimulation.

Even if it were possible to establish exactly those lesions or biochemical disorders responsible for amnesia, however, it does not follow that those same areas would form the physical basis of normal memory functions. Indeed, if the study of amnesia has thrown any light at all on normal memory, it is to emphasize the complex nature of the process. Memory appears to involve not just the storage of sensory impressions or the establishment of psychomotor connections, but also alterations of behaviour, either overt (as in the acquisition of motor patterns) or internal (in the form of imagery). The greater the number of previously established behaviour patterns activated by a presenting stimulus, the greater seems to be the sense of familiarity associated with it. In amnesia there is little or no loss of actual memories apart from those immediately preceding loss of consciousness. Rather the situation seems to resemble that found by Lashley in the course of his experimental search for the engram in rats (Lashley, 1950); that is to say all aspects of memory are reduced. The situation has a parallel in the holograph (Pribram, 1968) but it does not follow that the same principle is used in both holography and memory.

4.6 CONCLUSIONS

At the end of Chapter 1, the part played by the brain in mediating consciousness and wakefulness was considered. It was suggested that activation of the cortex by the brain stem actually retards rather than facilitates the immediate response to individual stimuli, and thereby allows for a response to be influenced by previous habits based on past experience—memory.

In this chapter it has been pointed out that memory itself is an exceedingly complex function. For a sensory impression to leave an after effect which can be reactivated to influence behaviour it must be (1) integrated with other sensory impressions and (2) these integrations must be rehearsed (i.e. repeated in the mind) a number of times. Even then the traces so formed are unstable. They are subject to alteration by all later stimuli, and it is these alterations which are known as forgetting. Finally, (3) the traces must be reactivated for the memory itself to be present, and it is this reactivation which often seems to be missing in the amnesic.

Since memory involves the awareness and integration of sensory stimuli, the manner in which these processes themselves are carried out must now be considered.

5
Disorders of Visual Perception

Although it is never easy to distinguish between a disorder of simple sensation and one of perception (i.e. the interpretation of a sensation) this chapter will attempt to deal mostly with the latter. It is certainly true that many of the perceptual disorders which follow cerebral injury are accompanied by—and may to a large extent be dependent on—sensory deficiency; but the latter may be of an apparently trivial nature. Nevertheless, a brief description of the manner in which vision is normally mediated, and of the structures involved in it, might be helpful.

Vision comes about when excitation of the cells in the retina is conveyed via the optic nerves, the long fibre tracts forming pathways within the brain, to the striate area of the cortex and its surrounding areas. The course of the visual pathways, demonstrated diagrammatically in Fig. 21 is fairly well known. Because of the partial decussation of the optic fibres in the optic chiasma, each hemisphere receives impulses from one of the visual fields of both eyes: interruption of the optic tract beyond the chiasma will produce a defect of the visual fields the most usual of which, together with the lesions causing them, are demonstrated in Fig. 21.

Activation of the cells in the primary visual cortex does not in itself give rise to sensation. Nor is there any point-to-point localization of retinal cells in this area. The primary visual cortex merely acts as a relay station to the surrounding areas, where integration and 'interpretation' takes place. EEG records indicate that when in a state of rest or relaxation, the nerve cells in the visual cortex are firing off synchronously at the rate of about 10 per second (the alpha rhythm) but as soon as they are stimulated, this synchrony ceases.

Agnosia, as the perceptual disorders are called, occurs primarily for *visual, auditory*, and *proprioceptive* stimuli. Instances of the defects seen in the visual sphere—the subject of this chapter—will be discussed first in their clinical setting. An attempt will then be made to analyse the psychological defects related to them, followed by a review of the organic conditions most commonly associated with them.

Visual agnosia is frequently seen in conjunction with loss of sensory input such as blind spots (scotomata) and defects of the visual fields due to injury of the optic tracts. However, the perceptual defects consist not so much in non-awareness of the stimuli as in misrecognition of their meaning. Objects, faces, spatial configurations, pictures, and colours lose their sense of familiarity. Although each of these defects can occur in isolation, (and will be dealt with in this chapter as if they did so), it is more usual for a patient who shows difficulty in recognizing one type of stimulus to have difficulty in recognizing others too.

5.1 VISUAL OBJECT AGNOSIA

'A 60 year old man almost blind in his right eye from an old injury, woke from a sleep unable to find his clothes, though they lay ready for him close by. As soon as his wife put the garments into his hands, he recognized them, dressed himself correctly and went out. In the streets he found he could not recognize people—not even his own daughter. He could see things, but not tell what they were' (see Critchley, 1953, p. 289). This case first described by Bay in 1952 is an excellent example of a patient with visual object agnosia, a condition which had been recognized in dogs by Munk in 1877 and described in humans by Stauffenberg in 1914 and Goldstein and Gelb in 1918 (see Critchley, 1953, p. 276). Thus one patient described by Stauffenberg:

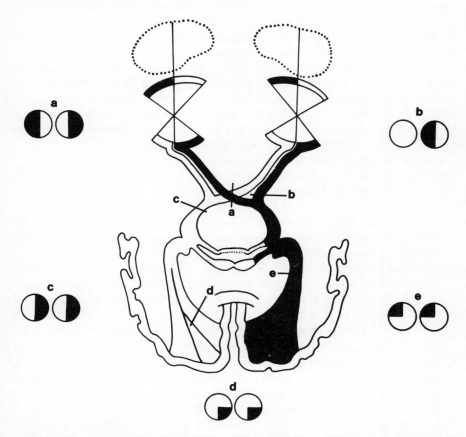

Figure 21. Diagram of visual pathways and the field defects produced by lesions at different levels

Could see objects, and avoid them when they constituted obstacles in her way, but she could not identify them surely, without recourse to the aid of hearing, touch, smell, or taste. At first indeed, she could not identify objects even by touch, but gradually she lost this disability. She could not recognize a sponge held before her until she felt it with her finger. She could not recognize a cigar until she put it into her mouth. A spoon was occasionally recognized, less often a knife and fork. A key, pocket knife, and wash basin were not recognized, or at any rate, their use was not described. Nevertheless after looking for a long time at a watch, she named the numbers correctly and told the time correctly.

It will be noted that in this condition the ability to recognize objects by touch is unimpaired although the ability to recognize them by their visual contours appears to be very largely lost. No defects of visual acuity were found in these cases by the above authors, but it has been argued that in the majority of cases showing visual object agnosia the symptom is largely attributable to general perceptual disorders. Indeed Gloning *et al.* (1968) found only three cases of visual object agnosia among the 241 patients studied by them, and in each of these cases the symptom was accompanied by a variety of perceptual disorders.

Care must be taken not to confuse inability to *recognize* objects (agnosia) with inability to *name* them (anomia or nominal dysphasia), especially as the two conditions sometimes occur together, or one disorder may appear to cause the other. Thus Marin and Saffran (1975) describe one patient who could perform quite complex perceptual tasks if he remained silent, but became very confused as soon as he started trying to describe what he was doing.

Geschwind (1965) gives an excellent summary of the criteria distinguishing true visual agnosia from other conditions—mainly aphasia—in his discussion on the disconnection syndromes, as follows:

1. The 'agnosic' disturbance is a circumscribed one: unlike the aphasic who tends to misname everything, visual agnosia may refer to a very limited area such as the naming of colours alone.
2. 'Agnosic' errors differ in character from 'aphasic' errors, the latter being linguistic and often taking the form of associations rather than misperceptions. For example, the aphasic might call a pen 'a pencil', whereas the agnosic might call it 'a knife'.
3. The 'agnosic' cannot choose the correct response, if various object names are suggested to him, whereas the aphasic usually can.
4. The 'agnosic' can often describe his difficulty, and will say that things look different to him. He may even 'offer dramatic descriptions of bizarre perceptions, this apparently providing direct evidence that he is experiencing distortions of his perceptions' (p. 587).
5. The 'agnosic' cannot show the use of the object, even though in certain circumstances he may actually use it correctly. For example, Geschwind describes one patient who, although unable to name or apparently recognize a glass of water, took it up and drank from it when thirsty.

5.2 PROSOPAGNOSIA

This, the inability to recognize faces, while frequently seen in all patients with visual agnosia, has been held by some authors to occur in isolation. Bodamen describes one patient to whom faces appeared:

Strangely flat; while with very dark eyes, as if in one plain, like white oval plates . . . all the same. He could see but not interpret facial movements and grimaces. Gazing in a mirror, he described the delineaments of what he saw, but could not recognize the face as his. Together with three other soldiers, he had his photograph taken, but he afterwards failed to recognize his face in the print. The features of his closest relatives, either in snaps or in real life, appeared quite foreign to him. He walked past his mother in the street, and he never got to know the looks of the other patients in the ward' (Critchley, 1953, p.293).

The connection between prosopagnosia and other forms of visual agnosia has been debated at length. While some observers believe that recognition of facial configurations is a specific act, and that it can be disturbed when all other visual functions remain intact, others regard it as only one aspect of the visual recognition process. Thus Warrington and James (1967b) found some difficulty in the recognition of faces (from photographs) in 62 patients with unilateral cerebral lesions (those with lesions on the right side being worse than those with them on the left), but since there was no correlation between the ability of the patients tested in the recognition of familar and unfamiliar faces, they were inclined to regard prosopagnosia as merely one constituent of an amnesic syndrome. De Renzi, Faglioni, and Spinnler (1968a) agree that prosopagnosia 'represents simply the most prominent aspect of a generalized visuo-perceptual disturbance' (and also that it occurs more frequently in the right than in left sided brain damage), but also follow other observers (Gloning *et al.*, 1966; Gloning, Harb, and Quatember, 1966) in pointing out that for the recognition of faces it is necessary to fixate and synthesize certain key parts—especially the eyes. If such fixation is difficult for a patient (for example, one quoted by Gloning *et al.*, 1968, described how the eyes of people he looked at seemed to be 'strange and permanently changing') facial recognition is likely to be impaired.

5.3 COLOUR AGNOSIA

An artist quoted by Holmes

No longer was able to use colours after he had sustained a stroke. He was not colour blind, however, for he could name most colours and pick out colours correctly to command. When tested with Holmgren's wools—(a test in which the subject is presented with skeins of wool in various different shades and from which he has to pick out and match those of the same colour as examples selected by the experimenter)—he could not sort colours, that is, pick out the various shades of say red or green. He could not associate colours with objects except by reference to rote memory. (Critchley, 1953, p. 276).

Another patient studied in detail by Stengel (1948) had difficulty in both matching and naming colours.

When requested to pick out coloured skeins to match the colours of an object named by the examiner, he succeeded as a rule, but not without considerable hesitation. In this test too differentiation between green and blue were the most difficult. Which colour is a pillar box? 'It would be a blue with a red—post office red' (patient picks out a brown-red skein first then a bright red). Grass ? (patient picks out light green). Sky ? (patient picks dark green). Blood ? (correct). Tomato ? (he hesitates, points to purple, then to orange, adding that the latter was the more likely to be correct).

In assessing colour agnosia it is important to make full allowance for the possible presence of dysphasia (see Chapter 8), for patients who have lost the ability to recognize or say words can often give a most misleading impression. Indeed colour agnosia and word blindness often occur together (Gloning *et al.*, 1968), and it seems quite possible that the patient described by Stengel above was suffering more from misrecognition of words than of colours. Another instance of colour agnosia has been described by Geschwind (see Chapter 9) and ascribed to 'disconnection' rather than true agnosia.

Critchley (1965) analyses the features of colour agnosia which distinguish it from true colour blindness of peripheral origin. In colour agnosia the colour boundaries of objects seem to be distinct from the form boundaries, sometimes shimmering, fluctuating, and even spreading to other areas. Critchley, in a review of the subject which stretches far beyond the immediate clinical environment, discusses this point in relation to the use of blue in the history of art and the development of language! He points out that in painting, blue only appears fairly recently as an object-identifying colour, and that a specific word for this colour appears later than for most others in the language of several different cultures.

5.4 SIMULTANAGNOSIA

This consists of inability to absorb more than one aspect of a visual stimulus at a time (Wolport, 1924; Weigl, 1964). For example, a 68 year old, right-handed patient studied by the present author had difficulty finding his way around because 'he couldn't see properly'.

It was found that if two objects (e.g. pencils) were held in front of him at the same time, he could only see one of them, whether they were held side by side, one above the other, or one behind the other.

Further testing showed that single stimuli including pictures, could be identified correctly and even recognized when shown again whether simple or complex (newspaper photographs or simple sketches), representing objects or faces. If stimuli included more than one object, one only would be identified at a time, though the others would sometimes 'come into focus' as the first one went out. If the stimuli were placed side by side, the right one was usually identified first, gradually giving place to the one on the left. Single letters were identified correctly, especially when in the right visual field. Those in the left visual field were sometimes neglected, sometimes overelaborated (P became B) and just occasionally fused with the one on the right. If long sentences were presented, only the most right-sided word could be read. If sentences were short, the right-hand words would be read first followed by those to the left of it. Thus 'the dog runs' was read as 'run dog'. If single words were presented, these were read without error. If a single word covered as large a visual area as a sentence which could not be read, the single word was read in its entirety, but a double-barrelled word was mis-read, only the last syllable being identified, even though the first part might leave some impression. Thus to the word houseboat the patient said, 'I see boat—but *not* houseboat'.

If the patient was shown a page of drawings, the contents of which overlapped (i.e. objects drawn on top of one another see Fig. 22), he tended to pick out a single object and deny that he could see any others. Moreover, the figure selected at the first exposure of such stimuli was seen again on all subsequent presentations. If shown a drawing which might be seen in two different ways, and which to the normal person appears first in one configuration and then in the other (reversible figures), he would pick out one configuration only and was quite unable to reverse it.

This man showed hardly any other mental disturbance. He was alert, fully orientated and on verbal tests of both comprehension and expression showed minimal impairment. Tunes and musical instruments were correctly identified.

This condition, first described by Wolpert in 1924, has led to considerable

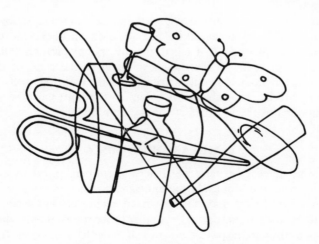

Figure 22. 'Mixed figures.' used in the
assessment of visual agnosia

discussion. Kinsbourne and Warrington (1963a) studied three cases of simultan-agnosia on the recognition of visual stimuli shown tachistoscopically. They found that whereas the recognition time of the first of any three successive stimuli were always within normal limits there was invariably a long delay to the second. If pairs of stimuli were shown together, the left was always seen before the right (in contrast to the case mentioned above). They believe this delay to be the basis of the disability—a conclusion also reached by Birch, Belmont, and Karp (1967) who found that if two stimuli were presented at time intervals differing by 300–600 ms both could often be identified together.

Although the condition of simultanagnosia bears some resemblance to the difficulties experienced by a normal person in a situation of stereoscopic rivalry (i.e when trying to fixate a different stimulus with each eye), it is different in that there is less fluctuation between perceptions in simultanagnosia than in the stereoscopic situation. Nevertheless, some of the conditions affecting dominance of perception in stereoscopic conditions might well be studied for their effect in cases of simultanagnosia. Is one item more likely to be seen than another if it is brighter, simpler, the right way up, meaningful, or emotionally loaded? (see Rommetveit, Toch, and Svendsen, 1968). These points have not been studied.

5.5 VISUAL INATTENTION

Simultanagnosia is somewhat similar to *visual inattention* though the latter is seldom recognized unless specifically looked for. In this condition the patient tends to recognize only one object if two are held up in different visual fields; that is to say he ignores the second object unless his attention is specifically drawn to it. Unlike patients with simultanagnosia, however, the patient who shows merely visual inattention is usually capable of seeing the two objects once his attention is drawn to them.

There is a tendency for patients to neglect the left side of visual space more than the right, just as they tend to neglect the left sides of their bodies more than they do the right, (see Chapter 6) and, if asked to draw or copy pictures will very often omit the left side or cram all the details of it on to the right of their paper (Chapter 7). This tendency is usually attributed to the fact that visuo-perceptual disorders appear to be associated with lesions in the right parietal area and so affect the functions of the left half of the patients body.

5.6 METAMORPHOPSIA

Although this is a defect of experience rather than of perception, metamorphop-sia is usually considered alongside the agnosias.

In this condition objects may be recognized accurately but seem to become distorted—either larger (macropsia) or smaller (micropsia), tilted (when walking one patient felt as though the pavements sloped to her left), inverted, fragmented, drifting, a long way away, or unfamiliar. Examples quoted by Critchley are as follows: 'the furniture seemed to be turned round'; 'my husband seemed too big and yet a long way away'; 'peoples faces would frequently change, their eyes would swell and contract . . . they looked terrible. The eyes go to nothing at all then come back like a pimple'.

Despite the nature of these distortions the patients can usually recognize and name the things which seem so strange to them. There is not so much agnosia for the objects as distortion of their visual contours.

Apart from the inability to recognize individual items as described above, there are other disturbances in the visual sphere.

5.7 VISUAL PERSEVERATION

Occasionally visual perceptions may seem to continue for an abnormal length of time (paliopsia) as after hashish and mescalin intoxication; or to recur after the stimulus object has been removed. Thus 'after a person had walked past the foot of the bed from left to right and then had gone away, she had a moment or two later the impression as if the same person had walked past as before' (Critchley, 1953, p. 304). One patient 'watched a man approach and then pass out of view. Then he seemed to see the man walking past again'. The special conditions associated with visual perseveration in one patient were studied in considerable detail by Kinsbourne and Warrington (1963b).

5.8 DENIAL OF BLINDNESS

This (Anton's syndrome) could be regarded as a special form of visual perseveration in which a visual image appears so clearly to the patient who has no visual perception at all, that he may maintain volubly that he can see all that is around him. If asked to describe a picture held by the examiner (who is holding nothing at all) he will confabulate freely. This condition is not common. Out of 708 patients with verified cerebral lesions, Gloning *et al.* (1968) only found eleven cases, and in ten of these there was also gross confusion. These authors, in fact, tend to attribute the symptom to loss of criticism, euphoria, and a tendency to fabricate in general.

Occasionally the denial applies to a blind half field only, the patient describing all the things he imagines to be present in it. Warrington (1962) has shown that a tendency to do this occurs in the majority of patients with left sided visual field defects, but King (1967) has pointed out that such completions tend to be common only on symmetrical figures where 'expectation' could give rise to the same sort of phenomenon as is common in the normal overlooking of a printer's error.

Word Blindness

Word blindness or dyslexia will be dealt with later, alongside other disorders of language.

5.9 VISUO-SPATIAL DISORIENTATION

This refers not so much to the misrecognition of objects as to their mis-localization in space. Patients have difficulty telling which of two things is above or below the other, which is nearest or further away, which is to the right or the left. A case described by McFie *et al.* (1950)

> began to leave food on the left side of her plate or to push it off on to the table. In reading she experienced difficulty shifting down to the next line. About the same time, she began to have great difficulty in finding her way about in places she knew well. This improved slightly but the patient noticed great difficulty in learning her way around in a strange house.

The defects in these cases are most obvious if the patients are asked to draw either from memory or from models shown to them. As will be described in greater detail in Chapter 7, they have particular difficulty in combining parts of objects into coherent wholes, in joining diagonal lines and in filling out the left side of a page.

5.10 PSYCHOLOGICAL ANALYSIS

What, exactly, is responsible for the above disorders? Can they all be attributed to a single 'basic defect'? These are important questions which have been discussed at length, and although the answers to them are still uncertain, some other facts have emerged from their consideration.

Although the phenomena described in the preceding pages are extremely varied, some factors are common to all, which may be listed as follows:

1. The defects tend to be worse in the left than in the right visual field.
2. They become more obvious the more complex the stimulus.
3. They are usually associated with some degree of sensory or motor defect (such as blind spots or faulty scanning).
4. They are associated with slowing-up of information-processing.
5. They are not usually associated with loss of visual imagery.

In order to understand what may have gone wrong, the disorders must be considered in relation to normal visual perception which, as the Gestalt psychologists were the first to demonstrate, is a constructional process leading to a total awareness much greater than 'the sum of its parts'.

Although normal visual perception cannot be discussed at length here, it must be borne in mind that the percept which finally reaches the awareness of the individual is dependent on:

1. The sensory stimulation experienced in the past by the individual at critical periods of his former life.
2. The verbal 'labels' he has learned to attach to percepts in the past.

3. His present state of maturation.
4. His 'set' or expectations for the future.
5. The restrictions and 'taboos' he has developed at an emotional level (leading to 'perceptual defence' unacceptable words or objects being recognized later than others).
6. The nature of the stimulus itself and the surroundings or 'ground' on which it is displayed.
7. The side or 'visual field' in which it occurs.

Before a percept takes up its final shape in a person's awareness, many of the characteristics of a stimulus will be recognized. This 'Vor Gestalt' is likely to contain many parameters of the final percept, some of which will be selected and others rejected at a preconscious level resulting in a final discrimination and generalization.

In visual agnosia, it seems as though perception is often cut short at the stage of this 'Vor Gestalt'. The subject has some awareness of the visual stimulus but the full processes of selection and rejection are lacking. He is like the patient with a 'blind spot' who is often able to define the angle at which a light is shining though not its exact distance (Perenin and Jeannerod, 1975; Warrington, 1962); or the normal person who is shown pictures in a tachistoscope at exposures too short to be correctly registered (Ettlinger, 1960; Underwood, 1977).

Faulty Visual Scanning

This may be one of the factors involved in visual agnosia and Bay, himself tends to accept this explanation. He observed how the patient described in Section 5.1 would enter a room cautiously, peering around, and turning his head from one side to the other. He did not fixate objects normally and would readily deviate his eyes towards any new stimulus. Abercrombie (1960) has also found evidence of grossly unsteady eye movements in cerebral palsied children, correlating with their poor performance on visuo-constructional tasks. It is also interesting to note that while omissions or neglect are almost always made to the left side of visual space, experimental work has shown that normal subjects tend to show a less pronounced but similar tendency, although the effects of laterality depend to some extent on the nature of the stimulus, words being recognized better in the right half of visual space than the left while faces are better on the left (Marcel and Rajan, 1975; Kimura, 1967).

The tendency for normal adults to scan systematically from left to right (thereby fixating more strongly on the right) has often been attributed to reading habits. Ghent-Braine (1968) studied Israelis with a view to seeing whether subjects whose reading habits had taught them to scan from right to left showed this same tendency. However, her work does not completely solve the problem. Whereas the adult subjects studied by her did recognize patterns shown to them tachistoscopically better in the left than on the right as predicted on the hypothesis of a learned scanning pattern, the difference only became evident in those who had attained at least the seventh grade of reading. Previously to this the right field predominated over the left, suggesting a more fundamental physiological basis for right visual field preference than mere habit formation—a suggestion substantiated by Orbach (1967) who also studied Hebrews and found that right-handed Hebrew subjects showed an even more marked tendency in this direction than left-handers.

Insufficient Integration

Another causal factor in visual agnosia is insufficient integration of the scanned parts which has also been suggested by Gloning *et al.* (1966, 1967) to account for some instances of prosopagnosia. Scanning defects could not alone account, however, for simultanagnosia or for visuo-spatial disorientation, in which conditions it is not the realization of the parts which appears to be lacking but the ability to see them as a whole. Moreover, faulty visual scanning has been identified by Luria *et al.* (1966) in patients with frontal (as opposed to parietal) lobe lesions, but in such patients leads to 'impulsive hypotheses about the contents of visual stimuli' rather than to the types of disorder that have been outlined here.

Faulty Visual Imagery

This is another postulated causal factor in visual agnosia. Loss of visual imagery plus loss of dreaming has been described in three cases of brain damage due to gun shot wounds by Humphrey and Zangwill (1952). But in the majority of patients who show visuo-spatial agnosia there appears to be no difficulty in visualizing the objects which the patients are trying to reproduce. They know what they want to draw, they can see them in their minds eye. It is the execution which is at fault.

Slowed Up Processing

Slowed up processing of visual data has been suggested by Kinsbourne and Warrington (1963a) as a basis for simultanagnosia and by Birch *et al.* (1967) for visual extinction. Whether such a process could be demonstrated in the other forms of visual agnosia mentioned here, such as object agnosia, prosopagnosia, etc. is uncertain and never appears to have been investigated. The mechanism postulated by Kinsbourne and Warrington seems to have a parallel in the changes which occur in normal ageing. Thus, Wallace (1956) found that while older subjects were nearly as good as younger ones at identifying simple visual displays, there is a progressive age decrement as the material becomes more complex. This is attributed by the author to the increased time taken to integrate stimuli by older subjects.

Faulty Integration

This does indeed seem to be the only factor common to all aspects of visual agnosia—but having said this has one said anything at all? Until we know what the processes are which underly or constitute integration of sensory stimuli we have only given another name to an observed phenomenon. It is true that the more items a subject has to integrate into a single percept (e.g. the complexity of the task) the more clearly his disabilities are shown up. The integration of input from two different modalities is often more difficult than the integration of many items from a single modality. Thus Ettlinger and Wyke (1961) report a careful study of one patient with visual object agnosia whose touch recognition was actually retarded when he was allowed to add visual to his tactile information. Mack and Boller (1977) describe another who was unable to recognize objects by sight, even though he showed no sign of dyslexia and could name objects after touching them.

Careful analysis of the conditions which do and do not assist behaviour in the brain-injured patient compared with stages through which normal visual perception is attained suggest that the two factors most commonly responsible for visual agnosia are (1) the speed with which visual sensory data are assimilated and decoded; and (2) the amount of visual sensory data which can be processed (i.e. integrated with other data) at any moment in time.

5.11 NEUROPATHOLOGY

Visual agnosia is closely associated with lesions in the parieto-occipital area (see Fig. 23). About this there is little controversy. But the extent to which lesions in the different hemispheres (right or left) cause different types of disorder is still debated.

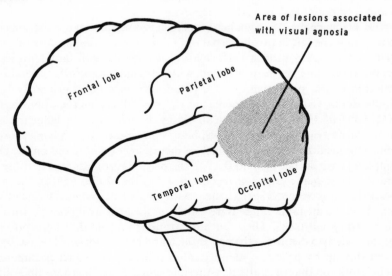

Area of lesions associated with visual agnosia

Frontal lobe

Parietal lobe

Temporal lobe

Occipital lobe

Figure 23. Location of area in which lesions are associated with visual agnosia

The hemispheres have traditionally been considered as dominant (or major) and non-dominant (or minor), the major hemisphere being that which controls the preferred hand, and, (since the neural tracts connecting the brain and the limbs cross over in the brain stem), being the one contralateral to it. Thus, in right-handed people, the left cerebral hemisphere is dominant and vice versa.

It might seem logical to assume that the hemisphere primarily concerned with skills and speech would also be the one most intimately involved in visual perception, especially as verbal labelling plays such an important part in the latter process. However, this does not seem to be the case. Much evidence has been accumulated in recent years suggesting that where the left hemisphere tends to specialize in the verbal and manual skills, the right specializes in visual and spatial ones. Hence in cases where visuo-spatial disorders are particularly severe, lesions tend to be 'exclusively or predominantly right-sided' (McFie *et al.* 1950). Critchley (1953) analysed the localization of 19 cases in which visuo-spatial disorders were not complicated by disorders of language. Eleven were solely in the right hemisphere, seven were bilateral and only one (unverified) was in the left.

Gloning *et al.* (1968) have published a large and well documented series of cases showing that disorders of visual perception are predominantly associated with lesions in the right parietal area in both right- and left-handed patients. Critchley draws attention to the possibility that in left-sided lesions, disorders of perception may not be absent so much as secondary to those of speech. In this connection Humphrey and Zangwill (1952) report an interesting case of a left-handed man with a right occipito-parietal gunshot wound. This patient showed all the usual symptoms of visuo-spatial agnosia (with severe neglect of the left side) and a minimal loss of verbal fluency.

Further evidence that the right hemisphere may control spatial functions in the same way that the left controls verbal ones comes from the number of reports comparing the WAIS subtest performance of patients with unilateral lesions. The common finding is that in patients with left-sided lesions the verbal scores are inferior to the performance ones (the latter depending primarily on the manipulation of visual data), whereas in right-sided lesions the opposite is the case (McFie *et al.* 1950). Warrington and James (1967a) tried to define the actual functions carried out by the two hemispheres more clearly by studying groups of patients with localized lesions on a task of picture recognition and on the Gollin (incomplete) figures. They found that on the picture recognition task those with left-sided lesions made errors of recognition. On the Gollin figures, those with right-sided lesions were worse than those with left. Where patients with left-sided lesions did make mistakes, these were usually associated with poor performance in other perceptual tasks. These authors argue from this that perception and recognition are two distinct activities. Bisiach and his co-workers (1976a, b) have followed this up by trying to identify more precisely the exact parameters of visual information that the patients with right-sided cerebral lesions find difficult to assimilate, while Kimura, studying patients with right and left temporal lesions on the perception of visual stimuli presented tachistoscopically found that the patients with right-sided lesions were only inferior to those with left on the recognition of unfamiliar (unnamable) material, suggesting that the disability of vision seen in right-sided lesions only becomes apparent when verbal identification is lacking. From this, she argues that true recognition nearly always involves some aspect of verbalization—a conclusion that Geschwind might agree with. Indeed Geschwind himself sees agnosia as a result not of direct visual disorder, but rather as the 'disconnection' of the visual areas of the brain from these underlying other mental processes, particularly speech and language (Geschwind, 1965).

This would suggest that patients with right-sided cerebral dominance as evidenced by handedness and speech could be expected to show less lateralization of visual performance than others—a fact which has been confirmed in a number of investigations.

The whole question of hemispheric specialization and the assessment of laterality will be returned to again in more detail in later chapters. Here it may just be mentioned that Warrington (1969) had discussed the subject in detail in her consideration of constructional apraxia, and agrees with the general conclusion that although much confusion still seems to exist regarding the functions involved in visual perception in general and in the activity of the two hemispheres in this skill in particular, the right hemisphere does seem to contribute more than the left to the perceptual components of skills. Semmes (1968) has put forward a neat model to account for the difference between the right and left hemisphere functions. She suggests that in the left hemisphere, focal representation may favour integration of *similar* units, thus giving rise to generalization and fine sensory motor skills including speech, whereas in the right hemisphere integration may consist of *dissimilar* units, accounting for multi-model co-ordination and discrimination. Whether these two different systems can actually be verified at a neuro-anatomical level remains to be seen.

6
Disorders of Bodily Awareness

The disorders to be described in this chapter are as different from simple sensory loss as are the visual agnosias from loss of visual acuity. Although, as will be discussed in Section 6.9, some loss of sensation may accompany them the total picture—often referred to as a body image disorder—is often extremely complex and may be very varied.

The main disorders can be listed and described as follows.

6.1 UNILATERAL NEGLECT

A patient with no serious weakness will sometimes ignore one side of his body (usually the left) or fail to carry out commands with it. When asked to lift his arms, he lifts one arm only. When dressing, he puts on only one shoe or combs only one side of his hair. This condition can be demonstrated by the 'glove test' in which the examiner tosses a pair of gloves into the patient's lap, telling him to put them on. The patient commonly puts on only one (usually the right hand) leaving the other aside.

Two points to note in this condition are that (1) the neglected half of the body functions quite well in spontaneous, automatic acts, and those in which the two sides of the body have to be co-ordinated; for example, in the glove test, the neglected hand may be used to place the glove on the accepted one and (2) while the accepted hand often crosses the midline of the body to help on the neglected side, the opposite seldom occurs.

Patients showing neglect, often also demonstrate a curious indifference about it. They appear unconcerned if the condition is pointed out to them, and although not euphoric will cheerfully laugh at themselves.

6.2 ANOSOGNOSIA

This might be regarded as an extreme form of neglect in which the patient not only fails to recognize his disability but actively denies its existence. Thus, if asked to lift his paralysed arm, the patient either moves the intact one and maintains that he has carried out the command, or if prevented from doing this will lie immobile and after a few seconds mutter 'well, there you are, that's done'.

In some cases the paralysed limb may be repudiated or attributed to the presence of someone else. One patient quoted by Critchley always referred to her hemiplegic leg as 'Toby'; another seen by the present author maintained that her own body was perfectly intact and that the hemiplegic limbs at her left side belonged to her husband.

6.3 ILLUSIONS OF CORPORAL TRANSFORMATION

These are sometimes seen, patients reporting that the shape of their bodies are changing or that the size of certain limbs have shrunk or become enlarged. Such sensations are usually transitory and frequently follow focal seizures.

6.4 ASTERIOGNOSIS

This consists of the inability to recognize objects from handling them, without the use of vision and other sensory cues. Care must be taken not to confuse this with a disorder of naming itself, especially as in cases where the two cerebral hemispheres are separated due to lesions of the corpus callosum, the disability may occur on one side only. Geschwind and Kaplan (see Geschwind, 1965), for example, describe a patient with such a lesion who:

When blindfolded, incorrectly named objects placed in the left hand. That this defect was one of naming was proved by several facts: (1) the patient would handle the objects correctly in the left hand while he was giving an incorrect name; (2) if the object was taken away and the patient was then instructed to select the object he had held from a group, he always selected the correct object either visually or tactually with his left hand; (3) similarly he could, after holding an object, concealed from vision, draw it correctly with his left hand although he had misnamed it. By contrast, after holding the object while blindfolded in his left hand, he could not afterwards select it from a group or draw it with the right hand. He correctly named objects held in the right hand and could draw such objects or select them from a group with the right hand but failed if he attempted to use the left hand for these tasks. That the disturbance was not one of transfer between limbs but rather between hemispheres was shown by the fact that he could draw with the left foot a pattern drawn on his left hand but not one drawn on his right hand. (p. 287).

This, and similar cases, will be discussed further in Chapter 9.

6.5 FINGER AGNOSIA

This consists of doubt and hesitation concerning the fingers only. This is a special and often isolated form of body image disturbance whose association with right-left disorientation, agraphia, acalculia, and colour agnosia was first noted by Gerstmann in 1924. Existence of the symptom may be elicited in a number of ways: (1) the patient may be asked to name a finger touched by the examiner;

(2) the patient may be asked to hold up a finger touched by the examiner; (3) the patient may be asked to point to a named finger on the examiner; (4) the patient may be asked to carry out complex commands such as 'put the third finger of the right hand on the tip of the second finger of the left hand; (5) the patient may be asked to point to the finger on a chart which the examiner touches on him; and (6) the patient has to touch or name on the examiner the same finger which the examiner touches on him.

It is usually found that the same errors are made on both hands, but that subjects do better on some of the tests than on others. For instance, a patient may have greater difficulty in indicating fingers than in naming them (apraxia) or vice versa (finger aphasia). It is also commonly noted that more errors are made on the two middle fingers (third and fourth) than on the thumb, index, or little finger.

Finger agnosia may occur in the absence of any other form of body image disturbance and it is noteworthy that agnosia for the toes is very rare indeed. Thus, finger agnosia cannot be attributed to the fact that it applies to the extremities of the limbs.

6.6 PHANTOM LIMBS

While phantom limbs are almost invariably experienced by all subjects at some period after an amputation (as will be discussed shortly), they are less rarely but still occasionally experienced by subjects in association with hemiplegic limbs. In the latter cases, the phantom limb is usually supernumerary to the healthy one and usually refers to the fingers of the hand, less commonly to the upper arm and very rarely to the lower limbs. The phantom limb appears to mirror movements carried out by the normal one and tends to vanish as soon as the hemiplegic limb is moved or located visually. Total hemiplegia of the affected limb is not essential. Walsh describes a patient who 'would imagine that his left arm was behind his back as if the two hands were clasped; that is, as if he were a soldier standing at ease. His immediate impulse was always to grope and determine the whereabouts of his real arm in case he should accidentally hurt it. As soon as he found the arm, the phantom feeling would disappear'. (Critchley, 1953, p. 234).

The vividness of supernumerary phantoms can, according to Critchley, 'be manipulated pharmacologically. It can be restored after spontaneous disappearance by mescalin, and it can be oblated by cocainization of the real limb' (p. 244).

Prosthetic limbs replacing those that have been amputated often modify but seldom actually decrease the sensations of the phantom and, like the hemiplegic limb, may alter the latter's position when in view. Indeed, sometimes the presence of the prosthetic device actually confuses a patient and may be left off for this reason. One patient seen by the author, whose phantom was accompanied by acute spasmodic pain, complained that when wearing his artificial arm, the only alteration was that the pain usually felt as being in the fingers of the phantom, moved up into the wrist of the artificial arm, and intensified.

6.7 ASYMBOLIA FOR PAIN

This was first described in 1928 by Schilder and Stengel and has since been discussed by a number of people. Although these patients can correctly distinguish sharp from dull sensations and respond appropriately to verbal threats or threatening gestures, they deny feeling any physical pain. Denny-Brown (1962) maintains that the defect lies not so much in unawareness of pain itself, but in its lack of biological importance to the subject.

The association between the disorders described above, and the development of a normal body image must be considered.

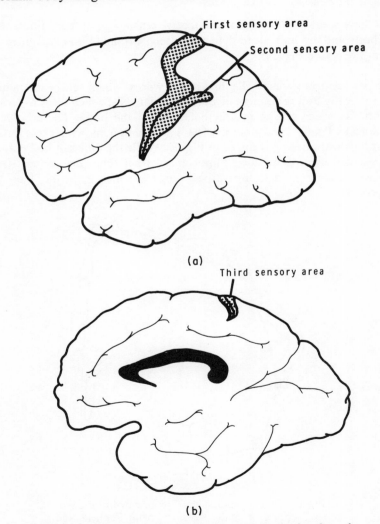

(a)

(b)

Figure 24. (a) The sensory-cortical areas of the brain—lateral view, (b) The sensory-cortical areas of the brain—medial view

6.8 PSYCHOLOGICAL MECHANISMS INVOLVED

Most healthy people are unaware of their body images, and remain so till something goes wrong. Hence it is when the body image fails to match up to reality that we become conscious of it.

Most of our knowledge about the normal body image comes from two sources; (1) studies of the sensory cortical areas, and (2) the study of phantom limbs following amputation.

Studies of the Sensory Cortical Areas

That is those areas in the cortex which receive sensory input from different parts of the body and are difficult to define precisely. Brodal (1969) recognizes three different areas (see Fig. 24).

1. The post-central gyrus or the 'first sensory area' which can be distinguished anatomically by a prominent layer of granular cells, which serve as terminals to fibrous tracts arising in different areas of the body. These latter were mapped by Penfield and Boldrey (1937), whose well known representation of their localization is reproduced in Fig. 25. While the different body areas are represented in order of their importance rather than their actual size, the general scheme is a comparatively orderly one, with the hind limbs uppermost.

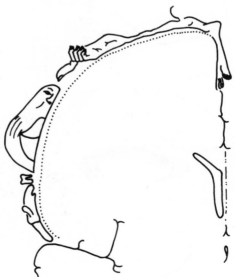

Figure 25. The 'homunculus' represented in the sensory cortex of man. Redrawn from Penfield and Boldrey (1937), 'Semantic and sensory representation in the cortex of man', *Brain*, **60**, 432

2. An area beneath the lower end of the first sensory-motor one, and sometimes referred to as the 'second somatosensory area'.
3. The medial aspect of the hemispheres.

Brodal points out, however, that none of these areas are exclusively sensory, since motor effects can be obtained from them as well. Moreover, although each hemisphere appears to receive most of its input from the contralateral side of the body, there is some overlapping or 'collaboration' of systems as yet poorly understood.

Study of Phantom Limbs

A good deal of information regarding the normal body image comes from the study of phantom limbs which, as already mentioned, follow the sudden loss (usually through amputation) of limbs with previously normal sensation.

Phantoms following amputation have been noted since the beginning of medical history, but it was Weir Mitchell (Mitchell, 1871) who first established the almost universal occurrence of this phenomenon in adults. The phantom is often so real that a patient on awaking from the operation refuses to believe that a limb has been amputated (Simmell, 1963) but with the passage of time both the vividness and the form of the phantom undergo modification. From a phantom of the whole limb as it is used to be (though not necessarily according to Simmell in the position it was in at the moment of loss or injury) parts begin to drop out and those that remain become telescoped or smaller in size. It is important to note that the first parts to go are the upper arm and thigh; then follows the lower limbs and calf and after them, the knee and elbow. The fingers and toes are the last parts to remain and often feel as though they are attached to the stump. Even in deformed limbs (amputated for aesthetic or practical reasons), it is the terminal parts (hands and digits) which are most strongly represented in the phantom. An interesting point here is that the phantom of the congenitally deformed limb resembles the deformity rather than a normal limb. (Weinsten, Sersen, and Vetter, 1964). Thus visual influences may play a large part in deciding both the original shape of the phantom as well as in the alterations it undergoes, but there is a close and striking parallel between the importance of a body part in the phantom and the area of cortex involved in its normal control, as demonstrated by Penfield and Rasmussen (Brodal, 1969).

The two most common factors affecting phantoms are (1) age at amputation, and (2) nature of the limb lost. Simmell (1962) has studied the phantoms of children after limb amputations and has found that the longer the subject has had and used the amputated limb the more frequent and the more persistent is the phantom experienced. Children under four years old seldom claim to experience phantoms and phantoms are never experienced for congenitally absent limbs. On the other hand, phantoms of the sex organs tend to decrease as sexual potency decreases (Weinsten, *et al.*, 1968), and after amputation of the breast the most detailed descriptions were given by 'the younger more intelligent women attuned to their environment' (Simmell, 1963). It seems, in fact, that the phantom reflects the degree to which the limb has been integrated into the body image in the past and is a part of current life problems and activities.

For a phantom to occur at all, it has been consistently noted that the limb has to (1) have had previously good sensation, and (2) be removed suddenly. Those digits which have been absorbed slowly as a result of leprosy may not appear in phantoms, but—and this seems to be an important point—if a half-absorbed digit is amputated the full digit may appear in the phantom (Simmell, 1956, 1961) and is often painful (Price, 1976). Explaining this Simmell (1963) suggests 'The new schema that has developed as a result of progressive absorption lacks the stability of the earlier schema' and may be superseded by it.

Phantom limbs which have faded with the passage of time may recur after cerebral lesions. L'Hermitte describes an interesting case of one patient whose left leg had been amputated at the thigh some years before and who subsequently developed a left hemiplega following a cerebro-vascular accident. After this the patient not only denied the amputation but insisted that he had an intact and useful left leg which he could see and feel. One patient seen by the present author who lost his right leg in the Second World War and whose phantom had since disappeared, had a renewed appearance of the phantom in association with right-sided Jacksonian epileptic attacks.

Theories to Account for Body Image Disorders

In trying to account for phantom phenomena and for body image disorders in general, three different types of mechanisms have been considered: (1) dynamic, (2) derivatory, and (3) organic.

The Dynamic Concept

This attributes phantom phenomena and anosognosia to the patient's reluctance to admit to bodily loss. Argued forcibly by Schilder (1950), stress is laid on the not infrequent traits of personality disorder which accompany these phenomena. Finger agnosia is similarly explained. It is argued that since the hand is the extension of thought into space, the disorder must be primarily mental rather than physical.

While the fact that reluctance to accept disability may be present in most patients showing these defects, there is no evidence that it is not also present in those who do not; and the fact that anosognosia and finger agnosia are most commonly associated with lesions to the right hemisphere is a serious argument against dynamic factors as being solely responsible.

The Derivatory Hypotheses

This attributes body image disorders primarily to defects in other spheres of mental activity, notably verbalization. Thus Weinstein, Cole, and Mitchell

(1964) conclude that 'the predominance of anosognosia for the left side is an artefact of the method of study usually employed'. From a close examination of 28 patients with right-sided sensory motor defects, they found anosognosia in 15. There was, moreover, an inverse correlation between anosognosia and aphasia, from which the authors argue that anosognosia may occur on the right side just as often as on the left but in these cases is usually unrecognized owing to the patient's inability to describe it. They admit that the descriptions by those with left-sided anosognosia 'are in general more bizarre' and are more often associated with unilateral neglect than those on the right, but they attribute the bizarreness to the florid language often used by patients with right-cerebral lesions and regard it as due to a linguistic rather than a perceptual disorder. Thus Weinstein *et al.*, would tend to avoid a purely organic basis for body image disorders and although not as committed as Schilder to a dynamic interpretation, would see it more in terms of a resultant of other disorders.

In this connection Critchley's analysis of the salient features of Gerstmann's syndrome (agraphia and acalculia with finger agnosia) is interesting and challenging. Asking why the hand should be the most affected body part, and what its connection may be with calculating, writing and right-left disorientation, Critchley points out that counting begins—historically as well as in each individual—with the fingers and is still linguistically associated with them (thus the numbers 1 to 10 are called the digits.)

The close connection between verbal, motor, and perceptual activity is further emphasized by Halnan and Wright (1961) who, in an amusing, but well presented paper, draw attention to the fact that while the thumb, forefinger and little finger have the largest areas of cortical representation and are also the most affected in finger agnosia, they are also the only digits to have specific names in the English language. Nonetheless, perceptual awareness and indeed right–left orientation can occur without their verbal equivalents, and even precede verbalization in childhood. Thus, Jambor and Williams (1964) found that for some years before they are able to give directions in verbal terms, children are able to find their way around simple mazes and complex corridors, indicating directions by naming landmarks instead of laterality.

The Organic Hypothesis

This relies for most of its evidence on neuropathology and argues that body image disorders are caused by disruption of the physiological processes carried out by discrete anatomical areas.

6.9 NEUROPATHOLOGY

Disorders of body image are, with very few exceptions, seen only in association with lesions in the parietal area. Anosognosia is usually confined to lesions in the right or non-dominant hemisphere, and finger agnosia to those in the left or dominant one. From the summaries of 28 published cases of Gerstmann's syndrome reported by Critchley it appears that only five were in the right hemisphere and amongst these, two of the patients were left-handed or ambidextrous (see Table 6). Predominance of left-sided lesions was also found by Gloning *et al.* (1968) in their survey of cases with focal cerebral lesions. Of the 241 patients studied by them 53 showed some aspects of Gerstmann's syndrome. In 49 of these the lesions were in the left hemisphere, and in all except one, were localized in the parietal area. Gerstmann himself was convinced that the lesion responsible for his syndrome lay 'in the region of the parieto-occipital convexity (of the dominant hemisphere), particularly in that part which is represented by the transitional region of the angular and the middle occipital convolutions' (Critchley, 1953, p. 224).

In the case of anosognosia and other body image disorders, localization of the lesion is less precise. Critchley, in fact, after very careful consideration of the data believes one can go no further than to relate it to the parietal area in general. To try to localize lesions further, he submits would be unjustifiable. To discriminate between superficial and deep lesions or to narrow them down to lesions of a particular gyrus he does not believe to be warranted.

In the case of asymbolia for pain, a somewhat different situation may be presented. As pointed out by Geschwind (1965), the situation here is not so much one of sensory loss as of its misinterpretation. He believes this is due to disconnection between the parietal sensory area and the limbic system.

Semmes *et al.* (1963) raise an interesting question of the relationship between disorientation of the body and that for external objects. Thus they distinguish bodily disorientation from external disorientation. From a study of 76 US veterans who had sustained localized gunshot wounds of the brain, they concluded that while there was a close correlation between the two forms of disorientation (independent of other factors such as aphasia or dementia) the two were not related to the same cerebral areas. Left hemisphere lesions of the anterior parietal area affected personal orientation more severely than external, but right hemisphere lesions of the posterior area affected external more than personal orientation.

In summarizing the content of this section, one sees that the name usually given to the disorders described here—namely body image disorders—is really unjustified. The body *image* of the patients described is undisturbed. The concept

Table 6
Location of lesions associated with Gerstmann's syndrome. Reproduced by permission from M. Critchley, *The Parietal Lobes*, 1953, London, Edward Arnold

| Handedness | Location of lesions | | |
	L.hemisphere	Bilateral	R.hemisphere
R. handed	18	4	3
Ambidextrous	1	0	1
L. handed	0	0	1

they have of their bodies, the image due to past experience, is still present. It is awareness of the real body and its present position which seems to be at fault. Information relating to the real body is failing to reach consciousness; it is not becoming integrated with other mental acts. The patient is carrying around, as it were, a phantom of himself, and in the absence of severe or prolonged external stimulation, lives with this phantom instead of with reality.

Why it should be that lesions in the right hemisphere cause this to happen more often than those in the left is unclear. It could be that the size and nature of body part representation in the sensory motor cortex is different in the two hemispheres. If the right hand and fingers are represented over a greater area in the left hemisphere than are the left hand and fingers in the right, then the frequency of finger agnosia with left hemisphere lesions and anosognosia with right could be understood: but as yet there is very little evidence to suggest that such a neat relationship occurs.

7
Disorders of Motor Skill

Motor movements of the body are controlled by a network of nerve cells which run from the posterior part of the frontal cortex via the spinal cord to the muscles. Within the motor cortex, as in the sensory cortex, different parts of the body are represented in different areas as shown in Fig. 26.

From the cerebral cortex, the motor pathways pass via the internal capsule (Fig. 27) into the brain stem and the spinal cord, receiving impulses throughout the major part of their journey from other areas of the brain, especially the basal ganglia and the cerebellum. Injury or damage to any part of this system may cause motor disorders, varying from diminution of activity (paralysis or weakness) to its opposite—excessive and poorly controlled movements such as tics, tremor, jerks, and spasm.

If the injury is confined to the motor system, the patient is usually fully aware of his disability and may be able to take steps to minimize or compensate for the inconvenience it causes him. For example, in the case of paralysis the patient may use a walking aid. In the case of unilateral tremor, he may use the unaffected arm

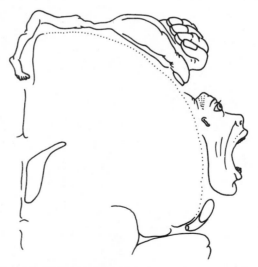

Figure 26. The 'homunculus' represented in the motor cortex of man. Redrawn from Penfield and Boldrey (1937), 'Semantic and sensory representation in the cortex of man', *Brain*, **60**, 432

to guide and control the affected one. If the damage also affects areas of the brain outside the motor system, the problem may be very different. A number of motor disorders are caused by degenerative diseases affecting the basal ganglia such as Parkinson's disease, Huntingdon's chorea, and senility. If the degeneration becomes widespread, the patient may be unable to make compensations. Such patients will be considered in greater detail in Chapter 10.

Another common cause of motor impairment is rupture or occlusion of blood vessels (strokes) supplying the internal capsule. The damage is seldom confined to this area alone and may involve many neighbouring structures. One result of this may be that while the movements themselves are spared, the patient loses the ability to combine them into the skills which had been developed during the course of life. The patients usually know what they are supposed to do and recognize their inability to do it, shaking their heads in perplexity and cursing their own foolishness. For example, a patient when asked to touch the top of his head, might touch his nose instead; if asked to comb his hair, might turn the comb over in his hands two or three times, and put it on the table; if asked to light a cigarette, might put the packet in his mouth and the cigarette on the table. Under emotional stress, or if the act is part of an automatic sequence, it may be completed adequately; but its execution is no longer under voluntary control.

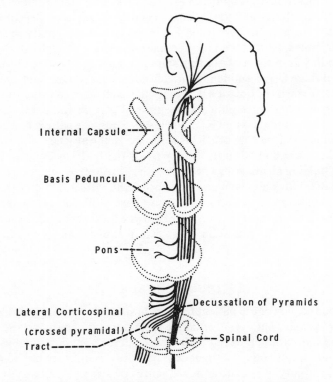

Figure 27. Diagram of the motor pathways in the brain

The harder the patient tries to carry it out, the more he concentrates, the more likely he is to fail.

Apraxia, as such disorders are called, must be distinguished from ataxia; in the latter, knowledge of the movements required is quite intact, it is the control of the limbs which is at fault—the finger overshoots the mark; the man with a broom sweeps near the target area but constantly misses it. In apraxia, fine muscle control is usually unaffected; it is the sequence of acts constituting the skill which is lost. It is apraxia only which will be considered here as the other motor defects come more into the province of the physician than the psychologist.

Apraxias were divided by Liepmann into ideotional (inability to plan an act) and ideomotor (inability to execute it), but this distinction has been seen by many authors to be more confusing than helpful.

7.1 IDEOMOTOR APRAXIA

Typical instances of Liepmann's ideomotor apraxia have just been described above. The disturbances are clearly recognized by both the patient and those looking after him, and need no special tests to elicit them. They refer to simple everyday tasks. Usually there is a relationship between the patient's ability to complete a task and the complexity of the task itself (the number of different isolated acts involved), and to the frequency with which it has been performed in the past; but the main defect always lies in the patient's inability to produce the act at will. Thus a patient who is quite unable to take a match out of a box and light a candle put in front of her on command, may still be able to carry out the same acts if there were a sudden failure of the electricity. One who cannot put on her spectacles when the doctor asks her to may well do so in order to read. There are also frequently in such patients disorders of gesture and pantomime such as those noted by Goodglass and Kaplan (1963). Thus, if a patient is asked to show how he would stir a tea cup, brush his teeth, etc. in the absence of the utensils, the patient, like a small child, uses some part of the body to indicate the utensil. Instead of holding an imaginary spoon to stir, he will stick a finger out and rotate it. Instead of holding an imaginary toothbrush, he will scratch his forefinger over his teeth. Besides demonstrating the 'body part as object' characteristic, these patients also tend to accompany their gestures with verbal commentaries (verbal overflow) and find the imitation of a gesture easier than its production from memory.

7.2 DRESSING APRAXIA

Inability on the part of the patient to dress himself is probably just one aspect of ideomotor apraxia, but as it is often the most obvious aspect and the one which attracts most attention, it has sometimes been described as an isolated symptom. As in ideomotor apraxia the patient does not lose the ability to put on his clothes, but only the ability to organize the sequences of acts necessary to do so. When trying to put on a coat, he cannot remember how to get his arm into the sleeve and ends up with it back to front. Tying bows and doing up buttons present particular difficulty, and it is in his attempts to carry out these acts that the patient suffering from apraxia is most easily distinguished from the one suffering from dementia, even though the end results are often the same in each case. Thus patients in both categories may finish up with their clothes on back to front, inside out, and upside down; they may try to pull their stockings on over their shoes or put on a coat before a shirt. Their reasons for doing so are different in the two diagnostic categories, and further investigation is usually necessary before an ill-dressed patient can justifiably be said to demonstrate apraxia for dressing rather than neglect of one side of his body or a more generalized mental disorder.

7.3 FACIAL APRAXIA

Inability to carry out movements of the face to command (e.g. screwing up the eyes, puffing out the cheeks) was first recognized in 1878 by Hughlings Jackson in certain patients with aphasia—especially with severe expressive disorders or Broca's aphasia (see Chapter 8). This, indeed, seems to be the most common form of apraxia in aphasics, some of whom will perform elaborate acts with other parts of their body to achieve the same ends as the act demanded of them. For example, a patient, 'may pretend to stub a match in an ashtray or stamp on it with his feet when asked how he would blow out a match' (Geschwind, 1965, p. 618).

7.4 VERBAL APRAXIA

The inability to carry out the movements necessary to articulate speech is comparatively common, and must be distinguished from expressive dysphasia—i.e. the loss of ability to find and select words themselves. This can usually be done by asking the patient to write instead of phonate. Although patients with verbal apraxia often have severe and profound hemiplegia involving the writing hand, they can usually use the contralateral hand to write fluently, even though some word finding difficulties may be present.

Verbal apraxia of insufficient severity to cause complete aphasia may produce slurring of consonants (dysarthria) or changes of melodic tone (dysprosody) and can occur as a single isolated symptom (Whitty, 1964).

7.5 CONSTRUCTIONAL APRAXIA

In contrast to the conditions described above, wherein the patient shows inability to carry out skills that have been acquired and practised over a lifetime, constructional apraxia consists of the loss of ability to apply practised skills to new situations—e.g. copy a design, draw a map of the ward, make a three-dimensional model with bricks, etc. To elicit constructional apraxia, the patient must be faced with these tasks; hence while ideomotor and dressing apraxia are easily observable in a ward setting and are usually recognized by medical and nursing staff, the discovery and measurement of constructional apraxia is usually the prerogative of the psychologist with his battery of tests.

Tests commonly used to elicit constructional apraxia are described by Critchley (1953) and by Warrington (1969) and may be mentioned briefly here.

1. Paper and Pencil.
    a. Copying test. The subject is asked to copy designs of varying difficulty and complexity which involve at least two figure or lines in contact with one another, and some diagonals.
    b. Free drawing tests. The patient is asked to draw a clock face, house, or a map from memory (see Fig. 28).
2. Stick tests.
    The subject is presented with sticks of various lengths and is asked to copy a design made by the examiner. If he finds this too difficult, the task may be simplified by removing all those sticks except the ones essential for the task.
3. Brick building (three-dimentional) tests.
    The subject is presented with a group of blocks of different shapes and sizes and asked to make them into a set of patterns (tower, bridge, etc.), or to copy patterns made by the examiner.

Figure 28. Typical drawings of a patient with
constructional apraxia

4. Block design.

The subtest from the WAIS is a useful method of eliciting this defect. Subjects with constructional apraxia usually show undue difficulty with the very first of these designs, and break down on this test much earlier than would be expected from their performance on other subtests.

Scoring of apraxic disorders is most satisfactorily based on (1) the presence of signs of abnormality, and (2) the difficulty (complexity) of the item eliciting them. The signs themselves have been well described by Critchley (1953) and by Warrington (1969). They are:

1. The copy cannot be placed in an appropriate place on the sheet of paper or the table. It may be started so close to one side that it must be pushed close together or fall off.
2. There is difficulty in bringing two lines or two designs together without overlapping, overshooting, or remaining disconnected.
3. In line drawings the copy may be smaller or larger than the original.
4. There is a tendency to place vertical lines either too close together or too far apart. Single lines may be reduplicated.
5. The copy may be rotated in space (rotation) or placed on top of the original (crowding). In the stick and brick tests, the subject will remove parts of the

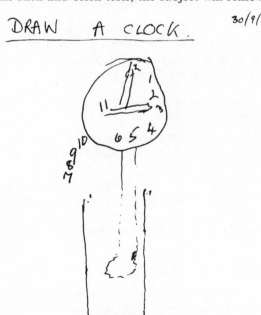

Figure 29. Drawing of a clock face by
a patient with constructional apraxia

original to make his own copy, and has difficulty in selecting those of the right size or length.

6. Sections may be omitted without the subject apparently noticing it. This is particularly common if visuo-spatial agnosia is also present, for then the patient tends to include in his reproductions only the right side of the model or the object that he is attempting to draw, omitting the left. If asked to place the numbers on a clock face, or the hand at a certain time, the numbers will be crowded together on the right or written underneath one another in a column. The big and little hands may be confused or placed on top of one another (see Fig. 29).

7.6 PSYCHOLOGICAL VARIABLES IN APRAXIA

As has already been mentioned, the degree of disorder seen in a patient may vary with a number of factors, some of which are as follows.

Complexity of Task

In general, the simpler the task in terms of the number of different acts involved in it, the more likely it is to be carried out successfully.

Emotional Setting

The importance of this has again been mentioned in considering ideomotor apraxia. Acts will often be carried out appropriately in response to emotional demands, which cannot be performed voluntarily.

Modality of Command

As pointed out by Geschwind, there are some patients who, although unable to use objects correctly if given verbal commands to do so, may be able to copy the examiner or handle them correctly.

Care must be taken not to confuse such patients with those showing 'disconnection syndromes' which will be discussed in Chapter 9, and whose condition is probably due to the disruption of neural connections between the speech areas and those controlling the contralateral limbs.

The Parts of the Body to be Used

It is possible for movements involving the whole body to be perfectly well preserved in some patients with otherwise widespread apraxic disturbances. Geschwind (1965) describes several such patients, one of whom

Was asked to assume the position of a boxer. He immediately assumed the boxing stance, leading correctly with the left fist. When asked to punch he looked perplexedly at his fist. Several different terms were then used—'punch', 'jab', 'uppercut', but none of these succeeded in eliciting a response. This situation set sharply in relief his ability to perform whole body movements in the face of marked difficulty with movements of individual limbs. (p. 622).

The accurate performance of motor skills probably depends on two factors: a 'cognitive map' of the skill and its aims (corresponding to Liepmann's ideotional system) and the 'stimulus-response' sequences by means of which the goal is reached (corresponding to Liepmann's ideomotor system). Whether one is more important than the other, or whether the two are interdependent (alternative sides of the coin, so to speak) are points which are much debated among psychologists. Neuropsychology does not appear as yet to have provided an answer to the question which may in fact, in the end, turn out to be unimportant.

Of far greater practical interest is the possibility that different patterns of breakdown may be associated with different locations of lesion.

7.7 NEUROPATHOLOGY

There is a fairly conclusive evidence that apraxia is associated with lesions in the parietal area (see Fig. 30), and a further distinction can be drawn between those

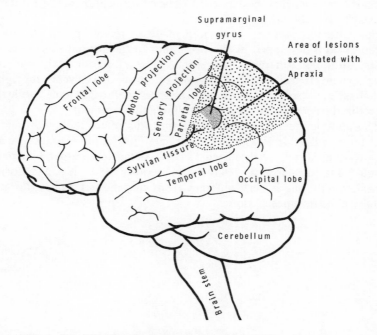

Figure 30. The location of area in which lesions are associated with apraxia

associated with left, those associated with right, and those associated with bilateral hemisphere lesions. Leipmann himself believed that the area responsible for all apraxias lay deep below the left supramarginal gyrus and suggested that the defects seen were due to severance of the connections between the posterior parts of the left hemisphere and the motor regions. Warrington (1969), however, believes that both hemispheres may be involved, but that each produces a slightly different picture. She has listed the differences under three headings: (1) the incidence and severity of the disability; (2) its qualitative aspects; and (3) the associated disabilities.

The incidence of constructional apraxia appears to be almost twice as common after right as after left-sided lesions but this is closely related to associated disabilities, notably slow reaction time, unilateral neglect and loss of topographical memory, all of which occur more often after right than after left hemisphere lesions. Many authors have argued that inability to carry out constructional tasks may be due to these associated disabilities rather than to any direct interference with the skill. Indeed analysis of the errors made by right as opposed to left hemisphere lesion patients support this conclusion to some extent (Heilman, 1975). Patients with right-sided lesions tend to copy designs in a fragmented and disjointed manner whereas those with left-sided lesions simplify them and can only succeed at all by slavishly reproducing the lines. While right-sided patients include all the details but often put them in their wrong places, the left sided patients miss the details out. The quantification of these differences has proved extremely hard.

Few attempts seem to have been made to relate apraxic disorders to the different skills developed by the two hands in the normal execution of manual tasks, although differentiation seems to start at an early age in human development (Ingram, 1977). Thus even by the age of 3–4 years, the right-handed child has developed greater strength and speed in the right hand, while the left has specialized in control of finger posturing and placement.

The apraxic conditions associated with 'disconnection syndromes' and the split brain will be dealt with in greater detail in Chapter 9 and those associated with dysphasia will be discussed in more detail in Chapter 8. It may just be pointed out here, however, that the bilaterality of the lesions associated with apraxic conditions is very different from the marked lateralization of those usually affecting speech alone.

8
Disorders of Language and Associated Skills

Disorders of speech (dysphasia or aphasia) are a common sequel to cerebral injury and have been noted for many years. The most obvious impairment refers to word finding. Rochford (1969) in a short history of aphasiology, writes:

> An early example was a case described by Napoleon's surgeon Baron Leary. In the Battle of Waterloo a soldier received a 'wound of the brain' after which his intellect was said to be impaired and he could not remember proper names or substantives. He returned to work as a drill sergeant but found himself unable to teach 'naming of parts' without consulting the manual, nor could he call his men by name.
>
> However, this loss of the ability to name objects (anomia, nominal aphasia, or amnesic aphasia) is not always associated with the inability to find nouns—only inability to associate them with the objects to which they usually refer. Bateman (in 1890) quotes a case of Trousseau's who said 'pig, brute, stupid fool' to a visitor pointing to a chair, and one could not say that such an outburst involved inability to find nouns even though there is clearly a lack of naming as such. Moreover, it is frequently noted that patients who may not be able to find a name at the moment it is requested can find it in another context. 'But Doctor, I can't say no' exclaimed a patient of Hughlings Jackson. Thus as Schuell and Brown (in 1950) point out the disorder refers to the inability to find words as required not just to name objects.

Speech is disturbed in psychiatric as well as focal cerebral lesions, but in general the psychotic speech disorders can be distinguished from those due to focal cerebral lesions by the following points:

1. Adults with speech disturbances of organic origin are seldom completely dumb. Unlike those due to some psychotic illness' (e.g. catatonic schizophrenia), the adult dysphasic patient usually has a number of words or sounds left in his repertoire which he may repeat over and over again even if not in the right context.

2. The dysphasic patient nearly always tries hard to communicate and usually succeeds in doing so, whereas in the psychotic patient (senile as well as schizophrenic), communication seems to be irrelevant.

Table 7
Disorders of expression and comprehension

Type		Disorders of expression	Disorders of comprehension
Non-Fluent	Amnesic	Defect mainly in word finding. Speech tends to be circumstantial, but grammatically correct.	None or minimal
	Broca's	Severe loss of fluency and grammar, leading to 'telegraphic' speech. Sometimes accompanied by articulatory disorders.	Minimal
	Global	Limited to a few repetitive phrases or meaningless utterances.	Severe loss
Fluent	Jargon (Wernicke's)	Speech over abundant and rambling. Grammatical structure intact, and sentences often begin appropriately but wander off into neologisms.	**Difficult to assess but appears greatly impaired.**

The way and degree to which practical language is impaired by focal cerebral lesions varies. In some patients expression may be limited as mentioned above, to a few single words or stock phrases. In others, fluency and normal word sequencing are retained (in fact may even be over-abundant) but the words uttered do not make sense (neologisms) and the sentences are meaningless (jargon aphasia). In yet others it is not so much the knowledge of the words but the ability to articulate them which is absent.

Different observers have tended to classify the disorders in somewhat different ways, but most distinguish the categories shown in Table 7.

8.1 NON-FLUENT DYSPHASIA

Although the inability to find names as required may predominate over the ability to string words together in sentences (agrammatism) and vice versa, it is now generally agreed that the disorders of speech arising from cerebral injury in non-fluent aphasia are difficult to place in separate categories and especially to associate with different cerebral lesions. Head (1926) regarded the ability to find names as an important symptom, and referred to at least three cases in which it was the sole residual symptom; but even he, when classifying the speech disorders into separate categories, stressed that each of his groups includes disorders of wider extent. Weisenberg and McBride (1935) regarded dysphasia as classifiable only into expressive and receptive disorders. This conclusion is also reached by Rochford and Williams (1964) who studied 33 consecutive patients admitted to the neurosurgical wards at Oxford with organic speech disorders on a battery of tests measuring naming, the comprehension of names, reading and writing, all of which were equated for difficulty and scored in terms of age equivalents based on the performance of children between five and eleven years. They found only three patients out of the 33 who showed impairment on the object naming test as a sole symptom. If naming of objects was severely impaired in their patients, there was also gross impairment on all other tests. Comprehension of names was, however, unimpaired in 20 of the patients who showed disorders in other spheres. Impairment in the visual aspects of language (reading and writing) was closely correlated $(r = +0.74)$ and was the sole language impairment in two cases, suggesting that this aspect of language may be regarded as a separate disorder.

Investigating their patients further, Rochford and Williams found that the inability to name objects was paralleled by the inability to name actions (verbs) and colours. Thus, the naming of objects appears merely to be one aspect of a general word finding disability. Nevertheless, as it is a task which is easily studied, open to experimental manipulation and controllable, it can be used as a basis for investigating language disorders in some detail. Rochford and Williams (1962, 1963, 1965) tried to define some of the factors involved in the word finding of dysphasic patients, and to relate these to the linguistic processes of normal individuals. Their main findings were as follows.

Non-Linguistic Factors in Word Finding

Memory

Since nominal aphasia has often been considered as due to a basic disturbance of memory (indeed it has been called amnesic aphasia by Goldstein, 1948) a comparison was made between dysphasic patients and those in whom disorders of language accompanied other evidence of mental impairment such as senile dementia and schizophrenia. In contrast to the latter, the dysphasic patients made many errors of naming but few of recognition. Indeed several of the dysphasic patients remarked when picking out some of the previously presented pictures 'This was the one I couldn't tell you'. Memory impairment does not, therefore, seem to be necessarily associated with naming difficulty.

Perception

It has also been argued (and indeed in some cases clearly shown) that patients are unable to name objects correctly because they do not perceive them accurately. In the case of senile dements this is often so. The errors made by such patients usually indicate faulty perception as often as inability to find names. The errors of dysphasic patients, however, are quite different. Such patients can very often describe the use of an object they are trying to name or may indicate by other means that they know what the object is. For example, shown a picture of a windmill the dysphasic patient may say 'You know,—it goes round and round', whereas a senile patient may mistake its identity and call it 'a coffee pot'. Shown a picture of a drum, the dysphasic patient may say 'In jazz-bands—they beat it', while the senile one may mistake it for a tea cup.

Comparing the number of errors classifiable as perceptual or semantic in 16 seniles and 29 dysphasic patients, Rochford and Williams found significant differences (see Table 8).

These observations suggest that while naming disorders in senile patients may arise from perceptual difficulties, those in dysphasics do not. To substantiate this hypothesis, the above two groups of patients were then asked to name parts of their bodies touched by the examiner. In this task, where the identity of the object to be named did not depend on visual perception, the senile patients, as predicted, made hardly any mistakes at all. (Table 9) (Rochford, 1971). The difficulty a dysphasic patient has in finding names cannot, therefore, be justifiably attributed to a disturbance of perception.

Intellect

Arguments have been put forward especially by Goldstein (1948) that dysphasia is associated with and dependent on loss of intelligence and what he calls ability

Table 8

Errors indicating failure of recognition, in an object naming task for dysphasic and senile patients

	Correct recognition, wrong name	Mis-recognition	Don't know	blank	% failures
Dysphasic (n = 33)	44	12	47	34	51%
Senile (n = 16)	11	41	14	5	55%

Table 9

Errors on two naming tasks made by dysphasic and senile patients. Reproduced by permission of G. Rochford

	Number of errors	
	Objects	Body parts
Dysphasics (n = 10)	41	42
Seniles (n = 10)	42	2

for 'abstract thinking'. The comparisons made between the dysphasic and senile patients mentioned above must surely refute this argument, for whereas most of the dysphasic patients studied in this research showed little loss of general intellectual ability the senile patients were grossly impaired on all intellectual tasks. Yet it was the seniles who in general made fewer mistakes on the naming task than the dysphasics.

Fatigue

The variability of dysphasic patients has often been attributed to fatigue. If this is so they should succeed more often at the beginning of a task on which they are asked to name a series of different objects than towards the end, but this is not found to be the case.

The number of errors made on the first half of a 20-item task, when compared with that made on the second half in a group of ten dysphasic patients, showed no difference.

Linguistic Factors

Frequency of Word Occurrence

Turning now to the variables within language itself one of the easiest to study is frequency—i.e. the relative number of times a word is spoken. The first count of word usage was that published by Thorndike and Lorge in 1944, column G, of which was compiled from a comprehensive sample of written language. This word count uses the following notation:

AA, indicates words occurring more than 100 times per million words.
A, indicates words occurring between 50 and 100 times per million.
Other words are given a number indicating the number of occurrences per million words.

In the studies of Rochford and Williams 18 objects were drawn in simple outline each on a plain white card. The names for these objects ranged from words occurring 100 times or over, or between 50 and 100 times per million (AA, or A words) to words occurring only eight times per million. They were all common objects which normal adults can name without difficulty and which have one unequivocal name in the English language.

There was a close correlation ($r = +0.79$) between the word frequency of an item and the number of errors made by dysphasic patients. There was still a positive but smaller ($r = +0.34$) correlation in the senile patients whose performance was very variable. Word frequency was also seen to affect the ease with which items other than common objects were named. Thus the names for actions (verbs), colours and even body parts varied with word frequency. In each of these tests a relationship was found between errors and word frequency in the dysphasic patients.

Sequencing

Once a single word or name is found, those that 'go with' or follow it in practice seem to be aroused automatically. The English language contains many composite nouns which are largely descriptive of the objects they name—e.g. wheelbarrow. These composite words can be divided into four groups depending on the word frequency of the different syllables: common-rare (e.g. sundial, pennyfarthing, hedgehog), common-common (lighthouse, penknife, horseshoe), rare-common (spinningwheel, padlock), and rare-rare. The proportion of errors made by dysphasic patients when asked to name such objects, depends on the frequency of the first syllable only. If this is common, the whole word is easy to find, if it is rare, the word is difficult to find.

Context

Similar, perhaps, to the effect of sequencing is also the fact that patients are often able to find words in their common verbal contexts when not able to do so in their less common ones or without a context at all. A group of dysphasic patients was asked to name a number of objects and for each one that they failed to name they were offered a variety of cues or prompts. One of these was a verbal sentence in which the word sought would normally be the last item. Thus for the word hand, the cue was 'We have feet and—', for the word teeth 'We bite with our—'. This cue was found to be effective in eliciting the word required in many cases (Rochford and Williams, 1963).

The situation in which a word is being sought and the frequency with which it has been used before in *that situation*, is another factor found to be important. There are many words in the English language which are used in a number of different contexts and denote completely different things in each one. For example, the word bat refers to a cricket bat or a flying mouse. Dysphasic patients are able to find the word in its common context (as deduced from the Thorndike–Lorge Semantic Count, 1938) more easily than in its rare one.

Prior Arousal

It is seen from the above two investigations that sequencing and context both appear to give dysphasic subjects a lead-in to the required word and so help them to find it. Does arousal of the phonetic elements of the word itself help?

Arousal by Rhymes. In the prompting investigation described in the subsection on Context above, one of the prompts used was a rhyme to the required word. Thus for the word hand they were told 'it rhymes with band'. These cues were found by Rochford and Williams to have no significant effect on the dysphasic patient's ability to find words; in fact, in not a single instance was a word found in response to this cue alone. The generalization of words on the basis of rhyming patterns seems to be a phase through which normal children pass between the ages of five and ten, but thereafter dies out (Rochford and Williams, 1963).

Arousal of the Word in its Common Context. If a word is aroused in one situation or by one means it is thereafter found more easily in another. Thus, once the word has been found in its common usage it can then often be applied to its rare one. 'Of course, those are the teeth too'.

Arousal by Spelling. Finally, a cue well known to be very effective is that of beginning to spell out the word sought 'It begins with H', 'It's a HAN—'.

From the above investigations it becomes clear that the word store of dysphasic patients is not so much destroyed as relatively inaccessible. Access to individual items can be gained either by some form of lead-in (semantic or contextual) or by arousal of the required item which immediately lowers its threshold to reproduction (de-blocking, Weigl, 1963). The effectiveness of the letters used to spell the word in writing suggests that words are coded in their written and spoken forms close together. However, it must be remembered that rhymes did not assist production. Perhaps the failure of a rhyme is due to the fact that a rhyme only arouses the last sound of a word, not its beginning, whereas the first letter of a word arouses its beginning rather than its end. The relative effectiveness of the first syllable of a composite word (as against that the last syllable) also indicates that it is the initial lead-in to the word that is the difficulty for the dysphasic patient, not its production once it has been, so to speak, located. The same is certainly true for normal people. Any crossword puzzle enthusiast will know that the assistance given by the first letter of a missing word is infinitely greater than that given by the last.

8.2 FLUENT (JARGON) DYSPHASIA

Quite different from the dysphasia described above and characterized by (1) its poor communication value, and (2) its overabundance of output, jargon or fluent dysphasia has been recognized as a separate category of speech disorder by most observers. First identified by Wernicke in 1874, it is much rarer than any of the non-fluent aphasias, although Geschwind (1974) found it to be present in 5% to 10% of all new aphasic admissions to the Boston Veterans Administration Hospital. An example of speech is given below. The patient is attempting to describe the 'telegraph boy' picture from the Terman–Merrill Test (see Fig. 31).

The telephone man in the process of describing the existence and spectator-ship of . . . in the West Country (Yes). The tunnership here . . . the form utterige of the er vessel, it really is what's in its front tyre plus not, are you with me? (No—would you explain). In order to find the tyreship there you'd run the tyre into the front wheel and then you'd weigh it, and then you'd

104

Figure 31. Picture of 'telegraph boy' from the Terman–Merrill Test. Reprinted by permission of Houghton Mifflin Company. All rights reserved. Copyright 1937 by Lewis M. Terman and Maud A. Merrill

have the weight of the front tyre, er it may be there's no great problem there as far as I see it. The, the, the, the cycle tube for the front tyre hasn't had a bad break down, isn't going to have one and it can't have one anyway, so your piterist is quite alright. (Rochford, 1974 Reproduced by permission of G. Rochford).

When asked to name a series of objects another patient gave responses as shown in Table 10.

The verbal output of such patients has been described by Valpeau (1843) as 'intolerable loquacity', by Jackson (1866) as 'peculiar and outwardly meaningless language form', and by Freud (1891) as 'impoverishment of words with abundance of speech impulse'. As with non-fluent dysphasia, many attempts have been made to attribute the disorders to some function other than the linguistic one, but nearly all can be refuted. Impoverishment of general intellectual ability and visual perceptual disorders were not found in the two cases of jargon aphasia described by Kinsbourne and Warrington (1963c) and although memory is difficult to assess in these patients, and may indeed be poor, there is no certain evidence that it is.

Weinstein *et al.* (1966) attribute jargon to lack of self-awareness (monitoring)

Table 10
Responses given to a series of objects

Object	Response
Book	"Book, a husbelt, a king of prepator, find it in front of a car ready to be directed"
Candle	"Craft candlestick"
Drum	"Drum"
Rake	"Walking stick, would have been designed"
Dice	"Dice"
Scarecrow	"We'll call that a three minute resk witch, you'll find one in the country in three witches"
Anchor	"A martha argeneth"
Whale	"Ship painted, shoereen or a shoecream"

or anosognosia, but both Kinsbourne and Warrington, and Rochford, believe that jargon aphasics are able to understand their own output if this is played back to them after very short time intervals, and occasionally they show some insight into their errors. Although the comprehension of others may be impaired, it is certainly not totally absent, and is usually much better preserved than in the three patients with word deafness described below who, however, almost totally avoided jargon in their speech. Thus the tendency to talk jargon cannot be *due* to comprehension loss.

Factors within the speech of jargon aphasia itself have been studied by Weinstein *et al.* (1966) and by Rochford (1969). Rochford described four cases, one of whom, a traumatic aphasic, was seen on five different occasions during the three months he took to recover and another who was seen on three different occasions during the course of recovery. The points noted by Rochford were:

1. There was a close relationship between the total number of errors made on a naming test and the total number of words emitted during the course of it (see Fig. 32).
2. There was less correspondence between word frequency and errors in these patients than is seen in non-fluent aphasics.
3. There was often some associative relationship between the words that were uttered and the words that were sought, even though this could not always be recognized immediately. Thus Rochford concludes 'it is prudent to suggest that any failure to relate the response to the stimulus seems more likely to be a failure of interpretation by the investigator than a randomness in the patient's verbal behaviour' (Rochford, 1974).
4. There was considerably more perseveration in patients with jargon aphasia than with those of standard aphasia, and the perseverative disturbances spread over a longer time interval.
5. The speech of jargon aphasics was similar in certain respects to that of psychotic patients. Thus jargon aphasics like schizophrenic patients often refer to themselves in the third person, use many personal references, and often resort to original metaphor.

106

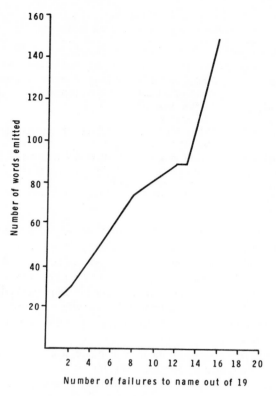

Figure 32. Graph showing relationship between number of words emitted and naming
errors in jargon dysphasic. Reprinted from
Rochford (1974), 'Are jargon dysphasics dysphasic?', *British Journal of Disorders of
Communication*, **9**, 35

6. Although flashes of insight may be apparent occasionally, it is much more
common for the patient to appear unaware of his mistake. Thus one patient
described by Rochford, when asked if he had any difficulty finding words,
replied: 'No, none at all. I come out of my speech making to everything like
that, quite quite comfortably, thank you'. He then proceeded to utter a stream
of jargon when attempting to describe the telegraph boy picture. (Fig. 31).

In their interpretation of jargon aphasia, both Weinstein and Rochford
stress the failure of monitoring: whether failure is due to the fact that too much
output is present for adequate filtering, or whether it is inadequate filtering that
allows the excessive output is impossible to say. Kinsbourne and Warrington
believe the speech of the jargon 'approximates quite closely to the patient's
uncorrected and unexpurgated inner speech' and Rochford's conclusions are
somewhat similar. Rochford points out that a characteristic of most patients

with organic cerebral involvement—and clearly shown in his own cases—is inability to give words associations as required. Thus, when Rochford's patient was still trying to name every object shown to him with a flood of associative answers, he was reduced to almost complete dumbness when specifically asked to *give* associations to the same words. This paradox is explained by Rochford in the following way. In non-fluent aphasia the threshold of all items in the word store is raised, so that in order to find any one at any time excessive stimulation is required. In jargon aphasia the threshold is lowered so that all are aroused and the difficulty lies in sorting out the appropriate item from the mass of words presenting themselves. The direction of 'spread' in both cases follows normal associational patterns. Thus, according to Rochford 'the jargon dysphasics inability to name does not lie behind his verbal excitement, but is the result of it'.

8.3 DYSPHASIA IN CHILDHOOD

The disorders of language shown by children who suffer brain damage of the dominant hemisphere are different from those of adults in that:

1. Residual speech is much rarer and seldom contains the paraphasias, stereotypies, and perseverations seen in adults.
2. Reading and writing is nearly always severely impaired alongside any loss of expression.
3. Articulatory disturbances are commonly seen alongside loss of word finding.

Thus the brain damaged child tends to remain mute or to emit only the simplest, most automatic phrases when questioned, saying most of the time 'I don't know' or 'I can't'.

Alajouanine and L'Hermitte (1965) noted that this gross loss of speech tends to be replaced by the adult type of dysphasia as the age at which trauma is sustained increases. The speed of recovery, however, shows an inverse relationship with age—the younger the child at the age of trauma, the quicker and more complete is its recovery. Other factors of prognostic importance are the aetiology and the presence or absence of epilepsy.

8.4 RELATIONSHIP BETWEEN EXPRESSIVE DYSPHASIA AND NORMAL SPEECH PROCESSES

Although expressive dysphasia renders its sufferers unable to retrieve or find access to words, the rules which govern dysphasic speech production appear to be the same as in normal people (Howes and Geschwind, 1961). Moreover, if the intellectual activity or alertness of normal people is temporarily reduced, they are found to show many of the features common to dysphasia. For example, ECT reduces the naming ability of patients in exactly the same way as it is reduced in dysphasia, access to the lower frequency words being the last to be regained. (Rochford and Williams, 1962) (see also Chapter 2). Distraction (on a dichotic listening task) not only reduces word finding (again the loss is relative to word frequency) but the errors made by normal people under these conditions are closely related to the errors made by dysphasics (Rochford and Williams, 1962). Finally, Oldfield and Wingfield (1965) found the same parallel between word frequency and naming latency in normal people as occurs between word frequency and name finding in dysphasia: the rare words taking longer to find by normal subjects just as they are less likely to be found (without cues) by the dysphasic patients.

Not quite so clear is the relationship between aphasic disturbances of grammatical structure (syntax) and the rules which govern normal syntactical structures. Chomsky's (1972) analyses of the latter have provided a useful framework within which to study the subject, and using this as a basis for their analyses Kerchensteiner and Huber (1975) conclude that the disorders seen in acquired (or traumatic) aphasia are different from those in normal childhood and in developmental aphasia. In the former, inhibition of faulty structures is removed, whereas in the latter it has never developed. Andreewsky and Seron (1975), however, conclude that even if agrammatism is exhibited in free speech, the retention of 'rules' can still exist, since the utterance of grammatically ambiguous words remains regulated by their syntactical roles. Gardner, Denes, and Zuriff (1975) found however that semantics are usually more important than syntax in determining a subject's recognition of an error, especially when reading.

These findings all indicate that the loss of word finding in dysphasia represents an exaggeration of a condition common to all linguistic expression. By focusing attention on some of the factors and conditions influencing dysphasia the study of brain damaged patients has also drawn attention to some of these factors in the normal—particularly the effect of frequency and the effect of sequency constraints. It has also told us a little about how the processes of language are mediated.

This is not the place to discuss the development of normal language in children—but it may be noted in passing that the pattern of breakdown in dysphasic children does indicate that the mechanisms used by adults to find and produce words develops only slowly over the course of time. The dysphasia shown by children also indicates that those skills least practised are the first to go. The close parallel between the age at which words are learnt by children and the difficulty with which they are found by dysphasic adults (Rochford and Williams, 1962) is another indication of the relationship between development and breakdown. To assume, however, that brain damage causes simple regression would be erroneous. Both development and breakdown are dependent on certain factors, one of these clearly being frequency of usage.

It has been pointed out above that language depends on (1) the presence of a store of words; (2) the ability to select any item from this store at a single moment in time (retrieval); and (3) the emission of words in strings or sequences (syntax). We still do not know where and how the items in the vocabulary are stored or the connection which exists between this store and cerebral activity in general. We do know, however, that the items are stored in groups rather than as individuals (since the arousal of one member of a group arouses others too); we also know that a single item (e.g. the word hands) is stored several times over for each of its contexts, but that there is some relationship between these independent stores, since arousal of a word in one context can arouse it in others too. And finally we know that the written and spoken forms of a word are stored separately and yet with connections between them.

We know too that with increasing age the groupings made between words is based on semantic rather than phonetic similarity although in the early stages of development this may not be so.

8.5 PHYSIOLOGICAL FACTORS IN DISORDERS OF EXPRESSION

That disorders of language are closely associated with injury to the dominant cerebral hemisphere is now well established. Within this area, further specialization seems to occur. While Broca's area (see Fig. 33) is concerned mainly with articulation, word finding difficulty is more often seen after lesions in the temporal lobe. In Wernicke's or fluent aphasia, Geschwind (1974) believes that the lesion is predominantly in the white matter, and involves principally the area below the first temporal gyrus. In general it is certainly found more often in posterior temporal lesions (i.e. those closest to the parietal association areas) than in fronto-temporal ones.

Where the disorder is due to a vascular lesion, Kerschensteiner (1977) believes

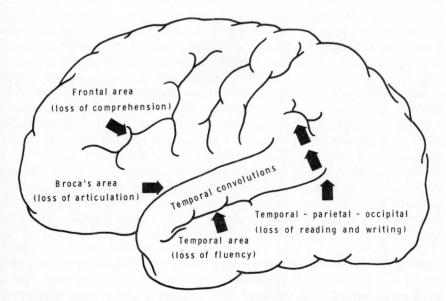

Figure 33. The location of cerebral areas associated with language—lateral view

that the different syndromes are related to lesions in the different arterial systems: Wernicke's aphasia (fluent aphasia) to rupture of the posterior temporal artery, Broca's to that of the precentral artery and global aphasia to the internal carotid. However, even if it were to be well established that lesions in clearly defined areas do cause clearly defined disorders it would not follow that the language function is necessarily 'stored' in those areas. Indeed, language can still be emitted to some extent even after complete obliteration of the left hemisphere in a right-handed person. Smith (1966b) describes a 47 year old right-handed man in whom the whole of the left hemisphere was removed for the treatment of a neoplastic lesion but who, six months after operation, was not only able to comprehend all that was said to him but was even able to utter short, simple stereotyped phrases, obey written, as well as spoken, commands and sing tunes to command. Hughlings Jackson's suggestion that whereas propositional speech may be confined to the dominant hemisphere, emotive speech can be carried out by the other, appears thereby to be confirmed. However, a clear understanding of the role played by the right hemisphere in speech is difficult to obtain, for as Archibald and Wepman (1968) point out, in most cases of right hemisphere injury other factors such as perseveration and general intellectual deterioration make the assessment of the language function extremely difficult. This is also the view of Serafetinides and Falconer (1963) from a study of the speech disorders associated with temporal lobe seizures.

One factor which throws doubt on all attempts to equate speech with particular discrete cerebral areas, is the improvement of function which may occur with time—i.e. recovery—even when the lesion which caused the loss is itself irreversible. In such cases, has the function been taken over by other cerebral areas, or is language itself really mediated by some other source? There seems to be little doubt that recovery from dysphasia and adequacy in the use of language are closely related to age and to the treatment or stimulation received post traumatically. The earlier a lesion is sustained the more complete is likely to be the restitution of function. Nevertheless, recovery can proceed surprisingly far in adults even if it does not begin immediately. Blakemore and Falconer (1967) followed up patients who had received left temporal lobectomies for the relief of epilepsy and found that while there was a considerable drop in verbal learning in the immediate post-operative period, and little improvement on this in the first two post-operative years, thereafter improvement became quite rapid.

The connection between handedness and localization of language has been discussed and debated at length (Zangwill, 1963; Russell and Espir, 1961). In general it seems fairly clear that language is more often mediated by the left than by the right hemisphere, in left-handed as well as in right-handed subjects, but left-handed people do appear to be less severely dysphasic than right-handed ones after equivalent left temporal lobe lesions, and recover more quickly. Gloning (1977) did find some difference in the 'type' of dysphasia, in that among left-handers there tend to be more 'unclassifiable' and mixed disorders. Thus in left-handed subjects it is surmised that language is more evenly represented throughout both hemispheres than it is in strongly right-handed ones, but that even in them there is a predilection for representation in the left cerebral hemisphere. Further evidence that in right-handers language is the prerogative of one hemisphere only comes from the work of Gazzaniga and Sperry (1967) on patients in whom the cerebral commissures have been sectioned (see Chapter 9). In such patients it is found that visual stimuli presented in the right visual field (and therefore entering the left hemisphere) may be named and described without difficulty, although those presented to the left, and therefore decoded in the right hemisphere, evoke 'only irrelevant confabulatory spoken responses or none at all'.

The possibility that language is affected by subcortical as well as by cortical lesions has been raised, and there is some evidence—derived from the operations that are performed for the relief of Parkinsonian symptoms (wherein electrodes are stereotactically inserted in the area around the basal ganglia) that this is indeed the case. Ojemann et al. (1968) found that stimulation of the left pulvinar and deep parietal white substance in the pericollosal region of both hemispheres through implanted electrodes, caused temporary inability to find names, even though automatic speech and consciousness were unaffected.

In summary, it seems clear that even though the left temporal region may not be the only cerebral area involved in verbal expression or the only area capable of mediating it, this area is particularly involved in the linguistic expressions of normal right-handed adults.

8.6 DISORDERS OF COMPREHENSION AND MUSICAL APPRECIATION

Inability to understand language is harder to recognize and assess. In the case of jargon dysphasia, the patient, as already mentioned, may appear to have little appreciation of the nonsense in his own output and yet respond relatively appropriately to commands. There are some conditions, however, in which loss of comprehension (word deafness) may occur as an almost isolated symptom. Three such cases were studied intensively by the present author and can be described briefly. The first, a 65 year old right-handed man, was admitted to hospital suffering from cerebro-vascular disease with left–middle cerebral artery involvement.

Three months before admission, he had been walking through his bedroom when he stumbled but did not fall and began 'talking like a baby'. After sitting down for a little time he proceeded to the toilet but on his return found that he could not understand what his wife was saying.

Three weeks later the patient's speech returned and he could understand written words although he found he often called things by their wrong names. He could hear passing cars and other sounds.

On admission to hospital he said 'I can hear everything but can't understand what people are talking about'. He said he could hear music but could not recognize tunes. He could recognize different people's voices and even tell whether they were speaking with a continental, American, or English accent, but he could not distinguish what they were saying. He was orientated for person, place, and time, and intellect appeared to be unimpaired. He could still do the football pools but not crossword puzzles. In speech he used the odd jargon word or phrase and showed some disorders of grammar, but his output was fluent and he showed no difficulty in naming objects. Reading, writing, and arithmetic were good, as was his general knowledge.

His performance on the Raven matrices placed him in the ninetieth percentile for his age. Memory for personal experiences was excellent and on a non-verbal association learning task he performed extremely well. He was, however, quite unable to recall nursery rhymes and mathematical tables or to repeat any words or numbers after the examiner.

Pure tone audiometry showed a slight fall-off for high frequency tones but no defects within the sound range for normal speech. Although he could recognize and name various sounds such as a bugle, a fog horn, and a bird song, his recognition of tunes was considerably impaired. He could recognize and repeat rhythms tapped out with a pencil if these were given slowly but he made many mistakes if they were given fast. In this connection it was interesting that he had been a practised Morse Code transmitter. On testing now, he could transmit and decode messages accurately *if they were given slowly*, but made many mistakes on those given fast, usually omitting the last dot. His recognition of amplitude modulation was normal but frequency discrimination was poor and variable.

His ability to comprehend the written word was almost perfect, although he had some difficulty understanding the meaning of prepositions. He could not recognize symbols (plus, minus, division) and also had some difficulty on a sentence completion task, showing a tendency to associate to single words rather than to deal with the sentence as a whole.

Writing showed little abnormality and he managed to write a number of words to oral dictation.

It was in the comprehension of spoken words that this patient showed a defect quite out of proportion to all the others. He was able to distinguish single phonemes without a great deal of difficulty and in this sphere followed the normal rules of phoneme distinction, having greater difficulty with the voiced–unvoiced distinction than with others. He could recognize some short words in that if presented with a limited number of objects—e.g. pictures—he was able to match an object with its spoken name. He could not do this with two or three syllable words. Words of high frequency of usage were better recognized than those of low. It was in the ability to recognize string of words, whether these were presented in a grammatical sequence or as a non-grammatical word string, that the patient had particular difficulty. Sentences of more than two words were completely ignored.

It was also striking that the patient appeared often to be quite unaware of sudden sounds or unexpected interruptions. Thus, if a person interrupted when the patient's back was turned to him, the patient appeared to have no knowledge of any auditory stimulus at all. Startle response was completely lacking to loud noises.

In contrast to normal subjects, the patient's response to delayed auditory feedback was absent. In this situation, a subject is fitted with earphones through which he hears what he himself is saying after his words have passed through a delaying filter. Thus he hears each syllable only as he is about to pronounce the next. Whereas most normal people's initial reaction to this situation is one of marked disturbance, this patient showed very little awareness of any inconvenience. It must be concluded that he was almost entirely lacking any feedback from his own output.

This patient made a slow but steady improvement over the next six months and on discharge could understand and obey short, spoken commands ('Put out your tongue').

In conclusion this man with little in the way of general neurological or intellectual disturbance, no peripheral deafness and whose powers of linguistic expression were very well preserved, had almost completely lost the ability to understand spoken (in contrast to written) language. In association with this (but not necessarily causing it) there were defects of musical appreciation and of sound-sequence appreciation, while monitoring of his own output seemed to be absent.

The second case was that of a 38 year old, right-handed housewife who was diagnosed as suffering from disseminated sclerosis. She had been quite well until four years before her admission to hospital, when she began having transient episodes of 'her speech going off at a tangent'. She would go out shopping but when starting to ask for what she wanted would find herself saying irrelevant things. She was fully aware of the defect but unable to control it, became embarrassed, and sought psychiatric advice.

Six months after this, she had an episode of life sided twisting of her face. At the same time she was only able to utter repetitive phrases ('what's the matter') and could not understand what people said.

Her defect of comprehension had persisted almost unchanged until the time of her admission, but her ability to speak had somewhat improved. There had been occasional episodes of weakness of the left leg and of diplopia, but she was able to cope with her housework. About six weeks before admission she had a sudden complete paralysis of both legs and of the right arm, all of which cleared up after a few weeks. Her hearing appeared to be erratic in that on some occasions she would respond to faint sounds (such as her kettle boiling) but on other occasions would show no sign of hearing a gong sounded immediately behind her.

Intelligence appeared to be well retained. On the matrices she scored slightly above average and her score on the WAIS performance scale gave her an IQ of 105. Visuoconstructional tasks were well executed, and there were no defects of visual retention.

In the sphere of language she had some difficulty in word finding and in naming objects and considerable difficulty in formulating sentences. Her intonation was monotone and stilted and she characteristically finished each word with an 'er' sound.

Writing was seriously impaired but although she had difficulty in reading long words or complex sentences, she was able to read aloud and showed good understanding of simple written material.

In contrast to this the patient showed almost no recognition of any spoken speech, even though she could usually hear and even copy the sounds made by the examiner. Presented with a selection of written syllables she *was* usually able to pick out the one which was spoken to her (like the previous patient, her recognition followed the normal rules of phonetic distinction), but the words themselves seemed meaningless to her unless she could 'cue herself in' to their meaning by some method. Occasionally she would grasp the meaning of a word if she repeated it herself (thus her own output seemed to retain some meaning for her) but often she could only grasp what was said if given some clue by visual means. When asked to repeat after the examiner the words 'Monday, Tuesday, Wednesday, and then continue the sequence', the patient stared blankly, murmured 'Mon—Monday' and could go no further, but as soon as the word Monday was written down in front of her the patient exclaimed 'Ah, Monday' and complied with the instructions without error. Lip reading appeared to help her to some extent and she was often able to grasp the meaning of what was said by other stimuli within the general context.

This patient shows many of the characteristics of the first, but there was considerably greater disorder of expression along with the defects of comprehension. The third patient was a 19 year old right-handed airman who was knocked off his cycle and sustained a head injury in January, 1966. During the course of an ultimately complete recovery he went through a period of marked dysphasia in which disorders of comprehension were considerably greater than those of expression. While there was no evidence of hearing loss and non-verbal sounds were identified correctly, the patient was unable to carry out any complex commands. Simple questions regarding time, date, and place were often answered correctly. The patient comprehended words well enough to be able to supply simple opposites and synonyms to those spoken by the examiner, but was unable to give rhymes for single syllable words. He was able to repeat words up to those of two syllables in length and to match them with the appropriate objects or written material but he broke down on those of three syllables. The frequency of a word was of less importance than its length, but the frequency of the context was an important factor. Thus the patient could point to the hand on the body but not to that on a watch. He could point to the eye on the body but not that on the needle. If presented orally with a string of letters and asked what it spelt he could manage those up to five letters but no more.

Comprehension of written material seemed to be intact. He made no mistakes on a picture-word matching task (see Fig. 34) and only random errors when asked to read aloud a list of words, but if given written sentences to read he often missed out the prepositions and 'little' words.

In this case, as in the two others, the loss of comprehension of the spoken word was quite disproportionate to other mental defects and appeared to be independent of peripheral hearing loss.

Summarizing the findings of the above three cases, it seems that (1) the difficulty presented by the material is related to its length or amount; (2) the difficulty is related to the speed with which it is given; and (3) the ease with which the verbal input is decoded depends on other factors in the environment providing a context.

While the comprehension of speech is often considered to be dependent on, or at least closely related to, a patient's ability to monitor his own output it was seen in the first case described above, the only one unfortunately on whom the effect of delayed auditory feedback was studied, that the effect of his own speech on the patient's output seemed to be virtually lacking.

The connection between word deafness as presented in the cases mentioned above and comprehension loss in jargon aphasia is still unclear. The three cases just described have been selected because of their almost complete absence of jargon, and as has already been discussed comprehension loss cannot be regarded as the basis or even the most important symptom in jargon aphasia (Weinstein *et al.* 1966). In jargon dysphasia, moreover, there are usually other associated defects such as perseveration and over-abundance of speech which were absent in the above cases.

The fact that some children, although not deaf, never apparently learn to understand or respond to speech was first recognized by Worster Drought and Allen in 1928. Since then, word deafness in children has been a subject studied

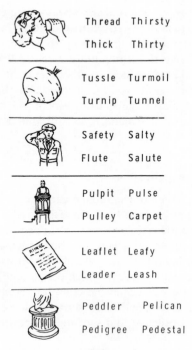

Figure 34. Sample of material
from the Gates reading test

much by neurologists but very little by psychologists. Tallal and Piercy (1975) have, however, found evidence in such children of reduced ability to appreciate brief auditory stimuli, and Tallal (1975) believes that a large part of their comprehension difficulty may be due to their inability to analyse rapid streams of acoustic information.

Amusia or the loss of musical appreciation, is a widely recognized symptom, often occurring in association with aphasia (as in the first case of word deafness mentioned above) but is by no means always associated with it. Thus many aphasic patients not only retain the ability to sing and recognize tunes, but may even be helped to find words themselves if these are accompanied by familiar songs or the compositions of melodies.

Amusia itself can occur as a result of a wide variety of defects, including the loss of appreciation of rhythm, of pitch, of volume, or of tone; loss of ability to read notation or loss of the emotional relationship to music itself. Gardner (1977) discusses the literature on the subject and the conclusions which can be drawn from it. He stresses (1) the wide variety of symptoms demonstrated under the heading, and (2) the wide variety of musical talents demonstrated by those who have been studied. He suggests that any conclusions drawn about the physical basis of musical ability from neuropsychological studies should consider the performance of highly trained and gifted musicians as well as those individuals with average musical ability.

In the case of the former, speech is nearly always affected in the early stages of the disrupting incident (usually a stroke), indicating involvement of the left hemisphere. This might seem contradictory to some of the findings to be discussed later (particularly those involving dichotic listening), but Gardner, suggests that in highly skilled musicians either the right hemisphere may have become predominant for speech as well as music, or that to become a really proficient and creative musician, the artistic elements must be combined with the constructive and creative ones which are usually under the control of the left hemisphere.

The Measurement of Comprehension

Loss of the ability to understand language can occur in very many different grades, from very severe to very mild. Appreciation and measurement of these is not easy, because if the patient fails to respond appropriately to a command or request, many reasons other than lack of comprehension could underly his failure. The first test to have been in general clinical use was that devised by Pierre–Marie, the 'three-paper test', in which the patient is presented with three pieces of paper and a variety of somewhat complex commands telling him what to do with them. Standards for the Pierre–Marie test have never been established inside or outside clinical practice and scoring procedure is entirely left to the administrator.

A more carefully designed and standardized test was first published in 1962 under the title 'token test' (de Renzi and Vignolo, 1962) and consists of nine tokens varying in shape, size and colour. These are placed in front of the subject who is then given a series of commands increasing in complexity from 'touch the red circle' to 'before touching the yellow circle pick up the red rectangle'.

In 1966 Boller and Vignolo presented the results on this test of a number of patients with left and right brain damage including those who did not show any clinical signs of dysphasia. It was demonstrated that defects on the test can still be seen with left hemisphere damage even when clinical signs of dysphasia are completely lacking.

The ability to 'transcend the literal meanings' of words by metaphor is a higher form of comprehension which is now being looked at for the first time. Winner and Gardner (1977) describe a simple test in which the subject was given a metaphoric sentence (e.g. 'He had a heavy heart') and shown four coloured pictures representing different possible interpretations of it including the metaphoric one (a person crying) and the literal one (a man carrying a heart and staggering under its weight). The subject is asked to select the picture which 'goes best' with the sentence. They found that whereas normal control subjects and those with left hemisphere lesions chose predominantly metaphoric interpretations, those with right hemisphere lesions and senile dementia chose predominantly literal interpretations.

The association between disorders of linguistic comprehension in adults and simple auditory acuity is not a simple one. Blumstein, Baker, and Goodglass (1977) found no defects of simple phonetic distinction in a group of patients with Wernicke's aphasia and suggest that the disorder is associated with inability to maintain stable phonetic configurations rather than simple perceptual acuity.

Psychological Mechanisms Involved

Thanks to the work that was started in the field of communication engineering during the two world wars, a good deal is known about the factors which affect auditory speech comprehension in normal people. This is not to say that we know exactly how the process is carried out; only that we know some of the factors affecting it.

The three most important factors in the comprehension of language by normal people seem to be (1) transitional probabilities; (2) filtering; and (3) chunking.

Transitional Probabilities

Because the number of different sounds available is smaller than the amount of information to be conveyed by them, and because the number of channels along which these sounds can be transmitted is limited, messages usually take the form of sound sequences, each sequence being a different signal. Thus, we speak in words and in sentences rather than in single phonemes. But this habit of stringing sounds together in sequences, governed by grammatical and syntactical rules, means that most of what is said becomes redundant. If we have heard how the sequence starts we can more or less guess how it will end. The signals at the beginning of the sequence limit the range of the ones that can follow, so that we do not have to hear many of the words in a sentence to comprehend its meaning. We seem to have at our disposal a built-in computer working out the transitional probabilities of word strings which tells us which word to produce or expect at any moment. Our knowledge of a language is based on programming of this computer by past experience.

Filtering

The importance of sound filtering in the comprehension process has mainly been studied by two-channel (dichotic) listening tasks. A subject listens through earphones to two simultaneous messages, one coming into his right ear and one to his left. He is asked to follow one of the messages only, and is able to do so by rejecting almost completely the sounds he hears in the other. It is presumed that the same process is involved in this task as when a person is trying to follow a conversation against a noisy background such as at a cocktail party. It is found that most of the rejected message is ignored completely, yet at the same time some aspects of it 'get through'. The subject can tell whether it is spoken by a man or a woman, in French or in English, fast or slowly and if individual words in it have special emotional value or fit in well with the message being followed, the hearer will switch over to the rejected message and let it in (Treisman, 1965).

To this extent, perception of a 'filtered out' message follows a similar pattern to linguistic perception in general; for the extent to which a normal (i.e. binaurally) presented message becomes recognizable depends on many non-linguistic factors (Boller and Green, 1972; Green and Boller, 1974). For example, the positions of speaker and listener *vis-à-vis* one another; the visual contact between them, and the presence or absence of a mechanical mediator (telephone or tape recorder) are important variables.

A great deal of work has been carried out in the 1960s and '70s to ascertain the relative efficiency of the two ears (representing by and large as they do, the two different hemispheres) in the perception of speech as compared to non-speech sounds. Much of this has again made use of dichotic tasks. There seems to be general agreement among investigators that while the right ear is better than the left at decoding verbal messages, the left is better than the right at appreciating musical and other non-verbal (especially tonal) sounds. There are, however, exceptions to this. Shankweiler and Studdert-Kennedy (1967) found that the difference between the right and left ears lay in the identification of consonants only. Whereas vowels were recognized equally well by both ears, it was only on the recognition of consonants that the right ear was superior. This suggests that the right ear is selectively attuned to the recognition of 'on–off' stimuli, and that it is in the *temporal sequencing* of input that its supremacy lies.

Much of the right ear supremacy depends on the message consisting of familiar material. (Hines, 1976). It is related to sex (Tucker, 1976) to socio-economic class (Borowy and Goebel, 1976), and it is often absent in people with a strong family history of left-handedness (Lishman and McMeeken, 1977), even though most ambidextrous people show the usual right ear supremacy. One difficulty here, however, lies in the distinction of handedness itself (Annette, 1975).

An interesting and ingenious method of investigating comprehension is that described by Heeschen (1977) who looked at the effect of priming on comprehension of single words. The target word was presented under masked conditions to make its comprehension harder; but it was preceded by a 'primer' in the form of another word connected with it by either associational or linguistic factors. While the comprehension of the left ear was related to the associational strength of the primer, that of the right was related to its linguistic distance.

Chunking

It appears that a listener does not deal with the sounds individually in the exact order in which they are received. He seems to store them up in chunks and then decodes the chunk as a whole rather than its individual elements. Thus, when we hear the word butterfly we do not think first of the word 'but', then reject this in favour of the word 'butter', and then reject both of those in favour of the whole word 'butterfly'. We seem to conceive the word butterfly as a whole right from the beginning. Recent work has shown the amount that can be stored and decoded in a single chunk increases with age and experience. One of the chief characteristics of the speech-retarded child lies in the small amount that he can deal with in a single chunk.

In the three cases of word deafness described in this chapter, the use of transitional probabilities seemed to be intact. The patients were still able to make use of contexts and, indeed, were even more reliant on them than before. It was in the spheres of chunking and filtering that the failure seemed to lie. Thus the length of word or sentence spoken was the most important factor in their comprehension, from which it can be supposed that the 'buffer store' in which this chunking takes place was severely reduced in these patients.

The other striking feature, especially in cases one and two, was the patients' apparent ability to *filter out* too much of the data provided. Loud noises, interruptions, bangs, etc. were completely ignored unless expected. The filter seemed, in fact, to have become a block.

Physiological Factors in Comprehensive Disorders

The sites of the lesions in the three cases of word deafness described in this chapter were not, unfortunately, able to be verified very exactly. A good deal of attention, however, has been devoted to ascertaining the parts of the brain involved in understanding both speech and music in other cases. The difference between defects of musical and verbal comprehension arising from cerebral lesions has been studied systematically in patients with temporal lobe lesions by the psychologists at the Montreal Neurological Institute. Milner (1962) reported a selective deficit in tone discrimination (measured on the seashore test) in patients with a dichotic listening task and at the same time found that patients with left temporal lesions made more errors than those with right in the repetition of digits. This latter deficit was further increased after left temporal lobectomy but was not influenced by right temporal lobectomy. Following this up Kimura (1964) compared patients with left and right temporal lobe lesions on dichotically presented melodies and digits, and confirmed the conclusion that melodies were more disturbed by right temporal lesions and digits by left.

Shankweiler (1966) further confirmed Kimura's finding in a careful study of 21 patients with left and 24 patients with right temporal lesions who showed no defect of hearing prior to the operation. Shankweiler and Harris (1966) found that in their ability to recognize single consonants or vowels or even clusters of phonemes, dysphasic patients followed the normal pattern of behaviour.

In children with retarded speech development, Springer and Eisenson (1977) found the size of ear asymmetry to be inversely related to the linguistic impairment, suggesting an impairment in left hemisphere specialization.

Investigating possible physiological mechanisms to account for ear asymmetry, Efron (1963) found that for two events to be judged simultaneously, the one directed to the non-dominant hemisphere had to precede the other by 2–6 ms. Efron suggests that signals reaching the non-dominant hemisphere have to be relayed to the dominant one, and that the matching or integration is carried out there. The study by Sparks and Geschwind (1968) of one patient with a surgically induced 'split brain' seems to add support to this suggestion, for their patient was totally unable to decode verbal signals applied to the left ear and hence only relayed to the right hemisphere.

When comparing the ability of patients with right and left hemisphere lesions to repeat sentences, Newcombe and Marshall (1967) found that the defect shown by the left hemisphere patients was mainly seen on the semantic constraints. Grammatical constraints were not important. On this task patients with right hemisphere lesions showed no deficit from normals. Gazzaniga and Sperry (1967) hold that although the right hemisphere may not normally be involved in decoding speech sounds it is still capable of so doing. In the three patients they studied after section of the cerebral commissures, they found that the right hemisphere could recognize object names as indeed it could also recognize written material. The patients, for example, could pick out an object by feel or vision whose name had been given to them in the left ear, but such disconnection syndromes will be discussed more fully in Chapter 9.

The recognition of sounds other than linguistic, i.e. the sound of a car starting, a telephone bell etc. have not been the subject of very extensive systematic study, but in 1966 Spinola and Vignolo reported an interesting study of patients with unilateral brain lesions who were asked to listen to tape recorded sounds and match them with pictures of the objects making them. Those patients with lesions in either hemisphere which did not affect speech made no more mistakes than normals; but the patients with speech disorders (dysphasia), especially those showing loss of comprehension made a significant number of errors (Spinola and Vignolo, 1966).

Another interesting study by Bender and Diamond (1965) concerns the localization of sound stimuli by patients with unilateral lesions. These authors found that the mislocalization of a sound source and a tendency to ignore the stimulus making it were predominant on the side contralateral to the hemisphere affected. These authors examined patients with known cerebral disorders but no defect in the peripheral auditory system. The defects noted concerned changes in volume, interruption, repetition, reverberation, roughness, and garbling of speech or music. All, or some, of these could occur in patients at different times and were very similar to the disorders which can result from peripheral deafness. The most striking disorder in the patients with intracerebral lesions was not in the nature of the disturbances reported but in the fact that these were reported almost always in association with the stimuli arriving in the half auditory space contralateral to the hemisphere affected. Occasionally stimuli which were presented in the affected half space would be localized in the other half space or would be ignored altogether. These signs were usually transitory and were closely related to other mental impairments (Bender and Diamond, 1965).

Of some importance to the physiology of comprehension are the observations made by Penfield and Perot (1963). Auditory experiences were often elicited by stimulation of the exposed superior first temporal convolution in patients undergoing craniotomy for the relief of epilepsy. Such phenomena were reported by 7.7% of the 520 patients in whom the exposed temporal lobe was stimulated. Some 62.5% of the experiences were reported by patients from stimulation of the non-dominant hemisphere. The experiences reported were usually the same as those experienced during the epileptic aura itself. While stimulation of the auditory sensory cortex (i.e. Heschl's gyrus, see Fig. 35) only evoked buzzing,

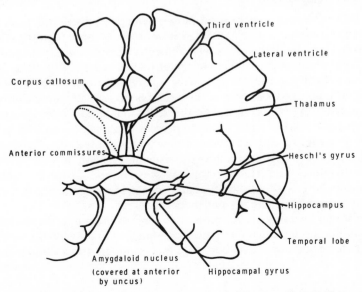

Figure 35. Transverse section of brain showing location of areas
associated with language

stimulation of the superior surface of the first temporal convolution evoked the same phenomena (voices, phrases or words) as were experienced during the epileptic aura.

Auditory plus visual experiences were also reported from 22 different points stimulated in 13 patients. Of these points, 13 were again in the non-dominant hemisphere and only nine in the dominant. Music was also experienced by eleven patients and more often again in the right than in the left superior temporal convolution. The authors dismissed the notion that this indicates the presence of 'engrams' in the temporal cortex itself by pointing out that stimulation of the area can still produce the experience even after the cortex has been removed. They do, however, suggest that this part of the cortex plays a part in the interpretation of sounds and renders the records of past experience available for this purpose.

8.7 DISORDERS OF READING AND WRITING

Since disturbances of reading (dyslexia) and writing (dysgraphia) are often seen in the same subject and at the same time, it seems reasonable to consider them together. This does not mean to say that they constitute a single function. Indeed not only do they sometimes break down independently of one another, but both reading and writing may each be disturbed for a number of different reasons.

The disorders of reading seen after cerebral injury can be divided into those of visual and those of verbal origin.

Dyslexia of Visual Origin

Many disorders seem to stem from purely perceptual disturbances and would have been considered in Chapter 5 had it not seemed more logical to deal with them here. Thus one patient may have difficulty fixating the stimuli and so miss out part of each word or sentence (Kinsbourne and Warrington, 1962). Another may have difficulty in following sequences from left to right so tending to see words in a haphazard way. Yet a third may be unable to recognize the visual aspects of letters or words but will be able to do so if he can move his hands over raised written material. Sometimes the perceptual difficulty can lead to writing errors. For example, a subject who can spell words orally without difficulty may be unable to do so in writing because the visual impression of what he puts on to the paper confuses him. He will stop half way through a word, unable to see which letters he has already written and repeat some again. He will miss out letters thinking he has already put them in.

The disorders mentioned above are not very often seen in the discrete form described. Far more frequently they are combined with difficulties in associating the visual forms of words or letters with their counterparts as will be described below.

Dyslexia of Verbal Origin

In these cases the difficulty lies not in recognizing the visual stimuli but in matching them to their appropriate verbal output. Thus written words can be matched to objects but not read aloud; or if the subject tries to enunciate them he may make the same paraphasic errors as he would in naming objects. Newcombe and Marshall (1966) describe one patient who read the word 'antique' as 'vase', 'canary' as 'parrot', 'gnome' as 'pixie', and the sentence 'put five shillings on a good horse' as 'five bob best horse'. Letters may be even harder to name than words, but in the case of the latter there is a close parallel between the words which children find hard to read (as judged by the age at which they are learned) and difficulty experienced after cerebral injury (Rochford and Williams, 1964).

The Assessment of Reading Ability

In the assessment of reading ability a clear distinction has to be made between ability to pronounce the words correctly and ability to appreciate their meaning. Thus in the paralexias mentioned above, comprehension of meaning appears to be relatively intact. Gardner and his colleagues (Gardner and Zuriff, 1975, 1976; Gardner *et al.* 1975a, b) have described a number of techniques for the assessment of comprehension which do not involve expression. Many of these are based on matching sentences to pictures or one sentence with another. They point out that adequate methods of assessment involve the recognition of syntactical (i.e. grammatical) as well as semantic constraints and hence must involve whole sentences as well as single words.

Using such techniques, they have been able to distinguish between subjects who read 'for meaning' (focusing on substantives and picturable elements) and who thus have difficulty understanding abstract messages, and those who do not. The former have difficulty with nouns but none with the little 'filler' words, whereas the latter tend to omit or alter the filler words but have little difficulty with nouns.

Dysgraphia

The disturbances of writing seen after cerebral injury can be divided into motor and ideational. The *motor* defects consist of (1) inability to put the letters of a word or the words of a sentence correctly in space (i.e. the lines become confused, run off the page, etc.); (2) perseveration (i.e. reduplication) of some letters (particularly those with loops such as l, m, or n); and (3) reversals (p for b). The basic disorder here is one of praxis, rather than of linguistics, and the same sort of mistakes are made as in drawing, building bricks, etc. (see Fig. 36).

The ideational defects are concerned mostly with spelling. 'I can't remember how it goes' a subject will remark. Kinsbourne and Warrington (1964) believe

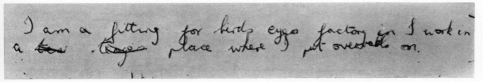

Figure 36. Sample of writing from a **dysgraphic** patient

that a large proportion of the spelling mistakes seen in dysgraphia can be divided into two groups: (1) those in which letters are added or omitted; and (2) those in which letter order is incorrect. While the former reflect 'an underlying disorder of language function' the latter reflect a more general difficulty in processing information in terms of spatio-temporal sequence. They believe that the second group is seen *par excellence* in Gerstmann's syndrome (see Chapter 6).

Relation between Dyslexia, Dysgraphia, and Dysphasia

As has already been mentioned, disorders of reading and writing may be seen in the absence of other linguistic disturbances. Where this is so they are predominantly of the sensory or motor type and do not involve impairment of the language function itself. Nevertheless, in the majority of instances dyslexia and dysgraphia *are* associated with dysphasia and do involve much more than loss of reading and writing alone. Thus out of 32 dysphasic patients studied by Rochford (1969), 21 showed impairment of reading and writing. There were only four patients who showed defects in reading and writing with intact expression, and seven who showed a discrepancy in the opposite direction. Again in children, as has already been mentioned, language impairment is almost always associated with marked loss of reading and writing, the loss being relative to the degree of past practice.

Nevertheless, two points are worth noting:

1. If the disorders of reading and writing are relatively more severe than the disorders in other language functions it is probable that a lesion is localized to the parieto-occipital area. The residual language skills shown by their dysphasic patients were all scored by Rochford and Williams (1964) on a scale standardized against the performance of children and rated in terms of age equivalence. Thus it was possible to give each subject a score for object naming, comprehension of names, picture-word matching, reading aloud, and writing. Each subject's own average score on all these tests was calculated and a note was finally made of the degree to which his performance on each of the subtests was above or below his own average performance—i.e. how good he was on each item relative to his own over-all performance. The 32 patients were then divided up into groups according to whether the lesion was predominantly frontal, temporal, or parietal. The results are shown in Fig. 37 and it will be seen that while inability to name is disturbed only in the temporal group, reading and writing are selectively disturbed in the frontal and parietal groups.
2. The defects in reading following cerebral lesions relate more to the execution than to the understanding of the word, just as the loss of speech relates to expression rather than to comprehension. Thus as will be seen from Fig. 37 patients with temporal or parietal lobe lesions are usually better able to match words to pictures or objects than to read the words aloud. This contrasts markedly with the performance of patients whose speech disorders

are accompanied by dementia or psychotic illnesses, in whom the opposite occurs. In these patients the ability to respond to the printed stimulus with the appropriate linguistic output is still present, even though the subject seems to have little idea to what the word refers.

Gardner and Zuriff (1976) in their early work found this difference tended to be associated with lesion site. However, from a more extended survey of ability beyond that of matching words to pictures, assessment becomes more difficult and they conclude that site of lesion is less important than the nature of the reading task itself for all aphasic patients.

Dyslexia and the Development of Reading

What relation does acquired dysphasia and dysgraphia have to reading back-wardness in children, and specifically to the conditions sometimes known as congenital dyslexia or word blindness? Backwardness in learning to read can have a number of different causes including low IQ, poor visual discrimination, language disorder, educational insufficiency, and emotional disturbances (Vernon, 1957). When all these factors have been discounted, however, there still remains a small group of children who seem incapable of learning to read and write, and in whom a variety of other features are nearly always found. These children may have difficulty in scanning systematically from left to right: they are often left-handed (or come from predominantly left-handed families), and tend to write from right to left instead of from left to right thus encouraging their scanning defects. They frequently have other language deficits (Denckla and Rundel, 1976) and poor visual imagery. Many of these children are known to have suffered some form of birth injury or to have been premature babies, and

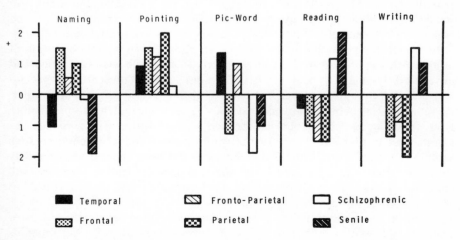

Figure 37. Differences from their own mean scores on various language tests by two groups of psychotic patients and four groups with localized cerebral lesions

several show features of Gerstmann's sydnrome including finger agnosia and right-left disorientation. According to Vernon, they 'belong to a class possessing a congenital disposition towards a set of defects of which reading disability is one'.

Attempts to elucidate some of the mechanisms involved have consisted of comparing dyslexic with normal children on a variety of specific tasks, and it seems as though the complexity of the task itself is one crucial factor. Thus on the recognition of isolated letters and words, dyslexic children show no difference from normal, but if the target is embedded in verbal material, differences become evident (Bauma and Legein, 1977).

Another feature commonly found in dyslexics—and even in slow adult readers—is very poor performance on tests of visual and verbal memory span. Compared to normal children of the same reading age, Ellis and Miles (1977) found dyslexic children only able to take in about half the data displayed for short exposures tachistoscopically. Slow reading adults are typically very poor at the common digit span task and these features suggest a general impairment in the 'chunking' or processing of incoming information.

Together with their inability to read, the writing of dyslexics is usually abysmal. Miles (1967) gives the following example:

Mary   IQ 131   Age 10.1.

Wlter rolgh was a yound menn m woust to rob sponsch treasure shreps and he was a grote fo (crossed out) fat (crossed out and t altered to v) fovout af the Quen and he bunnt the fleat of sbne in the horber and he co (crossed out) cone book and said he had bur the kens of a spoin bred.

A parallel between the defects shown by such children and those shown by patients suffering from traumatic dyslexia or dysgraphia is clear; but whereas in the latter cerebral pathology is almost always evident, there is as yet no conclusive evidence of a simple organic basis for the congenital defects.

In the teaching of congenitally dyslexic children and in the rehabilitation of adults with acquired dyslexia, a great variety of methods have been tried and advocated. The majority centre on devising some system of presenting letters and words so that the individual will learn how to distinguish them from one another. As yet there seem to be no hard and fast rules. While some individuals profit more from touching or moving an arm around a letter form, others do not. As summarized by Gardner (1977) 'Just as a variety of methods of teaching creative writing, athletics or mathematical competence has been evolved to suit widely divergent skills and personalities, so the therapist of reading disorders will similarly require an armementarium of techniques respectively suited to divergent kinds of disorder'. (p. 140).

Acalculia, or inability to carry out calculations, often accompanies loss of reading and writing and is also commonly associated with Gerstmann's syndrome, but is occasionally the outstanding symptom of cerebral dysfunction. Gloning *et al.* (1968) argue that disturbances of this skill are related more closely to the strategies a patient uses for calculation (whether he is a visualizer or a verbalizer) than to the site and nature of the lesion causing it.

Calculating, like reading, depends on a great many integrated functions—recognizing figures, remembering the tables, ordering numbers in rows and columns, etc. It is clear that a disorder which affects any of these functions will also affect a person's ability to calculate. However, it must be noted that patients who have lost the ability to recognize words or letters may still, on occasion, be able to recognize numerals and vice versa.

Psychological Mechanisms Involved

Although the defects of reading and writing seen in children cannot be tied down to a definite organic cause, the studies carried out on them have helped us to see a good deal more clearly the psychological mechanisms on which reading and writing depend. Systematic visual scanning from side to side (left to right in European and Arabic languages, right to left in Hebrew) seems to be an essential for reading and to some extent for writing, and where this is absent, either for congenital or traumatic reasons, the attainment or execution of these skills is impaired. Thus visual field defects usually lead to some reading deficits (Yeni-Komshian, *et al.* 1975).

At the same time association between visual and verbal systems must also be made. Phonetic elements and visual signals must be closely associated, as indeed they are in normal subjects (Conrad, 1964). Inability to make this association may be one of the bases for congenital dyslexia as well as for the acquired reading and writing disorders, and is one of the symptoms nearly always present in organic dyslexia and dysgraphia. Some interesting data in this field is emanating from the Japanese workers who have a unique opportunity for comparing the relative importance of visual and linguistic factors since two types of script are in current use in that country; Kanji (in which the word is represented as a single complex idiogram) and Kana (where it is represented as a series of phonograms as in European languages). Yamadori and Ikumura (1975) maintain that where writing disorders exist, they tend to be most severe in Kanji (idiograms) but reading ones are most severe in Kana (phonograms).

Physiological Mechanisms Involved

In searching for a physiological basis for dyslexia and dysgraphia it must be recognized that at least four functions are involved: the ability to control eye movements, the ability to co-ordinate these with hand movements, the ability to associate both these to words and finally the ability to understand what the words or letters mean.

The data supports a supposition that each of these functions is closely associated with a different cerebral area. The purely visual or motor disorders are most often impaired in lesions in the parietal lobes; the association between these and the motor processes of execution are disturbed by parieto-temporal lesions, and the ability to give meaning to the symbols is disturbed by frontal lesions. Moreover, studies of the disorders associated with congenital dyslexia or word blindness all suggest that functional impairment of the dominant parietal lobe is present in children showing this condition, and thus further emphasize the necessity for this area in the acquisition of the skills involved.

However, although these cerebral areas may be (and if present, apparently are) used for the specific functions listed, they are obviously not essential; for children in whom the entire left hemisphere is injured at birth (or removed for the prevention of epilepsy) can still learn to read and write adequately and may attain almost normal standards in these skills. That experience at an optimal period causes specialization of these areas seems, however, to be indubitable. Although some functions may be mediated by subcortical areas, the skills demonstrated are at a very elementary level. Moreover, as seen in 'split-brain' patients (see Chapter 9) stimuli presented to the right eye which cannot be transferred direct to the trained left hemisphere tend to remain unnamed, even when the subject is able to write the names with the left hand. Thus, the right hemisphere seems to be capable of some simple function but unless it is forced to take over the function and specialize in it at an early age it is unable to do so.

9
Disconnection Syndromes

Besides the dysfunction of individual skills and capacities, the integration or interaction between intact skills may become disturbed. These 'disconnection syndromes' may occur as the result of disruption between the two hemispheres (the 'split brain condition') or as the result of disruption between activities within the same hemisphere.

9.1 DISCONNECTION WITHIN ONE HEMISPHERE

Many aspects of this have already been considered and described. The agnosias and apraxias, which follow lesions in the sensory associations rather than in the primary sensory areas, often afford excellent examples. Geschwind in his classical paper on the disconnection syndrome (1965) describes patients who seem to behave almost as if they were different people in different circumstances. One patient with a colour-naming defect, but otherwise little word finding disorder, could match coloured papers, could sort slips of two slightly different shades of green correctly into different piles and could match seen colours to relevant line drawings of objects, but was quite unable to produce or even select the correct names for the colours themselves.

In reviewing other cases, Geschwind notes 'one striking feature . . . is the fact that the patient's ordinary behaviour is in marked contrast to the supposed perceptual disturbance. Thus . . . one patient who cannot "identify" a glass of water can yet a few minutes later pick it up and drink from it' (p. 593). In some patients the ability to name and recognize an object varies with its mode of presentation. Thus Ettlinger and Wyke are quoted as describing one patient who made many naming errors when objects were presented visually, but few when they were presented tactually. As Geschwind remarks 'We are constantly dealing with questions such as, if he can speak normally and he knows what he is holding in his left hand, why can't he tell you?' (p. 637).

For Geschwind the answer to this question is to be found in cerebral anatomy. In an abstract of his 1965 papers published in 1974 (p. 106) he outlines the evolution of the brain.

In the lower animals connexions between regions of the cortex may arise directly from the primary reception and motor areas. As one moves up the phylogenetic scale, these connections come to be made between newly developed regions of the cortex interspersed between the older zones. These regions are called the 'association cortex' . . . It follows that lesions of the association cortex, if extensive enough, act to disconnect primary reception or motor areas from other regions.

While connexions between primary receptive regions and limbic structures are powerful in subhuman form . . . in man the situation changes with the development of the association areas of the human inferior parietal lobule, situated at the junction of the older association areas attached to the visual, somasthetic and auditory regions. It is speculated that this new 'association area of association areas' now frees man from the dominant pattern of sensory limbic associations and permits cross-modal associations. It is particularly the visual-auditory and tactile-auditory associations which (allow for) the development of speech in most humans . . . In man the speech area . . . becomes the structure of major importance in the analysis of all the higher functions.

Although the term 'disconnection syndrome' was coined by Geschwind to refer primarily to lesions in the temporo-parietal association area causing agnosia, disconnection has been taken by some British workers to explain other phenomena as well, such as amnesia (see Iverson, 1977). Indeed it is language which Geschwind regards as primarily responsible for giving stability or permanence to both percepts and motor skills in man; hence whereas in animals disconnection syndromes seem to result mainly from cutting the sensory-limbic connections, in man they result from cutting the sensory-speech connections. This is often the result of lesions in the middle or posterior portions of the superior temporal gyrus (see Fig. 33), which according to Geschwind is the commonest cause of agnosias.

Very different from these disorders are those following section of the corpus callosum itself—an operation performed to prevent the spread of epileptic activity from one hemisphere to the other.

9.2 COMMISSUROTOMY AND THE SPLIT BRAIN SYNDROME

Early experiments with animals and observations on humans showed that the corpus callosum—the main subcortical connection between the two hemispheres—might be surgically sectioned or congenitally absent without causing any functional impairment (see Fig. 38). Callosum sectioned cats and monkeys are virtually indistinguishable from their normal cage mates under most testing and training conditions (Sperry, 1961). Thus the split brain monkey, like the split brain cat, can move about by all forms of locomotion as if his visual space perception were whole and unique and functioning at a normal pace (Trevarthen, 1974). However, using apparatus which ensures that both stimulus and response are confined to individual hemispheres, Sperry and his colleagues have been able to show that the two hemispheres can under certain conditions function as two quite separate brains, even to learning different and opposing tasks.

In humans, section of the corpus callosum causes the different functions of the separate hemispheres in language and perception to be highlighted, although special techniques are again essential for this purpose. The changes caused have been succinctly summarized by Zangwill (1976). 'There is . . . evidence that the two hemispheres may carry out concurrent tasks such as copying designs flashed simultaneously to the two visual half fields, without mutual awareness of each others' activities. Under conditions of unilateral input therefore, each hemisphere functions as an independent processor, producing results reminiscent of the behaviour of two separate individuals'. In Sperry's words, 'Each hemisphere . . . seems to have its own conscious sphere for sensation, perception and other mental activities and the whole realm of gnostic activity of the one is cut off from the corresponding experience of the other' (Sperry *et al.* 1969).

Sectioning of the corpus callosum seems to stop the sensory information which enters one hemisphere from being transferred to the other.

The split brain subject can only verbally report what he has seen when the stimulus appears in the right visual field. Stimuli presented to the left visual field, and therefore transmitted through the right hemisphere, cannot be

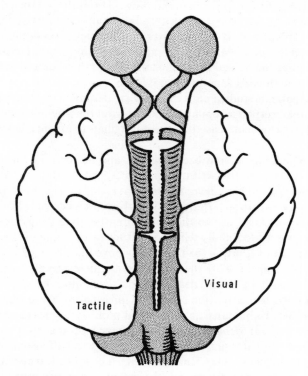

Figure 38. Diagram showing areas divided in split brain operations. From Sperry (1961), 'Cerebral organisation and behaviour', *Science* (June), **133**, 1749

described verbally although the subject can indicate the corresponding object with his left hand. Similar phenomena are observed with stereognosis. Sensory information about an object placed in the right hand is dealt with by the left hemisphere, and an unseen object placed in this hand can be named. The same object placed in the left hand cannot be described verbally but the left hand can retrieve an identical object by touch (Miller, 1972, p. 101).

If the eyes are closed an object actively explored by the left hand is not recognized by the right hand and vice versa. And similarly, the picture of an object exposed in the left half field of vision is not recognized when re-exposed in the right half field. These perceptual and discriminative tasks are carried out unilaterally and there is no apparent transfer of information between the hemispheres. (Zangwill, 1976).

Where hand-eye co-ordination is required however, matters are slightly different. Reaching and grasping seems to be performed as in the normal person. 'Each arm may reach to left or right of the sagittal plane of the body and visual events such as objects moving or lights coming on brightly and then disappearing either to left or right can be located as the goal for an accurate reaching response of either arm' (Trevarthen, 1974). However, the situation is very different when the hand is required to *recognize* the object rather than simply point to it. Each hand seems to recognize the objects independently just as they see and identify things seen separately with each separate hemisphere.

Three of the patients studied most carefully are described in detail by Gazzaniga (1970). Emotional responses could be elicited from both hemispheres and visual span for digits was even increased by presenting half to one hemisphere and half to the other.

One point which has seldom been stressed, and has certainly not been taken into account in any of the writings quoted above, is that the patients first described by Sperry and his colleagues were not tested in these tasks prior to their commissurotomy operations. Hence their performance can only be compared to that of normal controls—not to their own pre-operative behaviour. When the latter is done, as it undoubtedly will be in future cases, some of the conclusions regarding the effect of splitting the brain, may have to be revised. Even now, it is stressed by Gazzaniga (1970) that in order to illustrate any and all of the phenomena which have been described it is essential to use very special techniques devised to restrict the spread of information from one hemisphere reaching the other. In humans, as in cats and monkeys, observation shows few defects in the general behaviour or competence of the split brain subject (Akelaitis, 1944). Only if visual stimuli are exposed to a half visual field for times shorter than the subject is able to move his eyes (i.e. about 180 ms) are the results described above ever seen. Even then the deficits wear off with the passage of time. In discussing these observations Gazzaniga stresses three points which require special consideration: (1) the efficiency of ipsilateral hand-eye co-ordination is seldom if ever affected; (2) simple stimuli may 'get through' to the contralateral hemisphere even when all precautions to prevent spread are taken; and (3) the defects tend to improve with the passage of time.

Gazzaniga believes that subjects—both normal and split brain—can use a number of mechanisms for achieving cross-modal tasks and 'just as the experimenter thinks that one mechanism is isolated, the animal shifts to another' (Gazzaniga, 1970, p. 40). He believes that a simple conventional view is no longer tenable and that the corpus callosum should be seen rather as a filter of information from one hemisphere to the other than as a simple means of transference. When the corpus callosum is absent, cross queuing devices may be used or other forebrain commissures brought into play. With the passage of time these other mechanisms whatever they are, are improved so that cases two and three in the group followed up by him and his colleagues were able to 'speak' with their right hemisphere. Indeed a five to ten year follow-up of eight patients showed that residual deficits were restricted to mild dysgraphia and rapid alternating bimanual tasks (Zaidel and Sperry, 1977). However, although simple sensory data could be transferred or dealt with adequately by the commissurotomy patient there was still evidence that 'complex non-redundant' material could not (Zaidel, 1977).

In animals the situation is not quite so complex as in man but even here the amount of information transferred from one hemisphere to the other depends on the species, age, test, and type of response required. The nature of the reinforcement used in the learning situation is also relevant. Punishment by shock assists transfer of information whereas reward does not.

9.3 AGENESIS OF THE CORPUS CALLOSUM

In subjects in whom the corpus callosum is congenitively absent the deficits seen in the patients shortly after commissurotomy are hard to elicit. Patients with agenesis, however, seldom have a completely intact brain in other respects, and therefore tend to show a variety of intellectual deficits. According to Ferris and Dorsen, (1975) this may be because 'the corpus callosum is usually involved in accuracy, precision, and keenness of intellect' and facilitates learning in all spheres.

9.4 EVIDENCE FOR HEMISPHERIC SPECIALIZATION OF FUNCTION

Studies of split brain subjects have been popular as a means of checking conventional ideas about the localization of function within the two hemispheres, especially those concerned with dominance or handedness (Franco and Sperry, 1977). For example:

If displays such as photographs of human faces or other complicated designs difficult to specify in words are shown to both hemispheres simultaneously and the patient required to respond by pointing to its duplicate on a multiple choice array, the split brain subject shows a marked predilection to react to the right hemisphere input. It is only if a verbal response is demanded that there is a shift to the left hemisphere control. Moreover the efficiency of visual discrimination is greater when input is processed by the right hemisphere than by the left. Unless verbal coding is essential therefore, it seems likely that the right hemisphere typically takes the lead in processing complex visual information (Zangwill, 1976).

These observations however, far from providing ready answers to many of the questions already raised, do in fact raise further ones especially in the philosophical and ideological areas. Are, for example two brains better than one? And if the two hemispheres function as independently as has been suggested, wherein lies the personality or the soul?

These questions are not new. Nor are they really the concern of the present volume. That they have, however, been under consideration by psychologists throughout the history of the science, is illustrated in an anecdote related by the late Sir Cyril Burt and retold by Zangwill (1976).

McDougall more than once tried to bargain with the great Sherrington that if ever he (McDougall) should be smitten by an incurable disease, Sherrington should cut through his corpus callosum, that massive band of nerve fibres uniting the two hemispheres. 'If the physiologists are right,' said McDougall, 'the result should be a split personality. If I am right, my consciousness should remain a unitary consciousness.' And this, Burt comments, he seemed to regard as the most convincing evidence of something like a soul.

10
Disorders of General Intelligence

It used to be believed that since mental activity is mediated by the brain, general intellectual activity ('intelligence') would fall off if the latter were injured, and moreover, that the degree of deficit found would correlate with that of the organic impairment.

It might be thought that before such a contention could be either proved or disproved, an exact definition of intelligence itself should be made.

This latter is not easy (Heim, 1970), and in order to avoid becoming embroiled in controversies on the topic, this chapter will be confined to the consideration of the behaviour commonly found in the condition known as dementia. In the previous chapters it has been pointed out that disruption of specific cerebral areas often causes the disruption of specific mental skills, but a point that possibly has not been stressed sufficiently is that the loss of these skills does not inevitably reduce the individual's general competence. The dysphasic patient can still communicate; the amnesic one uses a notebook or some other form of mnemonic to organize his daily life. Even the patient with visuo-perceptual disorders can compensate for his losses by developing new cues to orientate himself by. 'One can always use geometry', said a mathematician, as he put the pieces of the WAIS object assembly together soon after having lost most of his right cerebral hemisphere as a result of a traffic accident.

In contrast to the above, the patient with true dementia is able to make no compensation for his disabilities. Often he seems to be unaware that compensation is required, but if he does possess 'insight' into his failures, his response is commonly one of depression often accompanied by agitation.

In addition to loss of over-all general intellectual ability, dementia is characterized by a number of 'positive' features which will be described briefly.

10.1 EMOTIONAL LABILITY

The demented patient may be in floods of tears at one moment, e.g. when talking about a dead spouse, and yet can be roused to merry laughter a few seconds later if the subject of conversation is changed. It is also typical of such a patient that in a test situation which is beyond his capacity he may appear severely disturbed and agitated but if given one within his capacity the next moment will be full of smiles and optimism. The speed with which such changes of mood can be brought about and the degree to which they can be controlled by the manipulation of the situation are important diagnostic criteria.

10.2 PERSEVERATION AND STEREOTYPY

The patient repeats a response appropriate to one stimulus in response to the next one even when it is not appropriate to that. Thus, asked to touch his nose, he does so correctly. Asked then to touch his ear, he again touches his nose. Asked to hold up his hand, he extends his fingers and places them on his nose. Or he may be asked to name a pen, and correctly says 'pen'. Shown a book, he again says 'pen'; an ashtray is also called a pen. The dysphasic patient often makes the same errors but realizes that he has done so and struggles to correct them, showing annoyance at being unable to do so. In contrast to this, the demented patient shows no insight into the errors he has made and appears to believe that he has complied with the instructions adequately.

Although perseveration may occur in association with any single cerebral lesion, it is most commonly seen in cases where the lesion is widespread and produces a variety of symptoms. Thus in all aphasics, some degree of perseveration is usually seen (Allison and Hurwitz, 1967) and is not correlated with any specific language defect. It is far commoner, however, in those showing jargon aphasia than in those with non-fluent aphasia (Rochford, 1969). Perseveration in patients with senile dementia often takes the form of a repetition of a word or an idea in a slightly altered context. Williams quotes the following conversation, 'How old are you? I was born in 1899. How old does that make you? 99. What is the date now? Would it be the 9th?' (Williams, 1965).

Allied to perseveration is inability to alter concepts—i.e. *stereotypy*. Seen particularly in the sort of situation where the subject has to categorize objects in a variety of different ways (e.g. the Weigl–Goldstein–Scheerer Test–see below) it is found that once the subject has achieved one form of categorization he cannot adopt any others.

The Weigl–Goldstein–Scheerer Test which is a useful method for eliciting this behaviour consists of twelve pieces in three different shapes (triangle, circle, square) and four colours (red, blue, green, yellow). The subject is asked to sort these pieces into groups so that all the objects in each group are alike according to some principle, but are different to those in the other groups. Once a subject has sorted the pieces according to one principle (e.g. shape) they are jumbled up and he is asked to sort them again according to another. The demented patient can typically sort them according to one category but is quite unable to change his frame of reference at the second attempt. Instead of resorting them, he typically places them in patterns, all the triangles in one row, the squares below, and the circles below that. Even if the examiner starts a group for him, he is likely to demolish it and revert to his previous system (Goldstein and Scheerer, 1941).

10.3 CONCRETENESS

This tendency first described and named by Goldstein may be evident in both verbal and non-verbal performance. Concreteness is 'an attitude which is determined by, and cannot proceed beyond, some immediate experience, object or stimulus' (Mayer-Gross, Slater, and Roth, 1960). Thus a subject responds to all stimuli as if they existed only in the setting in which they are presented. He cannot abstract them from their environment or their qualities from them. A knife cannot be grouped with any other objects because it is different from them. A word cannot be defined properly as it fails to call up any other words. (Definitions, therefore, tend to consist of either repetitions or of sentences in which the word itself features, e.g. bed = 'Yes, it's a bed, well just a bed you sleep on. Breakfast = 'When you have your breakfast. You eat your breakfast—sometimes we have bacon and eggs'.) Proverbs cannot be interpreted in terms of generalities but only in terms of the words they contain. (An interpretation of the proverb 'Still waters run deep' might be 'That's right; very deep and very still').

10.4 PERPLEXITY

Another sign of general intellectual impairment of organic origin is perplexity, first described by Goldstein (1939). Faced with a situation he cannot deal with, the patient tries to escape from it by indulging in irrelevant acts. Shown a picture he cannot name, he turns it over and looks on the back. Offered an object he cannot recognize, he puts it in his pocket or in his mouth.

10.5 THE CATASTROPHIC REACTION

This consists of an intense affective response with autonomic components (sweating, flushing, crying, restlessness) and has already been referred to. It is another typical response to a situation which cannot be coped with.

10.6 TESTS AND SITUATIONS ELICITING DEMENTIA

The presence of dementia especially in its early stages is not always readily apparent. The patient's responsiveness to all stimuli present at the moment, together with the retention of well-established skills, results in the fact that in an environment familiar to him, the patient can often continue to function without any apparent difficulty. It is only when he is removed from this (possibly for a holiday or for medical treatment) that his true limitations become evident. Various 'tests' to assist in diagnosis are available.

It has long been recognized that some mental functions 'fall off' with increasing age and in dementia before others (see Fig. 39). Those abilities developed in early age which stabilize on maturation, and classified by Cattell as 'crystallized', are retained better than those which are necessary for the continued adaptation to a changing environment (Cattell's 'fluid' abilities). Hence, on tests of general intelligence, items measuring vocabulary, information, and comprehension tend to 'hold up' whereas those measuring learning, speed and visuo-spatial construction 'don't hold'. Babcock (1933) was the first person to design a series of tests for the specific purpose of measuring the discrepancy

138

between these two groups of items, and her example was followed by many others (for example, the Shipley–Hertford and Hunt–Minnesota batteries).

The disadvantages of such tests are that they give no indication of the subject's ability to cope with everyday situations. Nor is there any satisfactory way of making allowance on these tests for past practice and life habits (Piercy, 1959). As is only to be expected the degree to which a skill of any sort deteriorates depends on the extent to which it was practised, so that it often happens that older people do better on some of the reputedly *don't hold* tests than on the *hold* ones (Williams, 1960).

Many people hence prefer to rely on the more familiar batteries of intelligence

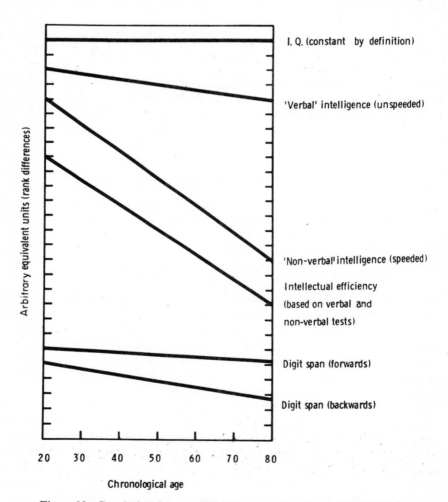

Figure 39. Graph showing age-differences in various mental functions expressed in arbitrary units. From Bromley (1966), *The Psychology of Human Ageing*, Penguin

test such as the WAIS, carefully analysing the qualitative as well as the quantitative pattern of a patient's performance on it (McFie, 1975). If considered necessary, specific tests of memory, linguistic ability, and visual discrimination are added to the battery.

Tests specifically designed to elicit the positive signs of 'brain damage' are also available. In 1947 Halstead developed a series of tests measuring essentially the sensory and motor functions on both sides of the body. These have since been refined and added to by Reitan. The final battery of tests making up the Reitan neuropsychological assessment include some of Halstead's original procedures as well as more general tests of intelligence (the WAIS) and personality (the MMPI) (Reitan, 1975).

Another very useful battery of tests aimed at eliciting specific 'signs' of impairment, is that put forward by Goldstein and Scheerer in 1941. It contains the following tests.

The cube test—the subject has to copy a number of designs in coloured cubes. The test is similar to the Kohs blocks and to the block design subtest of the Wechsler Scales.

The colour sorting test—woollen skeins of different hues and shades are presented to the subject who is asked to carry out a number of matching tasks with them.

The object sorting test—the subject is presented with a large variety of common and toy objects and is asked to select an object and then pick out all the others which go with it, or group all the articles together in various ways.

The colour-shape test (The Weigl–Goldstein–Scheerer Test)—this has already been described.

The Goldstein–Scheerer stick test—the subject is presented with a number of sticks of different length and is asked to copy designs made by the examiner, either beside the model or from memory.

The characteristic performance of patients with cerebral lesions have been described in detail by Goldstein and Scheerer and in more general outline by Williams (1965).

10.7 THE DIFFERENTIAL DIAGNOSIS OF DEMENTIA

Dementia and Normal Ageing

It used to be a common belief that dementia, especially in the senile and presenile conditions, was an exaggerated form of normal ageing. Because both conditions result in a loss of 'fluid' as compared to 'crystallized' abilities, the parallel is clear; but recent work has stressed the differences between these states rather than the similarities. Indeed, even in 1958 Welford and his colleagues were pointing out that the fall-off in speed which is undisputed in the older age groups (Birren, 1974) was often accompanied by increase in other qualities such as judgement and awareness, making the older worker no less efficient than the younger. Schaie (1974), from comparing short longitudinal and cross-sectional studies of different age groups, has even come to the conclusion that the intellectual changes usually attributed to ageing are the result of cultural bias rather than age as such. 'There is strong evidence', he writes, 'that much of the difference in performance on intellectual abilities between old and young is *not* due to decline in ability on the part of the old, but to the higher performance level of successive generations.' Miller (1977), although not going quite so far as this in discrediting the 'accelerated ageing' hypothesis in dementia does conclude that 'In the present state of knowledge it is difficult to gauge just how accurate it is' (p. 141). After his detailed analysis of the recent work on both normal ageing and dementia, this cautious conclusion seems justified.

In the examination of the individual patient, even the statistical differences which may show up between groups selected for research, are not so easy to identify. On the WAIS, the pattern of subtest performance in the demented patient is usually similar to that in the elderly, and it is mainly in the presence of Goldstein's 'positive' signs that dementia may be detected.

Specific Defects Due to Focal Lesions

In true intellectual deterioration or dementia the main trouble lies in the subject's inability to compensate for his losses, rather than in the nature of the losses seen. Indeed signs of all the specific impairments already noted in previous chapters (dysphasia, amnesia, apraxia, etc.), may be present in generalized dementia but affect over-all performance somewhat differently. These differences can be summarized in Table 11, in which the differences noted are listed along with the tests or situations which may be used to elicit them.

Table 11
The disorders associated with focal and general cortical impairment

	Focal	General
Disorders of memory (eliciting tests and situations: Bentons designs from memory test, Wechsler's memory scale, Williams' memory scale)		
Abilities lost	Retention (especially of recent events) and learning in all sensory modalities	Retention, learning and some established skills
Orientation	Poor for time and place	Retention learning and some established skills
Insight	Often quite good	Usually poor
Mood	Usually euphoric	Agitated, perplexed, confused
Response to cues	Usually good, tendency to confabulate if very severe	Confabulation and distraction
Disorders of speech (eliciting tests and situations: Rochford and Williams scale for measurement of dysphasia: Eisensons dysphasia test)		
Abilities lost	Expression and naming worse than comprehension. Reading aloud worse than recognition of written words. Errors indicate	Comprehension as bad or worse than expression. Recognition of written words worse than reading aloud.

	Focal	General
	correct recognition of objects	Errors indicate misrecognition of objects
Orientation	Good	Poor
Insight	Good	Usually poor
Mood	Distressed by failure to find right words	Appear perfectly satisfied by own performance
Response to cues	Assisted by any semantic or mechanical lead-in	Distracted by all cues
Perseveration	Some words repeated in identical form despite subject's awareness of their irrelevance, e.g. chair = 'chair', book = 'chair—no!—chair'	Portions of words or phrases often carried over from one sentence to another with elaboration or correction, e.g. chair = 'A sitting-on machine'. Book = 'A sitting on reading machine'

Disorders of perception (eliciting tests and situations: Bender-Gestalt, block construction, picture naming, picture-word matching, walking around ward!)

	Focal	General
Abilities lost	Inability to appreciate whole or relationship between its parts although individual parts recognized	Whole object misidentified. Parts regarded as adequate wholes
Orientation	Spatial orientation poor. Orientation for time and person usually retained	All poor
Insight	Subject often perplexed and worried; feels 'something is wrong', but may attribute his difficulties to 'madness' or 'poor memory'	Little insight. Subject usually satisfied with performance
Mood	Perplexed and distressed when disorder elicited	Undisturbed by errors, but agitated if lost in ward
Response to cues	May be helped by verbal directions, and can often learn to orientate themselves using verbal cues	Distracted and confused by cues

Disorders of motor skills (eliciting situations: dressing, tying a bow, lighting cigarette or candle, placing pegs in board).

	Focal	General
Abilities lost	Complicated sequencing of acts (apraxia)	Goal towards which act is directed
Orientation	Good	Poor
Insight	Good	Poor
Mood	Agitated by failure	Agitated when really confused —i.e. if clothes are on back to front
Response to cues	Little improved unless complexity of situation is reduced. Verbal directions do not assist	Improvement if continually reminded of goal

Depression

A further difficulty in the assessment of general dementia is that mental efficiency is influenced by many functional illnesses as well as by age, and differentiation between these in the older age groups is especially important but difficult. In particular the older age groups not infrequently see the onset of depression and paranoid illness, and the task of distinguishing between these and organic derangements is difficult but of great clinical importance. A summary of the differences found in the two conditions is shown in Table 12, but will be described in a little more detail in the following pages.

Emotional Lability

The nature of this has already been described in Section 10.1.

Psychomotor Behaviour

The demented patient usually responds to all tests and questions with little delay in contrast to the depressed older patient who usually exhibits retardation. The demented patient does not, however, necessarily respond appropriately. He often has difficulty in dressing himself, in finding his way round and in carrying out any truly purposeful task. This is not for lack of the necessary motor skills (as in apraxia) but appears to be based on poor goal-orientation. Thus the demented patient cannot remember whether he should be dressing or undressing himself and hence puts some clothes on at the same time as he is taking others off. His

Table 12
The disorders associated with dementia and functional illness

Activity	Dementia	Functional illness
Emotional expression	Labile, dependent on immediate stimulus	Consistent with internal preoccupations; unchanging
Psychomotor behaviour	R.T. brisk. Actions repetitive and stereotyped. Tend to be restless. Non-goal orientated	R.T. slow. Little spontaneous activity. Goal orientated
Verbalization	Vocabulary and sentence structure usually intact, but statements contradictory or meaningless	Form intact, but content refers principally to preoccupation
Orientation	Poor for time and often also for place. Orientation for person best retained	Usually intact, but may depend of preoccupation
Perception	Misperception evident in response to visual and verbal stimuli	Respond to external stimuli appropriately, despite pseudo-hallucinations and delusions

difficulty in finding his way around is due to the fact that he cannot remember where he is going, not to the fact that he cannot find the way there.

Verbalization

The demented patient's answers to questions are usually given quickly but are typically relevant only to the immediate question and to no other aspects of a conversation or situation. Thus he often demonstrates gross inconsistencies which, if pushed, he will rationalize in a glib manner. The following may serve as an illustration:

Q. How old are you?
A. 48.
Q. Are you married?
A. Yes, I'm a grandmother.
Q. How old are your grandchildren?
A. The oldest is 50.
Q. How can you only be 48 if your oldest grandchild is 50?
A. Well he is married too.

Orientation

The demented patient is distracted from a task by any external stimulus and is often more inclined to concentrate on minute details of the situation than on the whole. Thus if asked to describe a picture, he will spend a long time describing minute details in it apparently oblivious of its implications as a whole, and will frequently break off an interview to wander around the room or building. If asked to explain his actions inconsistency is again the keynote of his responses. Thus a female patient may walk out of the interview room and if asked where she is going will say it is to prepare dinner for her husband. If asked the same question of arrival at the end of the corridor she may say it is to find her hat and coat as she is going for a walk. If asked the question again when she reaches the front door she may say that she has come to meet an expected visitor.

Perception

The demented patient often appears to misidentify visual and verbal stimuli. If asked to name objects he will show no difficulty in word finding but will name something perceptually similar. Thus, as has already been mentioned in Chapter 8, a picture of a windmill might be called a pepper pot, or a drum be called a powder puff. This is in contrast to the patient with a focal lesion in the speech area (dysphasia) who can demonstrate clearly that he knows the nature and functions of an object even when he cannot find its name. ('It's a thing that goes round and round'.)

The comprehension of words is often grossly defective in the demented patient but in view of his own fluent output this sometimes goes unnoticed. If patients are asked to match one of four words with the picture it names the senile patient will often be unable to comply with the instructions at all (Rochford and Williams, 1964). He may point to each word, read each word correctly, or attempt to put pictures and words into a single pile. The shorter a command, the better a demented patient understands it, but much depends on his orientation at the moment. Lengthy instructions may simply allow his attention to wander.

Reversible Confusion

Confusion in older patients, commonly follow extra-cerebral physical disorders such as cardiac or respiratory illness, but can be differentiated from true dementia by a number of points, listed for convenience in Table 13. Most of the psychological differences will be apparent in general conversation with the patient or from a simple clinical interview, and do not depend on particular tests to highlight them.

10.8 PHYSIOLOGICAL CAUSES OF DEMENTIA

Cerebro-Vascular Disease

Cerebral arteriosclerosis is common in older people, but is not necessarily accompanied by mental changes. If these do occur, they tend to be fluctuating and varied, and are most probably related to multiple small infarcts (Corsellis, 1977). If any of the major cerebral vessels are affected, the damage most commonly occurs in the posterior cerebral artery, which involves much of the medial temporal grey matter. This may cause particularly disorders of speech and memorizing rather than a general dementia.

Table 13
The disorders associated with confusion and dementia

	Confusion	Dementia
Onset	Acute	Insidious
Duration	Clears up with treatment of cause	Chronic and irreversible
Conscious level	Fluctuates	Remains clear
Perception	Visual hallucinations may be present	Agnosic distortion may be present
Orientation	Disorders show attempts to 'make sense' of situation	Contains denial of knowledge not immediately aroused by present situation
Delusions	Result from striving for coherence	Persecutory
Memory	May be intact for short periods	Gross impairment of retention

General Cortical Atrophy

In most cases of general intellectual deterioration, some degree of cortical atrophy is present; but although the correlation between the two is statistically significant, it is not particularly high.

The shrinkage seen in older patients predominantly affects the frontal and temporal regions, while the ventricles may also be enlarged (Corsellis, 1977). However, although some signs of 'focal' disorder (such as speech or memory disorder) may be evident, the losses seen in conjunction with atrophy are a general loss of Cattell's 'fluid' abilities. Positive signs such as perseveration, perplexity, concreteness, etc. are usually obvious on routine clinical examinations, and the only object of carrying out more specific psychological assessment is either to establish a baseline of performance (McFie, 1975) or to assist in differential diagnosis in the early stages of illness.

Senile and Presenile Conditions

As Miller (1977) stresses, many of the pathological changes that occur in senile dementia are not unique to this condition, but the brains of demented patients differ from those seen in normal ageing not only in showing exaggerated degrees of atrophy, but frequently in demonstrating the presence of neurofibrillary tangles and 'senile plaques'. While these latter may well result directly from neural degeneration, it is their presence which is often found to correlate most closely with intellectual deterioration (Roth *et al.*, 1967).

The mental changes seen in the senile and presenile conditions usually consist of general all round lowering of ability. On the WAIS, there are exaggerated losses on the 'don't hold' tests (McFie, 1975) but all functions are greatly reduced.

If the plaques are concentrated in the temporo-parietal areas (as in Alzheimer's disease) mental performance may indicate specific losses of linguistic and visuo-spatial functions, while their concentration in the frontal areas (Pick's disease) tend to cause specifically loss of fluency and euphoria. A concentration of plaques in the basal ganglia alone (often causing Parkinsonian symptoms) may cause little in the way of intellectual deterioration, although if the lesions extend to the third ventricle amnesic states may result.

Lesions in the Thalamus and Basal Ganglia

Small focal lesions in these areas occur comparatively commonly, especially in certain hereditary diseases (e.g. Huntingdon's chorea), after head injury, due to a concentration of plaques (e.g. Parkinsonism), or as a result of metabolic disorders (e.g. Wilson's disease). The predominant results affect motor behaviour causing tremor, spasticity, or athetoid movements; but if the lesions are widespread, intellectual deterioration and amnesia may also be present.

A chance to study the connection between subcortical lesions and mental activity has arisen in recent years as a result of the techniques developed for treating Parkinson's disease. In the 1950s and 1960s the treatment of preference was small stereotactically placed lesions in the central medial nucleus on one side of the thalamus, which usually obliterated the tremor and spasticity in the lesions on the other side of the body. A similar lesion could be placed in the other hemisphere at a later operation if required. Careful psychometric study of patients before and at different time intervals after the operation was usually carried out to ensure no negative post-operative *sequelae*.

Summarizing the findings in a large series of cases Jurko and Andy (1973) conclude that while lesions placed within the central medial nucleus 'result in relatively few deficits in cognitive skills' those placed outside, especially in the ventralis posterior, the pulvinar, and the ventralis oralis do tend to produce impairment, the degree of deficit seen being directly proportional to the complexity of the skill itself. The deficits noted covered abstraction (WAIS similarities), associational learning, emotional lability (increased colour responses on the Rorschach) and spatial-motor performance (the Bender—Gestalt), although only the latter was correlated to the hemisphere operated upon. This similarity between subcortical and cortical specialization of function parallels the finding already mentioned in Chapter 8 relating to left hemisphere thalamolysis and speech impairment reported by Ojemann *et al.* (see p. 111).

Since the arrival of levodopa (L-dopa) for the treatment of Parkinsonism, thalomolysis has become rarer; but the effects of levodopa itself on intellectual functions are not without interest. In a series of papers published mainly in French, Sevilla and his colleagues (Sevilla *et al.*, 1973) have described the psychometric performance of Parkinsonian patients before and after effective treatment with this drug, and describe improved speed of reaction and breadth of interest in the majority. According to others, this improvement is only transitory (e.g. Loranger, 1973), while Wolf and Davis (1973) describe one case which they felt to be typical of many of an already demented patient becoming hallucinated and confused after the onset of treatment, his condition eventually leading to stupor and death.

Closed Head Injuries

Although the long-term psychological effects of head injuries usually reflect the area of the brain actually damaged, confusional states in the early stages of recovery are usually accompanied by some loss of general intellectual efficiency characterized by a general lowering of performance in all spheres with loss of insight, slowing, and poor retention. The picture seen will depend on the extent of the injury, the age of the patient and above all on his previous experiences and skills and may differ widely between individuals (McFie, 1975).

Frontal Lobe Lesions

In strong contrast to the above is the picture seen typically in association with lesions to the frontal lobes. In such cases, most of the individual functions may be perfectly well preserved, but the patient almost incapable of switching from one mental process or strategy to another. For example, a middle-aged woman was, until one week before her admission to hospital (where she was found to have a large and well localized right frontal tumour), a reliable, and well-respected department manager in a large store. She had always been considered by her family to be an 'odd person' and when, some weeks before her admission, she began complaining of blackouts, dizzy spells, headaches, and occasional lapses of memory, her relatives and colleagues took little note of her symptoms. It was only a careful neurological examination which revealed the nature of her illness, but even this showed little more than early signs of raised intracranial pressure. During a detailed psychological examination carried out in hospital before her operation, this patient completed all the subtests on the WAIS at the level expected of a person of her age and average IQ. On a test of delayed recall (Williams, 1968) she showed some impairment, but it was not till she was asked to perform sorting tests that any definite disorder was noted. The patient sorted the Weigl quickly into shapes, but was quite incapable of switching from this categorization to colours. Even when the two red pieces were placed together and she was asked to complete this particular grouping, the patient was unable to do more than place all the other squares beside the red square and all the other circles beside the red circle.

The difficulty found by this patient, as by most of those with similar conditions, was not so much in forming an original classification as in letting go of it once it had been formed. There appeared to be a breakdown of the mechanism whereby a person rejects the response first aroused by a stimulus (that most ready to hand) and replaces it by others more appropriate to the total situation: a failure of some filter through which reactions must pass before being put into operation, and of some buffer store in which they are held and from which the most appropriate ones are selected.

If such a condition is specific to lesions in the frontal lobes, it should be seen after the operation of prefrontal leucotomy carried out for the relief of psychotic or neurotic states. The original operation of prefrontal leucotomy which aimed to divide the fibres in the centrum ovale separating the frontal cortex from the thalamus (see Fig. 40) was carried out on a large number of mental patients who were studied by a large number of psychologists and in a great variety of situations.

One of the most systematic psychological studies in this field was carried out by Partridge (1950). He studied 300 patients over a two-year period, and although he did not apply any standard psychological assessment procedures, the care he took in analysing and examining his data compensates for this lack. Considering only those patients who were regarded as having made a complete recovery from the mental illness precipitating the operation and only those in whom adequate pre-operative as well as post-operative information was available, Partridge was left with a small group of 35 patients on whom to draw conclusions regarding the effect of prefrontal leucotomy on intellectual functions. Concreteness, a tendency to perseverate (e.g. to incorporate the 'set' aroused by one stimulus into the

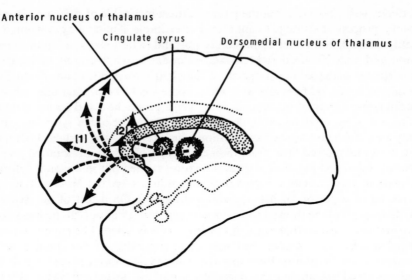

Anterior nucleus of thalamus

Cingulate gyrus

Dorsomedial nucleus of thalamus

Figure 40. Diagram of fibre tracts divided in orbital
leucotomy and cingulectomy

response to the next), and reduced planning performance were seen in nearly all patients immediately post-operatively, together with 'less ready orientation in time', diminished power of rapidly altering the attention and some difficulty in holding several items in mind at the same time. These defects tended to become fewer with the passage of time, but Partridge remarks that the patients' conversation remained 'factual, restricted, and unreflective' and that gross difficulty in repeating digits backwards persisted in 26 of the 35 patients for up to two years.

Tow (1955) subjected a group of subjects selected equally carefully to a large battery of more standardized procedures, but his assessment did not continue beyond twelve months post-operatively. He found significant falls on both verbal (vocabulary) and non-verbal (matrices) intelligence tests as well as on tasks of 'fluency' (the number of ideas triggered off by a stimulus), the ability to distinguish between abstract words (e.g. courage and boldness), an object sorting test and the porteus mazes. He found no significant differences on tasks assessing tempo (the speed of counting and dressing), persistence (the length of time a subject is prepared to hold up his leg), speed-accuracy (cancellation or tracing), and reversal of letters.

Both these authors were struck more by the qualitative than by the quantitative changes in their subjects' behaviour. Thus on the vocabulary test the patients post-operatively did not appear to have forgotten words but 'his short and often interrupted attempts never actually reached the point of definition. Usually the subject uses short phrases though he often repeats them'. (Tow, 1955). In giving the difference between abstract words, the same tendency was seen. Examples quoted by Tow are as follows:

Courage—you try to do a thing.   *Boldness*—you can't do it.
Thrift—you want more money.   *Avarice*—you spend money.
Murder—you kill a person.   *Manslaughter*—you couldn't kill him.

It was, however, on the object sorting test that Tow noted the most striking differences. The subject was presented with a tray full of common objects which could have been sorted according to four different principles—use, colour, material and shape. The first method of sorting adopted by most people ($n = 31$) was according to use, 21 managed to sort according to colour, 17 by material and twelve by shape. After the operation the number of people in each group fell significantly, but as well as this there was a striking tendency for most subjects to repeat their first sorting procedure over and over again, even though they might call it by a different name the second time and appear to believe that they had thereby found a new principle. Thus after putting the pen, pencil, and ink together 'for writing' one subject when asked to sort them differently put the pen, pencil and protractor together 'for drawing'. Tow concludes,

> There seems to be impairment in the powers of abstraction and synthesis; of perception of relations and differences; of the ability to deal with complex situations, planning, and thinking out the next action and its consequences; and appreciation of one's own mistakes. These are, of course, not several discrete functions but they are several closely related aspects of intellectual activity, which the tests show to be impaired. (Tow, 1955, p. 228).

A similar stereotypy and a tendency to adopt simple repetitive instead of more complex adaptive behaviour, has been noted by Luria *et al.* (1966) in non-psychiatric patients with frontal lobe lesions. If a normal person is asked to differentiate by touch between the letters E and H, he begins by feeling them extensively all over, but soon learns to single out the essential features. The original seeking movements and the subsequent abbreviation are both absent in frontal lobe patients, who repeat over and over their original rather cursory investigation and glibly give the first response that occurs to them. Again if such patients are asked to carry out motor activity based on the recording of information (e.g. 'When I lift my finger you will show me your fist, and when I lift my fist you will show me your finger'), they soon replace the required act by simple imitation of the examiner's movements. Asked to lift his right hand after a single knock and his left hand after a double one, the frontal lobe patient quickly reverts to a stereotyped sequence of movements (R–L–R–L) irrespective of the signals. (Luria *et al.*, 1966).

The frontal lobes have been referred to up till now as if they formed one homogeneous structure, but this is not the case. Pribram (1968) points out (see Fig. 41) that to consider them as such:

> May be one of the reasons for the confusion over their function. While the medial portion derives projections from the anterior thalamic nuclei, the

Lateral Surface   Medial surface

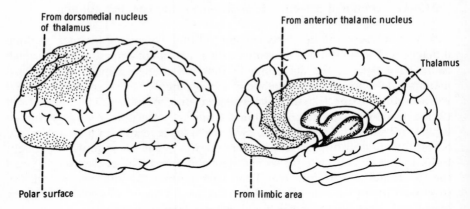

Figure 41. Diagram of thalamo-frontal projection areas

polar and lateral portions receive projections from the midline of the thalamus, and is reciprocally connected with the insular, amygdaloid and temporal cortices. Thus the frontal lobe can be divided into the medial, dorso-lateral and posterior orbital sections.

In trying to associate psychological defects with the cerebral lesions producing them, Tow concludes from his series of patients undergoing prefrontal leucotomy

The post central area . . . represents the more discriminative and more highly developed aspects of sensory function: the sensory cortex subserves all forms of discriminative sensation and the mechanisms by which all incoming sensory experiences are related to previous sensation. Similarly it seems that the prefrontal area subserves not a few specific abilities, but rather the more discriminative and more highly developed aspects of them all. (Tow, 1955, p. 236).

No exact physiological mechanisms by which this last process is carried out was suggested by Tow or by Partridge, but some hypotheses as to how they may be mediated are suggested at the end of the next chapter.

In the above studies and in one conducted by Smith (1960), no difference between the function of the two frontal lobes was mentioned, but a later study reported by Smith (1966a) suggests that the two frontal lobes do reflect to some extent the specialization of the two hemispheres as a whole. Thus the left frontal lobe appears to be more concerned with linguistic than with visuo-spatial data, and the right vice versa. Benton (1968) confirms this finding and mentions that the defects shown by frontal lobe patients often reflect those shown by patients having post rolandic lesions of the same hemisphere. In support of this hypothesis, Sylvester (1966) found a specific smallness of the parietal lobes, especially that associated with the posterior part of the callosal body, in the autopsy of 84 brains from subnormal subjects.

Experimental work with animals has not thrown as much light on the functions of the frontal lobes or on the factors underlying intellectual activity as might have been hoped, but it is nevertheless of some interest. Pribram has shown that lesions in the dorso-lateral region in monkeys can be distinguished from those in other areas in respect of their effects on some aspects of learning and problem solving behaviour.

Ever since experimental cerebral ablations of the frontal lobes have been carried out on monkeys, it has been noted that interference with the frontal lobe has impaired the animal's ability to perform the classical delayed retention problem—a task in which the animal has to remember, for specified periods, under which of two cups a reward has been placed. A 'normal' unoperated animal has no difficulty in retaining such information for long periods and will make few mistakes. The frontal lobe monkey, on the other hand, appears able to retain the information for only brief intervals. The reason for his difficulty, it has been demonstrated, is largely due to distractibility, perseveration, or lack of attention to the cues. (Mishkin and Pribram, 1955 and 1956). It has further been shown by Yoshii (see Pribram and Tubbs, 1967) that animals with frontal ablations fail to show the same EEG responses to cues that are seen in normals learning the task.

Alternation problems—those in which the animal has to take his reward first from the right, then from the left and so on—are specifically failed by animals with lesions in the fronto-limbic formation, but not by those with lesions in the sensory-motor projection areas. But this apparently simple task *can* be solved if each alternating pair (right–left) is separated from the next by a larger time interval. Thus the task, instead of being a continuous one— R–L–R–L–becomes 'parsed' or discontinuous R–L . . . R–L . . . (Pribram and Tubbs, 1967).

From these observations, Pribram and Tubbs argue that one important function of the fronto-limbic area may be that of 'chunking' incoming sensory information in such a way that it can be utilized to form a mental set. When the fronto-limbic area is removed, this chunking process has to be supplied from outside—i.e. from the environment.

11
Disorders of Personality

Personality can probably be viewed from as many different angles as there are viewers, and classified into as many different classes as there are classifiers. By and large all these different attitudes can be divided into two main groups: (1) those that consider the external manifestations of the person, i.e. his behaviour, and (2) those that consider his internal structure, his dynamics. The former is measured by traits and attitudes, the latter in terms of needs and drives. Psychometric assessment of the former is usually made by means of rating scales and questionnaires, while the latter is made by projective tests. The repertory grid and semantic differential techniques might claim to reflect both attitudes and needs to some extent.

Since any change in personality can only be seen by the observer in terms of altered behaviour, it is only the first of these aspects of personality which will be considered in this section, although to explain behaviour it is often necessary to postulate inner mechanisms as well. Moreover, assessment of personality on the basis of traits and attitudes alone is not always reliable. There is considerable evidence that although these alter to some extent in the normal course of ageing, the ageing person does not so much change as become a caricature of his former self.

11.1 THE EFFECTS OF FRONTAL LEUCOTOMY
AND CINGULECTOMY

The first recorded and best known instance of personality change resulting from physical injury was that described by Brickner in 1935. A farm labourer fell from a height on to a crowbar which penetrated his skull and destroyed a large part of his frontal lobes. The patient survived and made an apparently full physical recovery, but having been a conscientious, reliable, sober worker, he now revealed all the opposite characteristics. He was uninhibited, unreliable, euphoric, lacking in judgement, childish and lazy. Similar changes had been seen by Rylander (1939) following tumours in the frontal region.

Most of the evidence concerning the personality changes following cerebral lesions comes, however, from studying patients on whom operations have been performed for the relief of psychotic symptoms (see Chapter 10). Partridge's analysis of 60 recovered patients from 30 different mental hospitals in Great Britain (Partridge, 1950) sums up the results of the first few years findings most clearly.

Partridge divided his data on personality into three areas of function which he termed activity, affect, and restraint. A summary of his findings six months, twelve months and two years post-operatively is shown in Table 14. The tendencies noted in these patients were not seen under all conditions. For example, if the social situation truly demanded it, a patient with marked loss of restraint could control himself and behave in a conventional manner. Partridge's findings have been criticized on two grounds. Firstly, the operative technique to which these patients were subjected was a crude hit or miss affair, as a result of which the actual nature and extent of the lesions induced was often unknown. Secondly, the patients themselves were suffering pre-operatively from a wide

Table 14
Personality changes following prefrontal leucotomy (after Partridge, 1950) Reproduced by permission of Blackwell Scientific Publications

Number of patients showing changes at varying post-operative times		
	6 months	12 months	24 months
Activity			
More relaxed	52	41	?
Less active	49	33	?
Slower	44	37	15
Less spontaneous	41	18	12
Less persistent	39	34	28
Get up later	33	22	22
Combination of all above symptoms to some extent	60	56	52
Affect			
Worry less	60	54	?
Loss of 'feeling' for others	13	13 (less severe)	0
Fatuousness	12	7	?
Affect outwardly (but not subjectively) diminished	5	4	?
Less affectionate and more selfish	9	?	?
Restraint			
(Causing little concern to patient but much to relatives)			
Outspokenness	33	30	30
Snappishness	32	33	30
Selfish	31	30	30
Bad temper	16	12	?
Extravagence	15	15	15
Greedy	15	9	0
Bad language (swearing)	11	9	7
Inconsequential in conversation	11	14	?
Excessive smoking	7	4	4
Excessive alcohol intake	3	3	1
Violence	4	—	—

variety of mental and personality disorders, which had to be taken into account when the post-operative picture was considered. Lewin's (1961) observations overcome both these objections. He studied the effects of carefully controlled and circumscribed operations on patients with different and clearly defined pre-operative symptomatology. In one series of operations, he restricted his surgical procedure to undercutting the orbital surface of the frontal lobes thus only dividing the orbital cortex from the 'visceral brain' (orbital undercutting or orbital leucotomy). In another series, the anterior 4 cm of the cingulate gyrus was removed by suction on both sides, leaving the blood supply and the remainder of the frontal lobes intact (cingulectomy) (see Fig. 41).

Lewin considered his results only in relation to the pathological symptoms removed, not in relation to any other aspects of personality. It was clear from his paper (and from a further 59 cases reported in 1973), however, that while symptoms of severe psychotic disorders (including schizophrenic illness) were not influenced basically by either procedure, orbital undercutting was very effective in removing symptoms of anxiety and depression, while cingulectomy was effective in removing aggression and obsessional disorders. In the latter operation, it was not so much the habit which was disrupted, as the emotional state which the habit had been created to overcome. This was illustrated by one patient seen by the present author who had developed a ritual in which he had to hold on to every movable object he touched and who thus collected on to his person an immense and ever-growing mountain of rubbish such as empty bottles, cutlery, cigarette ends, etc. which he would occasionally take down to the hospital incinerator and burn, suffering intolerable feelings of guilt and anxiety afterwards. After the operation the patient remarked: 'I still sometimes find myself collecting things but now I just say to myself "Well, you had the operation, you can throw them away and you won't worry", and I do and I'm all right'.

Bridges and Goktepe (1973) maintain that prognosis in obsessional illness depends not only on the operation but also on the origin and length of the disorder. Good prognosis according to them depends on (1) the age at onset being 30 years or over; (2) the presence of depression; and (3) sudden onset. Especially good prognosis is seen in patients whose obsessions are related to pregnancy.

Petrie (1958) has compared the effects of a variety of different operative and pharmacological procedures on patients with different pre-operative symptoms and personality profiles, including patients treated for intractable pain rather than mental disorder. The findings are not always easy to follow, as she divides all her subjects along the dimensions of introversion and neuroticism (after Eysenck, 1947) and considers her results in relation only to these dimensions. Hence those who do not feel that this dichotomy has much to offer will find Petrie's work of doubtful value. Nevertheless her conclusions are interesting and thought provoking. She describes the patients after standard leucotomy as less inclined to blame themselves, more inclined to like sex jokes, less concerned with the future and more with the present, and setting themselves lower goals for attainment. These are characteristics of extroversion and thus Petrie concludes that after prefrontal leucotomy the subject becomes more extroverted. Hence leucotomy is likely to be (as is found to be the case) most effective in those subjects who were pre-operatively introverted. Local operations on specific areas of the frontal lobes (including orbital undercutting) were found to produce the same changes as leucotomy but to a lesser extent. Cingulectomy, on the other hand, was found to produce almost the opposite effects. Cingulectomy was found to increase the scores suggesting introversion and was only effective in subjects who were low originally on these scores. Petrie claims that temporal lobectomy carried out for the relief of epilepsy, as well as administration of chlorpromazine, have the same effect as cingulectomy. She also claims that the effects of stereotactic operations causing coagulation of the anterior nucleus of the thalamus are different from those causing coagulation of the dorso-medial nucleus; the former resembling the effect of cingulectomy while the latter resemble those of prefrontal leucotomy.

In subjects suffering from intractable pain, Petrie (1960a and b) found that leucotomy only gave relief to patients who originally showed high introversion scores, the relief being relative to the extent that the patients were rendered more extroverted. The tendency for orbital leucotomy to increase extroversion has not been substantiated by Levinson and Meyer (1965). These authors claim that increases are only seen in those people whose pre-operative scores were low and thus the observations show little more than a 'regression towards the mean'—a characteristic of any test repetition.

In summarizing the work up to 1970, Kalinowsky (1973) concludes there is little proof that individual psychiatric symptoms can be relieved by localized cerebral lesions. Despite the work reported above and many other projects that have been undertaken (especially the Columbia–Greystone Association project in the USA reported in 1949), the only consistent changes to be noted are a reduced concern over the symptoms. Accompanying this, there is nearly always a diminution of drive, interest and tact; so that the 'desirability' of the end result depends on the patients pre-operative state.

11.2 SELECTIVE ELECTROCOAGULATION

The technique used in selective electrocoagulation is described by Crow *et al.* (1963) as follows:

> Electrode sheaves are inserted through two frontal burr holes so as to lie in fans in both frontal lobes, the plane being 1 cm anterior to the anterior clinoid process. The aim is to produce controlled multifocal frontal leucotomy. After subsidence of the insertion effects, records are obtained for several days from all electrodes to eliminate the possibility of local pathology. The functional positions of the electrodes in relation to grey and white matter are then established by graded stimulation. Electrodes lying in cortical convolutions exhibit characteristic after-discharges at a threshold of about 4 V, while those in white matter show no after-discharges at twice or

thrice this level. From this information a chart of the electrodes in relation to cortical grey matter is prepared; attention is restricted to those in white matter.

The preliminary treatment is by polarization. The effects of polarization are brief but sometimes dramatic in relief of specific symptoms. The preliminary trials may last several weeks, since fifty or so electrodes may lie in frontal white matter and several days may be necessary to follow the temporary change in condition. When electrodes giving favourable results with polarization have been identified the current is raised to a level known to produce electrolytic coagulation and this is applied to each electrode in turn, again with periods of several days intervening to determine the extent of clinical remission.

In discussing the clinical changes brought about by this procedure, Walter (1966) stresses the fact that it has only been employed on patients who were carefully selected for 'good previous personality'. Indeed the importance of previous personality in determining the effect of psycho-surgical procedures has been stressed by nearly all workers. But what is a 'good personality'? Birley (1964) trying to define the term, found it extremely difficult. The only feature consistent among all his 106 cases was an absence of 'bad personality' features, among which he included aggression, bad work record, and addiction (see also Marks, Birley, and Gelder, 1966).

11.3 TEMPORAL LOBECTOMY AND AMYGDALECTOMY

The connection between functional disorders of the temporal lobes and disorders of personality have long been suspected, especially when epilepsy is present (see Chapter 1). The improvement which follows surgical removal of epileptic temporal lobe foci is often dramatic (Falconer, 1973), but has been followed, according to some observers, by changes of personality as well. Gibbs (1958), however, does not agree with this. He claims that apart from the changes that can be attributed to the cessation of the fits, little alteration can be noted. Green *et al.* (1958) give details of 43 patients who underwent temporal lobectomy and noted most improvement in those who were least disturbed. They summarize the psychological changes under three headings: (1) thinking; (2) feeling; and (3) acting. In 80% of the cases they noted considerable improvement in feeling or affect; acting improved in conjunction with it, although alterations to thinking were negligible. They suggest that much of the improvement they did find may have been due to 'stabilization because of increased security in the environment), rather than any actual alteration to cerebral function.

Temporal lobectomy for the relief of psychiatric symptoms where epilepsy was not involved has been discussed by Scoville (1973) who concludes that little benefit has been found, except where excessive anxiety or 'neurotic fixations' are present. 'This exaggeration of normal feeling tone or sensory input can be benefited . . . resulting in a lowering of such excess down to a normal level' (p. 35).

Observations on the beneficial effect of temporal lobectomy in cases of epilepsy led to the suggestion that ablation of some neclei within the amygdala might reduce aggressive behaviour in unmanageable, non-epileptic patients.

The results of stereotactic operations for this purpose have been described by a number of surgeons working in different parts of the world (Laitinen and Livingston, 1973), and have been clinically successful in a large number of cases. Ablation of the medial nuclei of the amygdala appears to produce the best results, especially if done bilaterally. As pointed out by Hitchcock *et al*. (1973), however, the operation does not cure all the patients' ills, but only removes occasional aggressive outbursts.

11.4 THE PSYCHOLOGICAL MECHANISMS INVOLVED

Although almost all clinical observers have agreed that the personality changes following cerebral injury are mainly seen in spheres of aggressiveness, spontaneity, and anxiety, very few of the people working in this field have tried to define what these words mean in operational terms. This does not mean to say that the words are not definable operationally, but what these definitions mean clinically it is often hard to see. Costello (1966) reviewing a great deal of work on the subject concludes:

Perhaps nowhere is the divergence between the clinician and the experimentalist more evident than in the area of anxiety. Most of the work that has been done, and which has been tied together by some attempt at theoretical formulation, has to do with issues (verbal conditioning, eyeblink conditioning, etc.) that are only quite indirectly related to the problem of anxiety facing the clinician.

Costello himself prefers to consider all such umbrella terms as aggression and anxiety under the headings of (1) the behaviour recorded, and (2) the conditions associated with it. In the case of aggression, a number of experiments have been conducted which seem to verify the hypothesis that aggressive behaviour is a response to frustration, and moreover, that the strength of an aggressive response is related to the degree of interference with the frustrated response and the number of frustrated response sequences. The strength of the primary drive whose satisfaction is frustrated is also of importance. The frustration of an aggressive response leads on to the condition known as anxiety (including self blame) and this is commonly dealt with by one of four different mechanisms: (1) putting the blame on something or someone else; (2) stereotyped repetitive behaviour; (3) regression to a more primitive mode of behaviour; and (4) physiological (autonomic) signs of stress.

Another common cause of anxiety is that first described by Festinger (1957) and named by him cognitive dissonance—an inharmonious, inconsistent, discrepant relationship between two things. According to Festinger the strength of the pressure to reduce dissonance is a direct function of its magnitude and three methods are commonly used to reduce it: (1) minimizing or ignoring one of the cognitions; (2) increasing or adding to one of the cognitions; and (3) decreasing the importance a person subjectively attaches to the dissonance itself.

Cognitive dissonance is regarded by many psychologists as a primary driving force in a great many social situations, and is somewhat similar to the double-bind situation which Bateson *et al.* (1956) have suggested underlines schizophrenic illness. A great deal of work has been done on individual differences in reaction to stress, frustration, and cognitive dissonance in normal people, and it has been found that although there is no consistent relationship between a person's level of anxiety and the effects of stress on his performance, most large groups of people can be divided into two broad categories: (1) those who react to frustration by externalizing their aggression, and (2) those who react by internalizing it.

Any direct association between the psychological mechanisms mentioned above and symptoms of mental illness has never been studied systematically. Nor have the effects of surgical operation been considered in the sort of experimental situations reviewed by Costello, but some of the work to be considered in the next section suggests that a closer investigation of the frustration tolerance of patients subjected to psycho-surgical procedures might be an important step in clarifying more precisely the personality changes which are so commonly reported following frontal lobe interference.

11.5 PHYSIOLOGICAL MECHANISMS

For some years it was fashionable to explain the connection between the frontal lobes and personality on the basis of 'long circuiting' of sensory impressions—a hypothesis first put forward by Cobb (1952). Greenblatt and Solomon (1958) quote in support of this suggestion the almost invariable sequences to frontal lobe damage: (1) a reduction in drive or energy; (2) the subject being less affected by past experience and more bound to immediate stimuli; and (3) his being less able to elaborate or sustain experiences. 'One way of looking at this', they conclude, 'is that the mechanism of prolongation in time is impaired.'

Closer investigation over the past years has, however, led to some modification of this view. In the first place the realization that identical procedures may lead to different results in different types of people has led to the conclusion that some different form of explanation is required. For example, Petrie (1960a) found that leucotomy for the relief of pain had different results not only in relation to the subject's pre-operative dimension of introversion but also in relation to the subject's responses to perceptual satiation. Thus if subjects are presented with a sensory stimulus for a certain time (e.g. asked to handle an object of a specific thickness) and then asked to make a judgements of its intensity (e.g. match the test object with others of the same subjective thickness) people generally can be divided into the augmentors and the reducers. The augmentors are those who tend to match the block with one thicker than itself, the reducers to one thinner. Augmentors also tend to be what Petrie calls extroverts, reducers to be introverts.

Tolerance to pain is generally greater in the reducers than in the augmentors. This is explained on the basis that 'a brief wave of intense pain could cause later pain to appear less severe' (Petrie, 1960a). It will be remembered that relief from pain was only produced in those subjects who also showed increased extroversion after the operation. Since neither increased extroversion nor relief from pain are brought about by cingulectomy, temporal lobectomy, or orbital undercutting, Petrie argues that a 'centre' for the processing and assimilating of incoming sensory data is probably present in the prefrontal lobes, which above all areas of the brain are specialized to carry out this function.

Walter (1966) comes to a somewhat similar conclusion from completely different data. Studying the EEG records from the scalp over the frontal lobes which follow when two signals occur together over a number of trials, Walter found that a characteristic response (the contingent negative variation, CNV, or expectancy wave) occurred between the two signals. He continues:

Our most exciting discovery is that when a person has to take some action, physical or mental (if there is a distinction), in response to the second or later signal a dramatic change appears in the electrical state of the frontal cortex. As the association of signals is repeated and the action performed, a new effect appears; a slow rise in the negative potential of the cortex that starts just after the first signal and continues until the moment of action or decision when it terminates abruptly.

We have found the CNV or E wave in a wide variety of situations. The simplest is in the establishment of a 'classical' blink conditioned reflex when a click is followed by a puff of air to the eye. In this case the E wave tends to appear during acquisition but declines when the conditional response is well established. (Walter, 1967, p. 259).

Studying the CNV in many patients before and after prefrontal leucotomy Walter (1966) found that habituation of the CNV did not occur with patients with chronic anxiety or phobic states: the CNV is almost absent in psychopaths and those who seem unable to learn from society, while in the obsessional patient it not only fails to habituate if the second signal is not reinforced, but may even increase its original amplitude. In psychotic subjects, especially schizophrenics, the results are irregular. Electrocoagulative leucotomy, where it successfully relieves symptoms, is usually followed by return of the CNV to the normally adaptive pattern.

When considering that the CNV represents Walter (1967) points out that it is essentially related to uncertainty.

In many people there is an almost linear relation between the maximum potential reached by the E wave and the arithmetical probability of signal association. This means that in such people the subjective probability and objective probability coincide. A very intersting complication appears here however. The E wave does not of course appear at once when an association of signals for action is presented; it grows steadily over a certain number of experiences. This number is usually (again in normal adult subjects) about 25 when the presentations are irregular at about one every 5–10 seconds. This means that the brain must, quite reasonably, acquire a certain number of samples before it 'decides' that subjective certainty is attained. In ordinary life, if two events occur together 25 times running one would probably consider their association a pretty trustworthy basis for action. However, the criterion of certainty as indicated by number of trials to E wave plateau is a very personal factor. This means that, in effect, the brain computes a running average of associations and if one takes the number of trials needed for full development of the E wave as the personal criterion of certainty used by a particular brain, the effects of uncertainty and of stress come out very tidily.

Thus for Walter the frontal lobes of the brain act not just as long circuiters but as highly skilled computers, calculating probabilities and preparing the rest of the body to take appropriate action. He maintains indeed that variations in evoked response patterns and CNV lead to the tentative identification of three main systems subserved by the frontal lobes. (see Fig. 42) One is related to the limbic regions and serves primarily as a warning system—'Something has happened'. Excessive or persistent activity in this system leads to the feeling 'everything is happening at once'. Another system seems to involve more directly the cingulate structures and is concerned with the maintenance of conditional attention. 'This may be worth remembering.' Here, over activity results in persistent recall and cyclic compulsion—'I can't get it out of my head'. The third system, engaging mainly superior frontal neocortex, provides the conceptual linkage between events—'There must be some connection between these experiences'. Exaggeration or persistence of this process leads to supterstitious conviction—'I don't care what you say, *I know*'.

Some revision or elaboration of Walter's theory may shortly be put forward as a result of findings reported by Kelley *et al.* (1973), Livingston and Escober

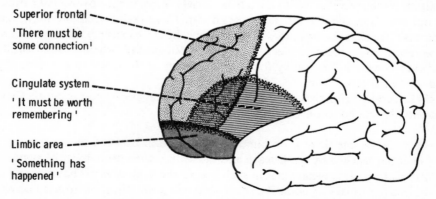

Figure 42. Functional areas of the frontal lobes, after W. Grey Walter

(1973), and Nauta (1973) of two chemically and anatomically distinct limbic systems—a medial (the original Papez circuit involving the hippocampus), and a basolateral or defence circuit (involving the hypothalamus amygdala) (see Fig. 43). The former is activated by acetylcholine (ACh) and seems to be mainly concerned with alertness; the latter is activated by dopamine and is concerned with motor activity. However, these are not the only major neurochemical pathways to have been isolated. A noradrenergic one with cell bodies located in the pons and a serotoninergic one with cell bodies located in the raphe area of the midbrain, pons, and medulla are also known to exist, even though their function is still somewhat obscure (Hornykeiwicz, 1973). Moreover, as Nauta (1973) pointed out, not only must all these systems be very closely interconnected, but their functional state is not solely regulated by neural afferents from the cerebral hemispheres. Other bodily functions have an important effect via endocrinological blood-born agents. The action of the frontal cortex, according to Nauta, is thus not only like that of a computer, but also 'like that of a friend who prevents us from making stupid, irreparable decisions when we have 'flu'.

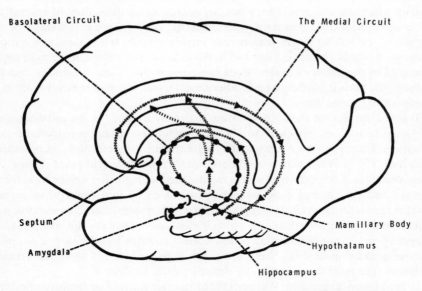

Figure 43. Diagram of two possibly distinct limbic systems, the medial and the basolateral

12
Final Conclusions

In the first paragraphs of this volume, it was pointed out that neuropsychology hoped that by studying the patterns of their breakdown it would be possible to reach a better understanding of mental mechanisms themselves. Has this been the case?

The old idea that by removing a specific area of the brain a specific function or skill would be lost, has not always been substantiated. It is true that a gross correlation can be established between some regions of the brain and impairment of certain mental functions, but replacing the jargon of phrenology by that of current anatomy and psychology has not overcome the difficulties of attempting to localize individual functions within specific cerebral areas. Damage to the cortex of the left temporal region may impair speech, but it does not remove individual words (the subject can still find words but not always at the right time). Damage to the memory centres does not remove individual memories, but the subject just finds it harder to remember recent events or may remember them at inappropriate moments.

It is not the present author's intention to get involved in the age old discussion of 'localization' as opposed to 'holistic' attitudes to brain-behaviour correlations. These have been discussed by a great many other authors, in particular Gardner (1977). What seems more important from a practical point of view is a consideration of the light thrown on mental mechanisms themselves by cerebral injury; and the general conclusion here seems to be that removal of certain cerebral areas far from eliminating a function, often seem instead to increase it; it is its relevance to external stimuli which is most commonly at fault. It tends to be inappropriate to the circumstances and would probably be inhibited or modified by the healthy individual. Acts are 'near approximations' to those actually required; the pool from which the desired would be drawn.

It is cogently argued by Werner (1956) that all normal or healthy stimulus-response behaviour begins with the arousal of a general pool of relatively appropriate behaviour (the Vor Gestalt), and that before the most appropriate response can be made, this pool has to be carefully sifted. The inappropriate responses have to be rejected (their threshold to production thereby being raised) before the most appropriate can be selected. It is via the rejection of the inappropriate responses that the appropriate one is selected. After organic cerebral impairment, the observations reported here suggest that it is precisely this process of inhibition and selection which breaks down. But how such a process is carried out may vary with different species and individuals. Rejection of an inappropriate response before it has even been actualized, must be based on some form of matching between possible responses and their outcomes. There must, therefore, in all adaptive behaviour not only be the ability to execute hypothetical activity, but also some feedback from it and from the external environment which are compared for 'goodness of fit'. But does this necessarily postulate a special organ or faculty for making judgements?

The selection and rejection of possible behaviour patterns has its parallel in the sensory field. For example, after injury to the peripheral nerves, the first stage of returning sensation consists of a general awareness (protopathic sensitivity) without the subject being able to differentiate heat, pain, or touch. Only later do these more specific qualitative differences (epicritic sensation) return. Henry Head believed that two distinct systems had to be evoked to account for such great qualitative effects, but it was later established that the difference is purely quantitative—'protopathetic characteristics being due to the response of a relatively thinned out mosaic of receptors'. (Fulton, 1949).

The fact that selection and rejection can be brought about be feedback systems (if these are complicated enough) without the need to postulate a separate organ, can be illustrated by a simple hydraulic model, such as that shown in Fig. 44. The first or top layer, A, is connected by pipes to a second layer, B, these being slightly out of phase with A. Thus each tank in layer B receives input from two tanks in layer A. The tanks in layer B are connected in the same arrangement to a further layer of tanks, C. The tanks in layer B are also each connected and flow into another whole similar structure, B′, the output of which is connected back to the input of the tanks in layer A, and to the output tanks in layer C. The middle layer of tanks in B′ is connected to a further similar structure, B″, and so on *ad infinitum* (see Fig. 45).

Now consider that some water is poured into tank 2 in layer A, Fig. 44. The water will flow into the two tanks connected to tank A2 in layer B, and from those into the three tanks connected to them in layer C. The motors connected to these

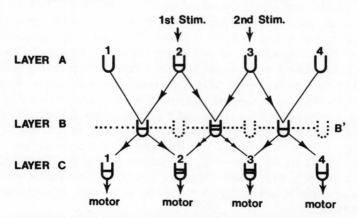

Figure 44. Hydraulic model illustrating possible mechanism for mediating mental activity

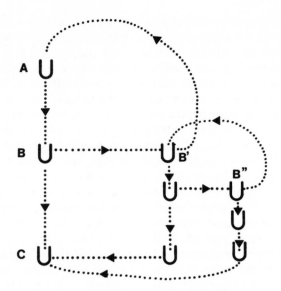

Figure 45. Hydraulic model illustrating possible mechanism for mediating mental activity

three tanks (C1, 2 and 3) will then be set in motion. Some water will also flow into the tanks in B′. The level of water in all these tanks will be raised and, if the pipes leaving these tanks do so at a point slightly above the ground level, some water will remain in these tanks after it has ceased to flow through the whole system.

Now consider that water is poured into tank A3, Fig. 44. It will flow as before, but as a result of the previous 'stimulation' of the system via tank 2, power will be driven into the motors connected to tanks C2 and 3 before it reaches a critical level in tanks C1 and 4. It can be said that the stimulation of tank 2 has left a 'memory' which is reflected in the behaviour of the whole unit. The same process repeated many times over in systems B′ and B″ will leave an impression in the whole system which might cause the sort of integration, suppression and selection of behaviour seen in normal mental states. The degree of arousal and retention in the system would depend on the width of the pipes connecting the tanks and on the distance up the sides of the tanks from which these pipes leave. Both these factors may depend on, and would be influenced by, the elasticity of the material with which both tanks and pipes are made. The efficiency of the system will depend on the number of units functioning in it as a whole, and particularly on those further away from the main stimulus-response area, A to C, i.e. it will depend on the complexity of systems B′ and B″. Should these be reduced in quantity, only those responses immediately evoked by a stimulus applied to a particular tank in layer A will result. Integration with past experience will be lacking.

Thus selection and rejection of possible behaviour patterns and the qualitative differences within behaviour is reduced to a quantitative basis, but despite the possibility that all mental functions could be carried out by all areas of the brain, there seems to be no doubt that in normal human beings different cerebral areas *are* specialized to control rather different forms of behaviour.

The greatest over-all anatomical distinction in the normal human brain is that between the two cerebral hemispheres. Whereas the left hemisphere specializes in the control of speech and language, the right hemisphere specializes in the visuo-spatial and constructive functions.

A second big distinction is that between the surface layers of the brain (the cortex) and the more basal aspects of it, midbrain and limbic system. Within the cortex itself, further specialization is usually apparent. The posterior (occipital) aspects of the cortex in both hemispheres specialize in the visual functions; the anterior (frontal) ones in foresight and anticipation; the lateral (temporal) ones in hearing and communication and the upper (parietal) ones in bodily activity. The midbrain and limbic systems themselves provide the powerhouse which keeps the whole process going, activates the different systems and provides the hardware for storing information.

This simplified concept has, however, to be constantly modified; for not only does each function depend for its actualization on the activity of all others, but each one can be carried out to some extent even when the area normally subserving it is damaged or obliterated.

This raises a point which has hardly been touched on in the present volume but may well serve as the major focus for future research—namely, the manner and pattern of restitution of function. Is the function taken over by other cerebral areas, or does the individual develop new strategies for coping with the problems?

That recovery of function does occur to a large extent is, of course, well recognized. Although little scientific research has been carried out into the processes involved, many accounts have been published both of what it feels like to suffer a particular loss and how some functions are regained. The most useful to date concern speech and language—a function whose absence is particularly disturbing to the sufferer and the return of which can be followed objectively as well as subjectively. Luria (1972) gives a detailed account of one such man who he followed for 25 years who, after a penetrating wound of the left parieto-occipital area originally lost not only almost all his symbolic and conceptual functions (including speech) but also demonstrated severe visual agnosia and apraxia. With time the patient regained some degree of speech and comprehension together with reading and writing, and was also able to compensate for the perceptuo-motor disorders.

The study and understanding of the substitute strategies adopted by the brain-damaged may not necessarily throw light on normal mental activity, any more than by watching an armless person using his toes to hold and hammer in a nail, one could learn much about the normal use of hands. The differences between a child learning to speak and an aphasic struggling to express himself are immense, and the final outcome will depend on different factors in the two cases. While practice may help the child, it has comparatively little effect on the aphasic or the apraxic; what these subjects lack is the ability to retrieve their skills at the required moment, and the means by which they can be assisted to do this is still a mystery. In the case of language, and to some extent memory, some of the factors affecting retrieval have been established; but how the individual can be trained to select and employ relevant retrieval strategies at the appropriate moment is still a problem. When this is understood, as it may very well be within the next few years, we may well reach a new phase in our understanding of mental behaviour.

Despite the title of this book, no attempt has been made hitherto to define or 'localize' the mind. It could be argued that if a mental act is performed, something must be performing it; and this 'something'—the me or the self—must have a basis somewhere. The identification (and even localization) of language, of memory, of perception and the other faculties is all very well, but none of these could be used without a self to use them.

Whether indeed the mind can be regarded as an independent, indivisible unit, or whether, like memory, perception, consciousness, or even life itself, it can be reduced in the long run to quantitative factors (above a certain value there is a mind; below it merely automata) is more a question for philosophy than psychology. Even those who lean towards a quantitative view, thereby avoiding the necessity for postulating extra-physical phenomena, still leave themselves with much to explain; for although the point of a pin and the seat of a chair may both be reduced in the long run to empty space held together by electrical forces, they are very different things to sit on.

References

Abercrombie, M. L. J. (1960). Perception and eye movements in cerebral palsy. *Cerebral Palsy Bulletin*, **2**, 142.

Abrams, R., and Taylor, M. A. (1973). Anterior bifrontal ECT: a clinical trial. *British Journal of Psychiatry*, **122**, 587.

Akelaitis, A. J. (1943). Studies of the corpus callosum. *Journal of Neuropathology and Experimental Neurology*, **2**, 226.

Akert, K., and Livingston, R. B. (1973). Morphological plasticity of the synapse. In L. V. Laitinen and K. E. Livingston (Eds.) *Surgical Approaches in Psychiatry*. Medical and Technical Publishing, Lancaster, Ch. 40, p.315.

Alajouanine, Th., and L'Hermitte, F. (1965). Acquired aphasia in children. *Brain*, **88**, 44.

Allison, R. S., and Hurwitz, L. J. (1967). On perseveration in aphasia. *Brain*, **90**, 429.

Anastasi, A. (1970). *Psychological Testing*, (Third Edition), MacMillan, Toronto, Ontario.

Andreewsky, E., and Seron, X. (1975). Grammatical rules in agrammatism. *Cortex*, **11**, 379.

Annette, M. (1975). Hand preference and laterality of cerebral speech. *Cortex*, **11**, 305.

Archibald, Y. M., and Wepman, J. M. (1968). Language disturbances and non-verbal cognition. *Brain*, **91**, 117.

Babcock, H. (1933). *The Examination for Mental Deterioration*. Stoelting, Chicago.

Baddeley, A. D., and Warrington, E. K. (1973). Memory coding and amnesia. *Neuropsychologia*, **11**, 159.

Bartlett, F. C. (1932). *Remembering*. Cambridge University Press, London.

Bateson, G., Jackson, D. D., Haley, J., and Weakland, J. (1956). Towards a theory of schizophrenia. *Behavioural Science*, **1**, 251.

Bauma, H., and Legein, Ch. P. (1977). Foveal and parafoveal recognition of letters and words. *Neuropsychologia*, **15**, 69.

Becker, J. (1974). *Depression: Theory and Research*. V. H. Winston and Sons, Washington DC.

Bender, M. B., and Diamond, S. P. (1965). Auditory perceptual defects and localization of function. *Brain*, **88**, 675.

Benton, A. (1968). Differential behavioural effects of frontal lobe disease. *Neuropsychologia*, **6**, 53.

Birch, H. G., Belmont, I., and Karp, E. (1967). Delayed processing and extinction. *Brain*, **90**, 113.

Birley, J. L. T. (1964). Modified leucotomy—a review of 106 cases. *British Journal of Psychiatry*, **110**, 211.

Birren, J. E. (1974). Psychophysiology and speed of response. *American Psychologist*, **27**, 808.

Bisiach, E., Nichelli, P., and Spinnler, H. (1976a). Hemispheric functional asymmetry in visual discrimination. *Neuropsychologia*, **14**, 335.

Bisiach, E., Capivani, E., Nichelli, P., and Spinnler, H. (1976b). Hemispheric functional asymmetry in visual discrimination. *Neuropsychologia*, **14**, 375.

Blakemore, C. B., and Falconer, M. A. (1967). Long term effects of anterior temporal lobectomy. *Journal of Neurology, Neurosurgery and Psychiatry*, **30**, 364.

Blumstein, S. E., Baker, E., and Goodglass, H. (1977). Phonological factors in auditory comprehension in aphasia. *Neuropsychologia*, **15**, 19.

Boller, F., and Vignolo, L. A. (1966). Latent sensory aphasia. *Brain*, **89**, 815.

Boller, F., and Green, E. (1972). Comprehension in severe aphasics. *Cortex*, **8**, 382.

Borowy, T., and Goebel, R. (1976). Cerebral lateralization of speech. *Neuropsychologia*, **14**, 363.

Brickner, R. M. (1935). *Intellectual functions of the frontal lobes*. MacMillan, New York.

Bridges, P. K., and Goktepe, E. O. (1973). A review of patients with obsessional symptoms treated by psychosurgery. In L. V. Laitinen and K. E. Livingston (Eds.) *Surgical Approaches in Psychiatry*. Medical and Technical Publishing, Lancaster, Ch.13, p.96.

Brierley, J. B. (1966). The Neuropathology of amnesic states. In C. W. M. Whitty and O. L. Zangwill (Eds.) (Second Edition) *Amnesia*. Butterworth, London, Ch. 7.

Brodal, A. (1969). *Neurological Anatomy*. (Second Edition). Oxford University Press, London.

Brody, M. B. (1944). Prolonged memory defect following ECT. *Journal of Mental Science*, **90**, 51.

Butters, N., Levil, R., Cermak, L. S., and Goodglass, H. (1973). Memory deficits in alcoholic Korsakov patients. *Neuropsychologia*, **11**, 291.

Butters, N., and Cermak, L. S. (1975). The memory disorders of alcoholic patients with Korsakoff syndrome. *Annals of New York Academy of Science*, **233**, 61.

Cairns, H. (1952). Disturbances of consciousness in lesions of the midbrain and diencephalon. *Brain*, **75**, 109.

Cairns, H., and Taylor, M. (1949). Tuberculous meningitis. *Proceedings of the Royal Society of Medicine*, **42**, 155.

Cattell, K. B. (1943). The measurement of adult intelligence. *Psychological Bulletin*, **3**, 153.

Cermak, L. S. (1975). Imagery in Korsakov patients. *Cortex*, **11**, 163.

Cermak, L. S. (1976). The encoding capacity of a patient with amnesia due to encephalitis. *Neuropsychologia*, **14**, 311.

Cermak, L. S., Butters, N., and Goodglass, H. (1971). The extent of memory loss in Korsakov patients. *Neuropsychologia*, **9**, 307.

Cermak, L. S., Butters, N., and Gerrain, J. (1973). Verbal encoding ability in Korsakov patients. *Neuropsychologia*, **11**, 85.

Chomsky, N. (1972). *Syntactic Structures*. Manton, Hague.

Clardy, E. R., and Hill, B. C. (1949). Sleep disorders in institutionalized children. *The Nervous Child*, **8**, 50.

Clyma, E. A. (1975). Unilateral electroconvulsive therapy. *British Journal of Psychiatry*, **126**, 372.

Cobb, S. (1952). *Foundations of Neuropsychiatry*. Williams and Wilkins, Baltimore.

Columbia-Greystone Association. (1949). *Selective Partial Ablation of the Frontal Cortex*. Columbia-Greystone Association, New York.

Conrad, R. (1964). Acoustic confusion in immediate memory. *British Journal of Psychology*, **55**, 75.

Corsellis, J. A. N. (1977). The neuropathology of dementia. *Age and Ageing (Supplement)*, **6**, 20.

Costello, C. G. (1966). *Psychology for Psychiatrists*, Pergamon Press, Oxford.

Critchley, Mc. (1953). *The Parietal Lobes*. Edward Arnold, London.

Cromwell, R. L. (1975). Assessment of schizophrenia. *Annual Review of Psychology*, **26**, 593.

Cronholm, B., and Lagengren, A. (1959). Memory disturbances after ECT. *Acta Psychiatrica Neuroligica Scand.*, **34**, 283.

Cronholm, B., and Ottosson, J.-O. (1963). Ultrabrief stimulus techniques in ECT. *Journal of Nervous and Mental Disorders*, **137**, 117.

Crow, H. J., Cooper, R., and Phillips, D. G. (1963). *Progressive leucotomy in current psychiatric therapies.* Grune and Stratton, New York.

Cutting, J. (1977). Personal communication.

d'Elia, G. (1974). Unilateral ECT. In M. Fink (Ed.) *The Psychobiology of ECT.* Wiley & Sons, New York.

Delgado, J. M. R. (1976). New orientations in brain stimulation in man. In A. Wauquier and E. T. Rolls (Eds.) *Brain-Stimulation Reward.* North Holland Publishing, Amsterdam Ch. 24, p. 481.

De Luca, D., Cermak, L. S., and Butters, N. (1977). Korsakoff patients recall following distractor activity. *Neuropsychologia,* **13,** 271.

Dement, W. C. (1972). *Some Must Watch While Some Must Sleep.* W. H. Freeman, San Francisco.

Denckla, M. A., and Rendel, R. G. (1976). Rapid automated naming in dyslexia. *Neuropsychologia,* **14,** 471.

Denny-Brown, D. (1962). *The Basal Ganglia and their Relation to Disorders of Movement.* Oxford University Press, London.

de Renzi, E., Faglioni, P., and Spinnler, H. (1968a). Face recognition and brain damage. *Cortex,* **4,** 17.

de Renzi, E., Pieczuro, A., and Vignolo, L. A. (1968b). Ideotional apraxia; a quantitative study. *Neuropsychologia,* **6,** 41.

de Renzi, E., and Vignolo, L. A. (1962). A token test for the measurement of dysphasia. *Brain,* **85,** 665.

Deutsch, J. A. (1976). Drive-Reward theory of Brain Reward. In A. Wauquier and E. T. Rolls (Eds.) *Brain-Stimulation Reward.* North-Holland Publishing, Amsterdam.

Dornbush, R. L., and Williams, M. (1974). Memory after ECT. In M. Fink (Ed.) *The Psychobiology of ECT.* Wiley & Sons, New York.

Dornbush, R. L., Abrams, E., and Fink, M. (1971). Memory changes after unilateral ECT. *British Journal of Psychiatry,* **119,** 75.

Ebtinger, R. (1958). *Aspects Psychologiques du Post-électrochoc.* Colmar, Imprimerie Asatie.

Efron, R. (1963). Perception of simultaneity. *Brain,* **86,** 261; *Ibid.* 285.

Ekstrand, B. R. (1972). To sleep, perchance to dream. In C. P. Duncan, L. Sechrist, and A. W. Helton (Eds.) *Human Memory.* Appleton-Centry-Crofts, New York, pp. 59–82.

Ellis, N. C., and Miles, T. R. (1977). *Visual and name coding in dyslexic and non-dyslexic subjects.* Meeting of Experimental Psychology Society. Oxford. July 1977.

Ervin, F. R. (1967). In A. M. Freidman and H. I. Kaplan (Eds.) *Comprehensive Textbook of Psychiatry.* Williams and Wilkins, Baltimore, Ch. 2.

Ettlinger, G. (1960). Interpretation of pictures in cases of brain lesion. *Journal of Mental Science,* **106,** 1337.

Ettlinger, G., and Wyke, M. (1961). Defects in identification in cerebrovascular disease. *Journal of Neurology, Neurosurgery, and Psychiatry,* **24,** 254.

Eysenck, H. J. (1947). *Dimensions of Personality.* Routledge and Kegan Paul, London.

Falconer, M. (1973). Pathological substrates in temporal lobe epilepsy with psychoses. In L. V. Laitinen and K. E. Livingston (Eds.) *Surgical Approaches in Psychiatry.* Medical and Technical Publishing, Lancaster, Ch. 17, p. 121.

Ferris, G. S., and Dorsen, M. M. (1975). Agenesis of the corpus callosum. *Cortex,* **11,** 95.

Festinger, L. (1957). *A Theory of Cognitive Dissonance.* Ron Peterson, New York.

Franco, L., and Sperry, R. W. (1977). Hemisphere lateralization for cognitive processing of geometry. *Neuropsychologia,* **15,** 107.

Freud, S. (1891). *On Aphasia,* translated by E. Stengel (1950). Image Publishing, New York.

Fuld, M. A. (1976). Storage, retention and retrieval in Korsakoff syndrome. *Neuropsychologia,* **14,** 225.

Fulton, J. (1949). *Textbook of Physiology.* (16th Edition). W. B. Saunders, Philadelphia.

Gardner, H. (1977). *The Shattered Mind.* Routledge and Kegan Paul, London.

Gardner, H., and Zuriff, E. (1975). *Bee* but not *be*: oral reading of single words in aphasia and alexia. *Neuropsychologia,* **13,** 170.

Gardner, H., and Zuriff, E. (1976). Critical reading of words and phrases in aphasia. *Brain and Language,* **3,** 173.

Gardner, H., Denes, G., and Zuriff, E. (1975a). Critical reading at the sentence level in aphasia. *Cortex,* **11,** 60.

Gardner, H., Albert, M., and Weintraub, S. (1975b). Comprehending a word. *Cortex,* **11,** 155.

Gazzaniga, M. S. (1970). *The Bissected Brain.* Appleton-Century-Crofts, New York.

Gazzaniga, M. S., Bogan, J. E., and Sperry, R. W. (1965). Disconnexion of the cerebral hemispheres. *Brain,* **88,** 221.

Gazzaniga, M. S., and Sperry, R. W. (1967). Language after section of the cerebral commissures. *Brain,* **90,** 131.

Gerstmann, J. (1924). Fingeragnosia. *Wien Klin. Wschr.,* **37,** 1010.

Geschwind, N. (1965). Disconnexion syndromes in animals and man. *Brain,* **88,** 237.

Geschwind, N. (1974). *Selected Papers on Language and the Brain.* Boston Studies in Philosophy of Science, Volume XVI, D. Reidd, Boston, U.S.A.

Ghent-Braine, L. (1968). Asymmetries of pattern perception in Israelis. *Neuropsychologia,* **6,** 73.

Gibbs, F. A. (1958). Abnormal electrical activity in the temporal region and abnormalities of behaviour. In *The Brain and Human Behaviour.* Proceedings Association Research Neurological and Mental Disease, Ch. 10 (Hafner edn., 1966), Illinois.

Gloning, K. (1977). Handedness and aphasia. *Neuropsychologia,* **15,** 355.

Gloning, K., Harb, G., and Quatember, R. (1966). Untersuchung der Prosopagnosie. *Neuropsychologia,* **5,** 99.

Gloning, J., Gloning, K., Hoff, H., and Tschabitsher, H. (1966). Zur Prosopagnosie. *Neuropsychologia,* **4,** 113.

Gloning, I., Gloning, K., and Hoff, H. (1968). *Neuropsychological Symptoms and Occipital lesions.* Collection Neuropsychologia Monograph. Gauthier-Villars, Paris.

Glosser, G., Butters, N., and Samuels, I. (1976). Failures in information processing in patients with Korsakoff Syndrome. *Neuropsychologia,* **14,** 327.

Goddard, G. V., and McIntyre, D. C. (1973). Lasting epileptogenic trace kindled by repeated electrical stimulation. In L. V. Laitinen and K. E. Livingston (Eds.), *Surgical Approaches in Psychiatry.* Medical and Technical Publishing, Lancaster, Ch. 15, p. 109.

Godden, D. R., and Baddeley, A. D. (1975). Context dependent memory in two natural environments. *British Journal of Psychology,* **66,** 325.

Goldstein, K. (1939). *The Organism.* American Book Co., New York.

Goldstein, K. (1948). *Language and Language Disturbances.* Grune and Stratton, New York.

Goldstein, K., and Scheerer, M. (1941). Abstract and concrete behaviour. *Psychological Monograph,* **53,** No. 2.

Goodglass, H., and Kaplan, E. (1963). Disturbances of gesture and pantomime in aphasia. *Brain,* **86,** 703.

Green, E., and Boller, F. (1974). Features of auditory comprehension in severely impaired aphasics. *Cortex,* **10,** 133.

Green, J. R., Stedman, H. F., Duisberg, R. E. H., McGrath, W. B., and Wick, S. H. (1958). Behaviour changes following temporal lobe excision. In *The Brain and Human Behaviour.* Proceedings Association Research Nervous and Mental Disorders, Ch. 11 (Hafner edn., 1966), Illinois.

Greenblatt, M., and Solomon, H. C. (1958). Studies in lobotomy. In *The Brain and Human Behaviour.* Proceedings Association Research Nervous and Mental Disease, Ch. 2 (Hafner edn., 1966), Illinois.

Halliday, A. M., Davison, K., Browne, M. W., and Kreeger, L. C. (1968). A comparison of bilateral and unilateral ECT. *British Journal of Psychiatry*, **114**, 997.

Halnan, C. R. E., and Wright, G. H. (1961). Fingers and toes in the body image. *Acta Neuroligica Scand.*, **37**, 50.

Halstead, W. C. (1947). *Brain and Intelligence. A quantitative Study of the Frontal Lobes.* University of Chicago Press, Chicago.

Head, H. (1926). *Aphasia and Kindred Disorders of Speech.* Volume I. Cambridge University Press, Cambridge.

Heeschen, K. (1977). *Sprachfunktionen den dominanten und subdominanten Hemisphäre.* Paper given to Arbeits Tagung für Neuropsychologie der Deutschen Gesellschaft für Neurologie. Aachen. May 12–14, 1977.

Heilman, K. M. (1975). A tapping test in apraxia. *Cortex*, **11**, 259.

Heim, A. (1970). *Intelligence and Personality.* Penguin Books, Harmondsworth.

Herberg, J. (1967). The hypothalamus and the aetiology of the migraine syndrome. In R. Smith (Ed.) *Background to Migraine*, Heinemann, London.

Herberg, L. J., Stephens, D. N., and Franklin, K. B. J. (1976). Catecholamines and self-stimulation. *Pharmacology, Biochemistry and Behaviour*, **4**, 575.

Hines, D. (1976). Recognition of verbs, abstract nouns, and concrete nouns. *Neuropsychologia*, **14**, 211.

Hitchcock, E. R., Ashcroft, G. W., Cairns, V. M., and Murray. L. G. (1973). An assessment scheme for amygdalotomy. In L. V. Laitinen and K. E. Livingston (Eds.) *Surgical Approaches in Psychiatry.* Medical and Technical Publishing, Lancaster. Ch. 22, p. 142.

Hornykiewcz, O. (1973). The subcortical monoaminergic systems. In L. V. Laitinen and K. E. Livingston (Eds.) *Surgical Approaches in Psychiatry.* Medical and Technical Publishing, Lancaster, Ch. 38, p. 293.

Howes, D. H., and Geschwind, N. (1961). Statistical properties of aphasic language. *Excerpta Medica International Congress.* **Series. No. 38** (VIIth International Congress of Neurology).

Humphrey, M. E., and Zangwill, O. L. (1952). Effects of rightsided occipito-parietal brain injuries in a left-handed man. *Brain*, **75**, 312.

Huppert, F. A., and Piercy, M. F. (1976). Recognition memory in amnesic patients: temporal context and familiarity. *Cortex*, **12**, 3.

Hutt, C., Hutt, J. T., Lee, D., and Ounsted, C. (1964). Arousal in childhood autism. *Nature*, **204**, 908.

Hutt, C., and Coxon, M. W. (1965). Systematic observation in clinical psychology. *Archives General Psychiatry*, **12**, 374.

Idzikowski, C. J. (1977). *Memory and Sleep.* Paper read to the Experimental Psychology Society. London.

Ingram, D. (1977). Motor asymmetries in young children. *Neuropsychologia*, **13**, 95.

Iverson, S. D. (1977). Temporal Lobe Amnesia. In C. W. M. Whitty and O. L. Zangwill (Eds.) *Amnesia.* (Second Edition). Butterworth, London, Ch. 6.

Jackson, J. H. (1866). Notes on the physiology and pathology of language. In J. Taylor (Ed.) (1932) *Selected Papers.* Volume 2. Hodder and Stoughton, London.

Jambor, K., and Williams, M. (1964). Disorders of topographical orientation. *Neuropsychologia*, **2**, 55.

Jurko, M. F., and Andy, O. J. (1973). Psychological changes correlated with thalamotomy site. *Journal of Neurology, Neurosurgery and Psychiatry*, **36**, 846.

Kalinowsky, L. B. (1973). Attempts at localization of psychological manifestations observed in various psychosurgical procedures. In L. V. Laitinen and K. E. Livingston (Eds.) *Surgical Approaches in Psychiatry.* Medical and Technical Publishing, Lancaster, Ch. 3, p. 18.

Kehlet, H., and Lunn, V. (1951). Retrograd amnesi ved electrochok befandling. *Nord Psykiat Medlemsbl.*, **5**, 51.

Kelly, D., Richardson, A., and Mitchell-Heggs, N. (1973). Technique and assessment of

172

limbic leucotomy. In L. V. Laitinen and K. E. Livingston (Eds.) *Surgical Approaches in Psychiatry*. Medical and Technical Publishing, Lancaster, Ch. 24, p. 174.

Kennedy, A., and Wilkes, A. (1975). *Studies in Long Term Memory*. Wiley & Sons, London.

Kerchensteiner, M., and Huber, W. (1975). Grammatical impairment in developmental aphasia. *Cortex*, **11**, 264.

Kerchensteiner, M. (1977). *Klinick der Aphasien*. Paper gives to Arbeitstagung für Neuropsychologie der Deutschen Gesellschaft für Neurologie. Aachen. May 12–14, 1977.

Kimura, D. (1963). Visual perception by patients with temporal lobe lesions. *Archives of Neurology Chicago*, **8**, 264.

Kimura, D. (1964). Left-right differences in the perception of melodies. *Quarterly Journal of Experimental Psychology*, **16**, 355.

Kimura, D. (1967). Asymmetry of the brain in visual perception. *Neuropsychologia*, **4**, 275.

King, E. (1967). The nature of visual field defects. *Brain*, **90**, 647.

Kinsbourne, M., and Warrington, E. K. (1962). Reading loss associated with right hemisphere lesions. *Journal of Neurology, Neurosurgery and Psychiatry*, **25**, 339.

Kinsbourne, M., and Warrington, E. K. (1963a). Limited visual form perception. *Brain*, **86**, 697.

Kinsbourne, M., and Warrington, E. K. (1963b). A study of visual perseveration. *Journal of Neurology, Neurosurgery and Psychiatry*, **26**, 468.

Kinsbourne, M., and Warrington, E. K. (1963c). Jargon aphasia. *Neuropsychologia*, **1**, 27.

Kinsbourne, M., and Warrington, E. K. (1964). Disorders of spelling. *Journal of Neurology, Neurosurgery and Psychiatry*, **27**, 224.

Laitinen, L. V., and Livingston, K. E. (1973). (Eds.) *Surgical Approaches in Psychiatry*. Medical and Technical Publishing, Lancaster.

Lancaster, N. P., Steinert, R. R., and Frost, I. (1958). Unilateral ECT. *Journal of Mental Science*, **104**, 221.

Lashley, K. S. (1950). In search of the engram. *Symposium Experimental Biology*, **4**, 454.

Levinson, F., and Meyer, V. (1965). Personality changes following orbital cortex undercutting. *British Journal of Psychiatry*, **111**, 207.

Lewin, W. (1961). Observations on selective leucotomy. *Journal of Neurology, Neurosurgery and Psychiatry*, **24**, 37.

Lewin, W. (1973). Selective leucotomy: a review. In L. V. Laitinen and K. E. Livingston (Eds.) *Surgical Approaches in Psychiatry*. Medical and Technical Publishing, Lancaster, Ch. 9, p. 69.

Lewis, S. A. (1976). Sleep. In S. Krauss (Ed.) *Encyclopaedic Handbook of Medical Psychiatry*. Butterworth, London, p. 509.

Lishman, W. D., and McMeeken, E. R. L. (1977). Handedness in relation to direction and degree of cerebral dominance. *Cortex*, **13**, 30.

Livingston, K. E., and Escobar, A. (1973). Tentative limbic system models for certain patterns of psychiatric disorders. In L. V. Laitinen and K. E. Livingston (Eds.) *Surgical Approaches in Psychiatry*. Medical and Technical Publishing, Lancaster. Ch. 33, p. 245.

Loranger, A. W. (1973). Parkinsonism, L-dopa and intelligence. *American Journal of Psychiatry*, **130**, 1386.

Luria, A. R. (1966). *Human Brain and Psychological Processes*. Harper and Row, New York.

Luria, A. R. (1969). *The Mind of a Mnemonist*. Jonathan Cape, London.

Luria, A. R. (1971). Memory disturbances in local brain lesions. *Neuropsychologia*, **9**, 367.

Luria, A. R., Karpor, B. A., and Yarhuss, A. L. (1966). Disturbances of visual perception in frontal lesions. *Cortex*, **2**, 202.

Luria, A. R. (1972). *The Man with a Shattered World*. Basic Books, New York.

McCurdy, J. T. (1928). *Common Principles in Psychology and Physiology*. Cambridge University Press, Cambridge.

McFie, J., Piercy, M. F., and Zangwill, O. L. (1950). Visuo-spatial agnosia. *Brain*, **73**, 167.

McFie, J. (1975). *Assessment of Organic Intellectual Impairment*. Academic Press, New York.

McGhie, A., Chapman, J., and Lawson, J. S. (1965). The effect of distraction on schizophrenic performance. *British Journal of Psychiatry*, **3**, 383; *Ibid.* 391.

Mack, J. L., and Boller, F. (1977). Associative visual agnosia and its related deficits. *Neuropsychologia*, **15**, 345.

McKinney, J. P. (1967). Handedness, eyedness and perceptual stability. *Neuropsychologia*, **5**, 339.

Marcel, T., and Rajan, P. (1975). Lateral specialization of words and faces in good and poor readers. *Neuropsychologia*, **13**, 489.

Marchbanks, G., and Williams, M. (1971). Factors affecting word selection in schizophrenic patients. *British Journal of Social and Clinical Psychology*, **10**, 241.

Marks, I. M., Birley, J. L. T., and Gelder, M. G. (1966). Modified leucotomy in severe agoraphobia. *British Journal of Psychiatry*, **112**, 757.

Marin, O. S. M., and Saffran, E. M. (1975). Agnosic behaviour in anomia. *Cortex*, **11**, 83.

Marshall, J. C., Caplan, D., and Holmes, J. M. (1977). The measurement of laterality. *Neuropsychologia*, **13**, 315.

Marsler-Wilson, W. D., and Teuber, H.-L. (1975). Memory for remote events in organic amnesia. *Neuropsychologia*, **13**, 347.

Mason, S. T., and Iverson, S. D. (1975). Learning in the absence of forebrain noradeneline. *Nature*, **258**, 422.

Mason, S. T., and Iverson, S. D. (1976). *Role of dorsal noradrenergic bundle in behaviour control*. Paper read to the eighth annual meeting of the European Brain and Behaviour Society, Copenhagen.

Mayer-Gross, W. (1943). Memory defects after ECT. *Lancet*, **ii**, 603.

Mayer-Gross, W., Slater, E., and Roth, M. (1960). *Clinical Psychiatry*. Cassell, London.

Meduna, L. von (1937). *Die Konvulsionstherapie der Schizophrenie*, Halle.

Miles, T. R. (1967). In defence of the concept of dyslexia. In J. Downing and A. L. Brown (Ed.) *The Second International Reading Symposium*. Cassell, London.

Miller, E. (1967). Psychological theories of ECT: a review. *British Journal of Psychiatry*, **113**, 301.

Miller, E. (1972). *Clinical Neuropsychology*. Penguin, Harmondsworth.

Miller, E. (1977). *Abnormal Ageing*. Wiley & Sons, London.

Milner, B. (1962). Laterality effects in audition. In V. B. Mountcastle (Ed.) *Interhemispheric Relations and Cerebral Dominance*. John Hopkins University Press, Baltimore, pp. 177–195.

Milner, B. (1966). In C. W. M. Whitty and O. L. Zangwill (Eds.) (First Edition) *Amnesia*. Butterworth, London, Ch. 5.

Mishkin, M. (1954). Visual discrimination following partial ablation of the temporal lobe. *Journal of Comparative Physiology and Psychology*. **47**, 187.

Mishkin, M., and Pribram, K. H. (1955). The effects of frontal lesions in monkeys, I. *Journal of Comparative Physiology and Psychology*, **48**, 492.

Mishkin, M., and Pribram, K. H. (1956). The effects of frontal lesions in monkeys, II. *Journal of Comparative Physiology and Psychology*, **49**, 36.

Mitchell, S. W. (1871). Phantom limbs. *Lippincotts Magazine of Popular Literature and Science*, **8**, 563.

174

Nauta, W. J. H. (1973). Connections of the frontal lobe with the limbic system. In L. V. Laitinen and K. E. Livingston (Eds.) *Surgical Approaches in Psychiatry*. Medical and Technical Publishing, Lancaster, Ch. 39, p. 303.

Newcombe, F., and Marshall, J. C. (1966). Syntactic and semantic errors in paralexia. *Journal of Neurology and Psychology*, **4**, 169.

Newcombe, F., and Marshall, J. C. (1967). Immediate recall of sentences by subjects with unilateral lesions. *Neuropsychologia*, **5**, 329.

O'Connor, N., and Hermalin, B. (1963). *Speech and Thought in severe Subnormality*. Pergamon Press, Oxford.

Ojemann, G. A., Fedio, P., and Van Buren, J. M. (1968). Anomia from pulvinar and subcortical parietal stimulation. *Brain*, **91**, 29.

Oldfield, R. C., and Wingfield, A. (1965). Response latencies in naming objects. *Quarterly Journal of Experimental Psychology*, **16**, 273.

Olds, J. (1958). Self-stimulation experiments and reward systems. Reprinted in D. Bindra and J. Stewart (Eds.) (1966). *Motivation*, Penguin, Harmondsworth, Ch. 40.

Olds, J. (1976). Reward and drive neurons. In A. Wanquier and E. T. Rolls (Eds.) *Brain-Stimulation Reward*, North-Holland Publishing, Amsterdam.

Orbach, J. (1967). Recognition of English and Hebrew words in the right and left visual fields. *Neuropsychologia*, **5**, 127.

Oswald, I. (1966). *Sleep*. Penguin, Harmondsworth.

Ottosson, J. O. (1960). The action of ECT. *Acta Psychiatrica Scand. Supplement*, **145**.

Owen, G. M., and Williams, M. (1977). Short term visual memory in amnesic and snile patients. In press.

Paivio, A., and Csapo, K. (1973). Picture superiority in free recall. *Cognitive Psychology*, **5**, 176.

Partridge, M. (1950). *Prefrontal Leucotomy*. Blackwells, Oxford.

Payne, R. W., and Friedlander, D. (1962). A short battery of tests for measuring over-inclusive thinking. *Journal of Mental Science*, **108**, 362.

Penfield, W., and Boldrey, E. (1937). Semantic and sensory representation in the cortex of man. *Brain*, **60**, 432.

Penfield, W., and Perot, P. (1963). The brain's record of auditory and visual experience. *Brain*, **86**, 595.

Penfield, W. (1952). Epileptic automatisms and the centrencephalic integrating system. *Association for Research Nervous and Mental Disorders*, **30**, 513.

Perenin, M. T., and Jeannerod, M. (1975). Residual vision in cortically blind hemispheres. *Neuropsychologia*, **13**, 1.

Petrie, A. (1958). The effects of chloroprazine and brain lesions on personality. In H. D. Pennes (Ed.) *Psychopharmacology*. Hoeber–Harper.

Petrie, A. (1960a). Some psychological aspects of pain. *Annals of New York Academy of Science*, **86**, 13.

Petrie, A. (1960b). Some psychological aspects of pain. *American Journal of Psychology*, **73**, 80.

Phillipson, O. T., McKeown, J. M., Williams, M., Baker, J., and Healey, A. F. (1977). A new rating scale for use in the correlation of clinical responses and plasma drug levels in schizophrenia. In press.

Piercy, M. F. (1959). Testing intellectual impairment. *Journal of Mental Science*, **105**, 489.

Piercy, M. F. (1977). Experimental studies of the organic amnesic syndrome. In C. W. M. Whitty and O. L. Zangwill (Eds.) *Amnesia*. (Second Edition). Butterworth, London, Ch. 1.

Plum, F., and Posner, J. B. (1972). *Diagnoses of Stupor and Coma*. Contemporary Neurological Series No. 10 (Second Edition). F. A. Davis, Philadelphia.

Pratt, R. T. C., Warrington, E. K., and Halliday, A. M. (1971). Unilateral ECT as a test of cerebral dominance. *British Journal of Psychiatry*, **119**, 79.

Pratt, R. T. C., and Warrington, E. K. (1972). The assessment of cerebral dominance with unilateral ECT. *British Journal of Psychiatry*, **121**, 327.

Pratt, R. T. C. (1977). Psychogenic loss of memory. In C. W. M. Whitty and O. L. Zangwill (Eds.) *Amnesia*. (Second Edition). Butterworth, London, Ch. 9.

Pribram, K. H. (1968). The primate frontal cortex. In A. R. Luria and K. H. Pribram (Eds.) *Frontal Lobes and the Regulation of Behaviour*. Academic Press, New York.

Pribram, K. H. (1969). The neurophysiology of remembering. *Scientific American*, **220**, 73.

Pribram, K. H., and Tubbs, W. E. (1967). The primate frontal cortex, *Science*, **156**, 765.

Price, D. B. (1976). Phantom limb phenomenon in patients with leprosy. *Journal of Nervous and Mental Disease*, **163**, 108.

Reitan, R. M. (1975). Assessment of brain-behaviour relationships. In P. McReynolds, (Ed.) *Advances in Psychological Assessment*. Volume 3. Jossey-Boss Publishers, San Francisco, Ch. 5, p. 186.

Ribot, T. (1885). *Diseases of Memory*. Kegan Paul, London.

Riege, W. (1977). Inconsistent non-verbal recognition memory in Korsakoff patients and controls. *Neuropsychologia*, **15**, 269.

Rochford, G. (1969). *The breakdown of language associated with organic brain damage*. Thesis offered for D. Phil. Oxon.

Rochford, G. (1971). *A study of naming errors in dysphasic and demented patients*. *Neuropsychologia*, **9**, 443.

Rochford, G. (1974). Are jargon dysphasics dysphasic? *British Journal of Disorders of Communication*, **9**, 35.

Rochford, G., and Williams, M. (1962). Studies in the development and breakdown of the use of names. I and II. *Journal of Neurology, Neurosurgery, and Psychiatry*, **25**, 222; *Ibid.*, 229.

Rochford, G., and Williams, M. (1963). Studies in the development and breakdown of the use of names. III. *Journal of Neurology, Neurosurgery, and Psychiatry*, **26**, 377.

Rochford, G., and Williams, M. (1964). The measurement of language disorders. *Speech Pathology and Therapy*, **7**, 3.

Rochford, G., and Williams, M. (1965). Studies in the development and breakdown of the use of names. IV. *Journal of Neurology, Neurosurgery, and Psychiatry*, **28**, 407.

Rommetveit, R., Toch, H., and Svendsen, D. (1968). A study of stereoscopic rivalry. *Scandinavian Journal Psychology*, **9**, 138.

Roth, M., Tomlinson, B. E., and Blessed, G. (1967). The relationship between dementia and degeneration changes in the elderly. *Proceedings of the Royal Society of Medicine*, **60**, 254.

Russell, W. R. (1959). *Brain, Memory and Learning*. Clarendon Press, Oxford.

Russell, W. R., and Espir, M. L. E. (1961). *Traumatic aphasia*. Oxford University Press, London.

Rylander, G. (1939). *Personality changes after operations on the frontal lobes*. Oxford University Press, London.

Sanders, H. I., and Warrington, E. K. (1971). Memory for remote events in amnesic patients. *Brain*, **94**, 661.

Sanders, H. I., and Warrington, E. K. (1975). Retrograde amnesia in organic amnesic states. *Cortex*, **11**, 397.

Schaie, K. W. (1974). Intellectual function (in ageing). *American Psychologist*, **29**, 802.

Schilder, P. (1950). *The image and appearance of the human body*. International University Press Incorporated, New York.

Schmidt, R. P., and Wilder, B. J. (1968). *Epilepsy. Contemporary Neurology*, Series No. 2. F. A. Davis, Philadelphia.

Scoville, W. B. (1973). Surgical location for psychiatric surgery. In L. V. Laitinen and K. E. Livingston (Eds.) *Surgical Approaches in Psychiatry*. Medical and Technical Publishing, Lancaster, Ch. 5, p. 29.

Seligman, M E. P. (1973). Depression and learned helplessness. *Psychology Today*, **7**, 43.

Seltzer, B., and Benson, D. F. (1974). Temporal patterns of retrograde amnesia in Korsakov disease. *Neuropsychologia*, **14**, 527.

Semmes, J. (1968). Hemispheric specialization. *Neuropsychologia*, **6**, 11.

Semmes, J., Weinstein, S., Ghent, L., and Teuber, H. L. (1963). Correlates of impaired orientation. *Brain*, **86**, 747.

Sem-Jacobsen, C. W. (1976). Electrical stimulation and self-stimulation in man. In A. Wauquier and E. T. Rolls (Eds.) *Brain-Stimulation Reward*, North-Holland Publishing, Amsterdam, Ch. 25, p. 505.

Serafetinides, E. A., and Falconer, M. A. (1963). Speech disturbances in temporal lobe seizures. *Brain*, **86**, 333.

Sevilla, M., Vernet, J. P., Beckle, J., and Darcourt, G. (1973). The Rorschach test in Parkinsonians. *Annales Medico Psychologiques*, **1**, 577.

Shankweiler, D. (1966). Dichotically presented melodies. *Journal of Comparative Physiology and Psychology*, **62**, 115.

Shankweiler, D., and Harris, K. S. (1966). Articulation in aphasia. *Cortex*, **2**, 277.

Shankweiler, D., and Studdert-Kennedy, M. (1967). Speech sounds in interaural competition. *Quarterly Journal of Experimental Psychology*, **19**, 59.

Sherwin, I. (1966). Seizures precipitated by the use of language. *Cortex*, **2**, 347.

Simmell, M. (1956). Phantoms in patients with leprosy. *American Journal of Psychology*, **69**, 529.

Simmell, M. (1961). The absence of phantoms for congenitally missing limbs. *American Journal of Psychology*, **74**, 467.

Simmell, M. (1962). Phantom experiences following amputation in childhood. *Journal of Neurology, Neurosurgery and Psychiatry*, **25**, 69.

Simmell, M. (1963). The psychological after effects of amputation. *Rehabilitation Council Bulletin*, **6**, 75.

Slater, E., Beard, A. W., and Clitherow, E. (1963). The schizophrenic-like psychoses of epilepsy. *British Journal of Psychiatry*, **109**, 95.

Smith, A. (1960). Changes in scores in brain-operated schizophrenics. *Journal of Mental Science*, **106**, 783.

Smith, A. (1966a). Intellectual functions in patients with lateralized frontal tumors. *Journal of Neurology, Neurosurgery and Psychiatry*, **29**, 52.

Smith, A. (1966b). Speech and other functions after left hemispheractomy. *Journal of Neurology, Neurosurgery and Psychiatry*, **29**, 467.

Sparks, R., and Geschwind, N. (1968). Dichotic listening after section of the neocortical commissures. *Cortex*, **4**, 3.

Sperry, R. W. (1961). Cerebral organization and behaviour. *Science*, **133**, 1749.

Sperry, R. W., Gazzaniga, M. S., and Bogan, J. E. (1969). Interhemispheric relationships: the neocortical commissures. In P. J. Vinken and G. W. Bruyh (Eds.) *Handbook of Clinical Neurology*. Volume 4. North-Holland Publishing, Amsterdam, Ch. 14.

Spinola, H., and Vignolo, L. A. (1966). Impaired sound recognition in aphasia. *Cortex*, **2**, 337.

Springer, S. R., and Eisenson, J. (1977). Hemispheric specialization for speech in language-disordered children. *Neuropsychologia*, **15**, 287.

Springer, S. R., and Gazzaniga, M. S. (1977). Dichotic testing of partial and complete split brain subjects. *Neuropsychologia*, **13**, 341.

Squire, L. R. (1975). A stable impairment in remote memory following electrovulsive therapy. *Neuropsychologia*, **13**, 51.

Squire, L. R. (1977). E.C.T. and Memory Loss. *American Journal of Psychiatry*, **134:9**, 997.

Squire, L. R., Chace, P. M., and Slater, P. C. (1976). Retrograde amnesia following electrovulsive therapy. *Nature*, **260:5554**, 775.

Stengel, E. (1948). Visual alexia and colour agnosia. *Journal of Mental Science*, **94**, 46.

Stones, M. J. (1970). *The effect of attention on memory following ECT*. Dissertation for BA at Brunel University, London.

Stones, M. J. (1974). *Sleep and the storage and retrieval processes in Humans.* Unpublished Ph.D Thesis. University of Sheffield.

Sylvester, P. E. (1966). Parietal lobe deficit in the mentally retarded. *Journal of Neurology, Neurosurgery and Psychiatry,* **29**, 176.

Symonds, C. P. (1937). Head injuries. *Proceedings of the Royal Society of Medicine,* **30**, 1081.

Tallal, P. (1975). The token test in developmental dysphasia. *Cortex,* **11**, 196.

Tallal, P., and Piercy, M. F. (1975). Developmental aphasia—the perception of vowels and consonants. *Neuropsychologia,* **13**, 69.

Talland, G. A. (1965). *Deranged Memory.* Academic Press, New York.

Thompson, R. F. (1967). *Foundations of Physiological Psychology.* Harper and Row, New York.

Thorndike, E. L., and Lorge, I. (1944). *The Teachers Word Book of 30,000 Words.* Bureau of Publications, Teachers College, Columbia University, New York.

Tow, McD. (1955). *Personality changes following frontal leucotomy.* Oxford University Press, London.

Treisman, A. (1965). Verbal responses and contextual restraints. *Journal of Verbal Learning and Verbal Behaviour,* **4**, 118.

Trevarthen, C. (1974). Analysis of cerebral activity in commissurotomy patients. In S. J. Dimond and J. G. Beaumont (Eds.) *Hemispheric Function in the Human Brain.* Elek Science, London.

Tucker, D. M. (1976). Sex differences in hemispheric specialization for synthetic visuo-spatial functions. *Neuropsychologia,* **14**, 447.

Underwood, G. (1977). Attention, awareness and hemispheric difference in word recognition. *Neuropsychologia,* **15**, 61.

Valenstein, E. G. (1976). The interpretation of behaviour evoked by brain stimulation. In A. Wauquier and E. T. Rolls (Eds.) *Brain-Stimulation Reward.* North-Holland Publishing, Amsterdam, Ch.28, p. 557.

Valpeau (1843). see Rochford, 1969.

Vernon, M. D. (1957). *Backwardness in Reading.* Cambridge University Press, Cambridge.

Victor, M., Adams, R. D., and Collins, G. H. (1971). *The Wernicke-Korsakoff Syndrome.* Contempory Neurology Series. F. A. Davis Philadelphia.

Wallace, J. G. (1956). Some studies of perception in relation to age. *British Journal of Psychology,* **47**, 283.

Walter, W. G. (1966). Electrophysiological contributions to psychiatric therapy. *Current Psychiatric Therapies.* Volume VI. Grune and Stratton, New York.

Walter, W. G. (1967). Electrical signs of association expectancy and decision. *Recent Advances in Neurosurgery and Physiology, Supplement,* **25**, 258.

Warrington, E. K. (1962). Completion of visual forms across the hemionopic field. *Journal of Neurology, Neurosurgery, and Psychiatry,* **25**, 208.

Warrington, E. K. (1969). Constructional apraxia. In *Handbook of Clinical Neurology.* Volume 4. North Holland Publishing, Amsterdam.

Warrington, E. K., and James, M. (1967a). Disorders of visual perception with localized cerebral lesions. *Neuropsychologia,* **5**, 253.

Warrington, E. K., and James, M. (1967b). Facial recognition and unilateral cerebral lesions. *Cortex,* **3**, 317.

Warrington, E. K., and Sanders, H. (1971). The fate of old memories. *Quarterly Journal Experimental of Psychology,* **23**, 432.

Warrington, E. K., and Weiskrantz, L. (1968). Long term retention in amnesic patients. *Nature,* **217**, 972.

Warrington, E. K., and Weiskrantz, L. (1971). Organizational aspects of amnesic patients. *Neuropsychologia,* **9**, 67.

Watts, G. (1976). ECT: How does it work. *World Medicine,* **January**, 27.

Wauquier, A., and Rolls, E. T. (1976). *Brain Stimulation Rewards*, North-Holland Publishing, Amsterdam.

Weigl, E. (1963). Deblockierung bildagnostischer Störrungen bei einem aphatiker. *Neuropsychologia*, **1**, 91.

Weigl, E. (1964). The problem of so-called simultanagnosia. *Neuropsychologia*, **2**, 189.

Weinstein, E. A., and Keller, M. J. A. (1963). Linguistic patterns of misnaming in brain injury. *Neuropsychologia*, **1**, 79.

Weinstein, E. A., Cole, M., and Mitchell, M. S. (1964). Agnosia and aphasia. *Archives Neurology*, **10**, 376.

Weinstein, E. A., Lyerley, O.A., Cole, M., and Ozer, M. N. (1966). Meaning in jargon aphasia. *Cortex*, **2**, 166.

Weinstein, S., Sersen, E. A., and Vetter, R. J. (1964). Phantoms in congenital aphasia. *Cortex*, **1**, 276.

Weinstein, S., Sersen, E. A., and Vetter, R. J. (1968). Phantoms after orchidectomy. *Neuropsychologia*, **6**, 63.

Weisenberg, T., and McBride, K. E. (1935). *Aphasia, a clinical and psychological study*. Oxford University Press, London.

Weiskrantz, L. (1966). In W. M. Whitty and O. L. Zangwill (Eds.) (First Edition). *Amnesia*. Butterworth, London, Ch. 1.

Welford, A. T. (1958). *Ageing and Human Skill*. Nuffield Foundation, Oxford.

Werner, N. (1956). Microgenesis and aphasia. *Journal of Abnormal Sociology and Psychology*, **52**, 347.

Whitty, C. W. M. (1964). Cortical dysarthria. *Journal of Neurology, Neurosurgery and Psychiatry*, **27**, 507.

Whitty, C. W. M. (1966). C. W. M. Whitty and O. L. Zangwill (Eds.) (First Edition). *Amnesia*. Butterworth, London, Ch. 2.

Wilkinson, R. T., and Morlock, H. C. (1967). Auditory evoked responses and reaction time. *Electroencephalitic Clinical Neurophysiology*, **23**, 50.

Wilkins, A. J., Andermann, F., and Ives, J. (1975). Stripes, complex cells and seizures. *Brain*, **98**, 365.

Williams, H. L. (1971). The new biology of sleep. *Journal of Psychiatric Research*, **8**, 445.

Williams, M. (1950). Memory studies with ECT. I and II. *Journal of Neurology, Neurosurgery and Psychiatry*, **13**, 30; *Ibid.*, 314.

Williams, M. (1952). A case of displaced affect following ECT. *British Journal of Medicine Psychology*, **25**, 156.

Williams, M. (1953). The effect of progressive prompting on memory after head injuries. *Journal of Neurology, Neurosurgery and Psychiatry*, **16**, 14.

Williams, M. (1954). *Memory defects associated with cerebral lesions*. Thesis submitted for D.Phil. Oxon.

Williams, M. (1960). The effects of past experience in the elderly. *Journal of Mental Science*, **106**, 783.

Williams, M. (1968). The measurement of memory in clinical practice. *British Journal of Social and Clinical Psychology*, **7**, 19.

Williams, M. (1973). Errors in picture recognition after ECT. *Neuropsychologia*, **11**, 429.

Williams, M. (1978). The Clinical Assessment of Memory. In P. M. Reynolds (Ed.) *Advances in Psychological Assessment*. Volume 4. Jossey-Bass, San Francisco, Ch. 10.

Williams, M., and Zangwill, O. L. (1952). Retrograde memory disturbances. *Journal of Neurology, Neurosurgery and Psychiatry*, **15**, 54.

Williams, M., and Pennybacker, J. (1954). Memory defects in tumours of the third ventricle. *Journal of Neurology, Neurosurgery and Psychiatry*, **17**, 115.

Williams, M., and Smith, H. V. (1954). Memory defects in tuberculous meningitis. *Journal of Neurology, Neurosurgery and Psychiatry*, **17**, 173.

Williams, R. L., Karacan, I., and Hursch, C. J. (1974). *EEG and Human Sleep: Clinical Applications*. Wiley & Sons, London.

Winner, E., and Gardner, H. (1977). Comprehension of metaphor.

Winocur, G., and Weiskrantz, L. (1976). Paired-Associate learning in amnesic patients. *Neuropsychologia*, **14**, 97.

Wolf, S. M., and Davis, R. L. (1973). Permanent dementia in idiopathic Parkinsonism treated with levodopa. *Archives of Neurology*, **29**, 276.

Wolport, I. (1924). Simultanagnosia. *Gez. Neurol. Psychiatr.*, **93**, 397.

Yamadori, A., and Ikumura, G. (1975). Central aphasia in a Japanese.*Cortex*, **11**, 73.

Yeni-Komshian, G. H., Isenberg, D., and Goldberg, H. (1975). Cerebral dominance and reading disability. *Neuropsychologia*, **13**, 83.

Zaidel, E. (1977). Laterality effects on the token test. *Neuropsychologia*, **15**, 1.

Zaidel, E., and Sperry, R. W. (1977). Some long-term motor effects of cerebral commissurotomy in man. *Neuropsychologia*, **15**, 193.

Zangwill, O. L. (1950). Amnesia and the generic image. *Quarterly Journal of Experimental Psychology*, **2**, 7.

Zangwill, O. L. (1963). The cerebral localization of cerebral functions. *Advancement of Science*, 20.1.

Zangwill, O. L. (1964). Psychological studies in amnesic states. *Proceedings of the Third World Congress of Psychiatry*, Vol. 3, 219.

Zangwill, O. L. (1966). In C. W. M. Whitty and O. L. Zangwill (Eds.) (First Edition). *Amnesia*. Butterworth. London, Ch. 3.

Zangwill, O. L. (1967). The Grünthal-Störrung case of amnesia syndrome. *British Journal of Psychiatry*, **113**, 113.

Zangwill, O. L. (1976). Thought and the brain. *British Journal of Psychology*, **67**, 314.

Zinkin, S., and Miller, A. J. (1967). Recovery of memory after amnesia induced by ECT. *Science*, **155**, 102.

Zubin, J., and Barrera, S. E. (1941). Effects of ECT on memory. *Proceedings of the Society for Experimental Biology and Medicine*, **48**, 596.

Index